The Laws of the Damascus Document

Studies on the Texts of the Desert of Judah

VOLUME XXIX

EDITED BY
F. Garcia Martínez
A. S. Van Der Woude

THE LAWS OF THE DAMASCUS DOCUMENT

The Laws of the Damascus Document
Sources, Tradition, and Redaction

Charlotte Hempel

Society of Biblical Literature
Atlanta

THE LAWS OF THE DAMASCUS DOCUMENT

Copyright © 1998 by Koninklijke Brill NV, Leiden,
The Netherlands

This edition published under license from Koninklijke Brill NV,
Leiden, The Netherlands by the Society of Biblical Literature.

All rights reserved. No part of this work may be reproduced or transmitted in any form or by any means, electronic or mechanical, including photocopying and recording, or by any means of any information storage or retrieval system, except as may be expressly permitted by the 1976 Copyright Act or in writing from the Publisher. Requests for permission should be addressed in writing to the Rights and Permissions Department, Koninklijke Brill NV, Leiden, The Netherlands.

Authorization to photocopy items for internal or personal use is granted by Brill provided that the appropriate fees are paid directly to The Copyright Clearance Center, 222 Rosewood Drive, Suite 910, Danvers, MA 01923, USA. Fees are subject to change.

Library of Congress Cataloging-in-Publication Data

Hempel, Charlotte.
　The laws of the Damascus document : sources, tradition, and redaction / by Charlotte Hempel.
　　　p. cm.
　Originally published: Leiden ; Boston : Brill, 1998. (Studies on the text of Judah, 0169-9662 ; v, 29).
　Includes bibliographical references and index.
　ISBN-13: 978-1-58983-256-5 (paper binding : alk. paper)
　ISBN-10: 1-58983-256-6 (paper binding : alk. paper)
　1. Damascus document. 2. Dead Sea scrolls. 3. Qumran community. 4. Jewish Law. I. Title.

BM175.Z3H46　　2006
296.1'55–dc22　　　　　　　　　　　2006026260

Printed in the United States of America
on acid-free paper

Meinen Eltern

TABLE OF CONTENTS

Preface xi

I	*Introduction*	1
1.1	The Damascus Document from Cairo and Qumran	1
1.2	The Damascus Document and the Origins and History of the Qumran Community	3
1.3	Source Criticism and the Damascus Document	8
1.3.1	The Admonition	8
1.3.2	The Laws	13
1.4	The Present Study	14
II	*Identifying Sources and Redactional Activity*	15
2.1	Frame of Reference	15
2.2	Vocabulary	16
2.3	Form	16
2.4	Polemical/Ideological Stance	18
III	*Halakhah*	25
3.1	Halakhah in the Legal Material of D that is Represented by CD and Parallels in 4QD	30
3.1.1	Halakhic Exposition of Scripture	30
3.1.2	Halakhic Exposition Lacking an Explicit Reference to Scripture	34
3.1.3	Discussion	35
3.2	Halakhah in the Additional Legal Material from 4QD..	38
3.2.1	Torot: Halakhic Exposition Dealing with Issues of Particular Concern to the Priesthood	38
3.2.1.1	The Disqualification of Various Categories of Priests	39
3.2.1.2	Skin Disease, Fluxes, and Childbirth	43
3.2.2	Various Agricultural Laws	50
3.2.2.1	Two Fragments Introducing Agricultural Halakhah, Gleanings, and Bread Offerings	50
3.2.2.2	More Agricultural Halakhah	54
3.2.2.3	Various Prescriptions on Tithing	56
3.2.2.4	Overall Assessment of the Agricultural Halakhah	58
3.2.3	Various Laws Dealing with Ritual Defilement and Purification	59

3.2.4	The Wife Suspected of Adultery and the Betrothed Slave Woman	62
3.2.5	The Jubilee Year, a Prohibition of Transvestism, Ethical Standards in Business, and the Arrangement of Marriages	64
3.3	Conclusions	70
IV	*Community Organization Part One: Admission into the Covenant Community*	73
4.1	Admission into the Covenant Community	73
4.2	Summary	90
V	*Community Organization Part Two: Administration of Justice*	91
5.1	The Procedure for Dealing with Lost or Stolen Property in the Camp	91
5.2	Witnesses	93
5.3	The Judges of the Congregation	100
5.4	Summary	104
VI	*Community Organization Part Three: The Organization of the Camps*	105
6.1	Announcement of Statutes for the משכיל	105
6.2	Questions of Authority	107
6.3	The Overseer over the Camp	114
6.4	The Meeting of All the Camps	131
6.5	Summary and Conclusions	140
VII	*Community Organization Part Four: The Penal Code*	141
Summary and Conclusion to Chapters Four-Seven		149
VIII	*Miscellaneous Pieces of Halakhah*	153
8.1	Rules on Entering the House of Worship	153
8.2	Prohibition of Sexual Relations in Jerusalem	155
8.3	The Spirits of Belial and Failure to Honour the Sabbath and the Festivals	157
8.4	Various Purity Regulations	159
8.5	The Fragmentary Beginning of CD 15	162
8.6	Conclusion	162
IX	*Catalogue of Transgressions*	163
9.1	The List of Transgressions	164
9.2	The Conclusion to the Catalogue	169

X	*Transitional Chapter Introducing the Laws* 171
XI	*Expulsion Ceremony and the End of the Document* 175
XII	*Conclusion* 187
12.1	Halakhah 187
12.2	Community Organization 189
12.3	Miscellaneous Halakhah 189
12.4	Miscellaneous Traditions and Redactional Passages 189
12.5	Outlook 191

Bibliography 193

Indices 205

PREFACE

This monograph is a thoroughly revised version of my doctoral dissertation. Without a large network of support offered in the course of my work on this book by my family, both old and new, friends, teachers, and colleagues this book would not have come to be or would be the worse for it. Responsibility for any remaining shortcomings lies, of course, exclusively with me. I owe thanks to a great many people who have read or heard all or parts of this material for their comments. My colleagues Mark Boyce and Daniel Falk have read my thesis and made a number of valuable comments. I have presented parts of this material at a meeting of the Oxford Forum for Qumran Research convened by Prof. Geza Vermes and, more informally, at the Orion Centre for the Study of the Dead Sea Scrolls and Associated Literature at the Hebrew University, Jerusalem. I thank the participants at both meetings for their interest and comments as well as the Academic Study Group, London, who awarded me a travel grant to visit Jerusalem in April 1996. Dr. Vanessa Davies, formerly director of the Language and Communication Centre at King's College London, offered tailor-made French tuition and much more. Prof. Joseph Baumgarten kindly informed me of a number of his readings and permitted me to read his transcriptions prior to the appearance of his edition of the Cave 4 fragments. Prof. Michael Knibb of King's College, London first introduced me to the scrolls as an undergraduate and later supervised my dissertation. He has been an exceedingly kind, learned, and demanding teacher for many years and continues to be a constant source of generous support for which I am very grateful. Profs. Graham Stanton of King's College London and George Brooke of the University of Manchester examined my thesis in December 1994, and I am grateful for their encouragement and helpful comments. I have been in regular contact with George ever since, and he has been and continues to be tremendously supportive, for which I am very grateful. I completed work on this book as Edward Cadbury Post-Doctoral Research Fellow in the Department of Theology at the University of Birmingham. My colleagues in the Department and beyond created a stimulating environment for research, and the Faculty of Arts supported my work in the form of a number of research grants. I am grateful further to Prof. Florentino García Martínez of the University of Groningen for accepting this volume for publication in the series *Studies on the Texts of the Desert of Judah* as well as for a number of suggestions for improving the work before you. I would also like to acknowledge the assistance by Hans van der Meij, Pim Rietbroek and Wouter Kool of E.J. Brill in the process of getting the work before you ready for publication.

I hope I may be permitted to write the next sentence in German. Dieses Buch ist meinen Eltern gewidmet als kleines Dankeschön für ihren moralischen und materiellen Beistand während meiner Arbeit an diesem Projekt. Finally, my fiancé Dick has been a long-standing source of strength and encouragement, and I look forward to our wedding next month as I write these lines.

Birmingham, July 1997

CHARLOTTE HEMPEL

CHAPTER ONE

INTRODUCTION

1.1 The Damascus Document from Cairo and Qumran

The Damascus Document was discovered in the form of two mediaeval manuscripts (MSS) at the end of the nineteenth century in the storeroom of a synagogue in Old Cairo (the Cairo *genizah*). The MSS were first published by Solomon Schechter under the title 'Fragments of a Zadokite Work' in 1910.[1] This title was chosen because the community behind parts of the document seems to refer to itself as 'the sons of Zadok', cf. CD 3,20b-4,4a.[2] The title that is most commonly used today, i.e. the Damascus Document (CD = Cairo Damascus Document), is based on several references to 'the land of Damascus' or 'Damascus' in the first part of the document, cf. CD 6,5.19; 7,15.19; 8,21; 19,34; 20,12.

The two mediaeval MSS from Cairo are usually referred to as manuscript A (MS A) and manuscript B (MS B). MS A is the longer and older of the two MSS. It contains sixteen pages and dates from the tenth century CE. Its contents can be divided into an Admonition (pages 1-8) and a collection of Laws (pages 9-16). MS B dates from the twelfth century CE and consists of two pages which partly overlap with MS A. The original editor of the document introduced the numbers 19 and 20 to refer to the two pages of MS B. Page 19 contains a different version of pages 7 and 8 from MS A, and page 20 contains additional material which constitutes the end of the Admonition as it is known from the Cairo text. The contents of CD can, therefore, be clearly divided into a section of Laws (CD 9-16) and an Admonition (CD 1-8; 19-20).

After the discovery of the Dead Sea Scrolls scholars soon recognized a connection between the Damascus Document and those discoveries. Such a connection was indicated firstly by the occurrence in the Biblical Commentaries from Qumran of the nicknames

---

[1] S. Schechter, *Documents of Jewish Sectaries*, Vol. I, Fragments of a Zadokite Work, Cambridge: CUP, 1910.

[2] For a critical discussion that emphasizes the lack of evidence for an identification of a Zadokite group behind the document cf. P.R. Davies, *Behind the Essenes. History and Ideology in the Dead Sea Scrolls*, Atlanta: Scholars Press, 1987, pp. 51-72.

'Teacher of Righteousness' and 'Spouter of Lies' known hitherto only from the Damascus Document. Secondly, a number of similarities in doctrine, vocabulary, and organization were recognized. Finally, the discovery of fragments of the Damascus Document in Caves 4, 5, and 6 of Qumran proved those scholars right who had argued that the mediaeval MSS were based on an ancient original. Since the discovery of fragments of the Damascus Document at Qumran the document has been studied in this context. The existence of fragments of the Damascus Document at Qumran was taken to indicate, moreover, that the work had been composed by the community responsible for the *pesharim* and other sectarian works. It is one of the achievements of P.R. Davies' work on the Damascus Document to question the former assumption on methodological grounds.[3] The place of the Damascus Document at Qumran continues to be a subject of scholarly debate, and it is the purpose of the present work to form a contribution to this ongoing discussion with particular reference to the Laws of the Damascus Document. For full bibliographical information dealing specifically with the Damascus Document the reader is referred to the helpful bibliographies by Fitzmyer[4] and García Martínez.[5]

Fragments of the Damascus Document were found in Qumran Caves 4, 5, and 6 (4QD, 5QD, 6QD). The material from Caves 5 and 6 consists of a small amount of text only. Both 5QD and 6QD were published already in 1962 by J.T. Milik and M. Baillet.[6] Cave 4, on the other hand, yielded a rich and significant amount of fragments belonging to the Damascus Document. In all, eight MSS of this document were found in Cave 4. These have recently been published by J.M. Baumgarten based on the transcriptions by J.T. Milik[7], and this edition provides students of the Damascus Document with a wealth of new material. Already before the edition of the fragments appeared Baumgarten had made available and commented upon a significant amount of material in scholarly journals

---

[3] Cf., for example, *The Damascus Covenant. An Interpretation of the "Damascus Document"*, Sheffield: JSOT Press, 1983, p. 2.

[4] *Prolegomenon* to the reprint of S. Schechter, *Documents of Jewish Sectaries*, Vol. I. Fragments of a Zadokite Work, New York: Ktav, 1970, pp. 9-37.

[5] 'Damascus Document: A Bibliography of Studies 1970-1989', in *The Damascus Document Reconsidered* ed. M. Broshi, Jerusalem: Israel Exploration Society, 1992, pp. 63-83.

[6] M. Baillet, J.T. Milik et R. de Vaux O.P., *Les 'Petites Grottes' de Qumrân: Exploration de la falaise, Les grottes 2Q, 3Q, 5Q, 6Q, 7Q à 10Q, Le rouleau de cuivre* (DJD III), Oxford: Clarendon Press, 1962, esp. pp. 128-31 and p. 181.

[7] *Qumran Cave 4. XIII: The Damascus Document (4Q266-273)* (DJD XVIII), Oxford: Clarendon Press, 1996.

and conference proceedings.⁸ Furthermore, Baumgarten had published a fairly comprehensive preliminary description of the contents of each of these eight MSS as well as a description of the contents of the Damascus Document as a whole taking into account both the mediaeval MSS and 4QD.⁹ These preliminary descriptions of the contents of D are now supplemented by the outline provided in the official edition of 4QD.¹⁰

A considerable proportion of 4QD is paralleled by the text of CD with minor variations. E. Qimron's edition of the text of CD includes restorations that are derived from parallels in 4QD as well as details of some variant readings in 4QD in the footnotes.¹¹

The legal part of the Damascus Document has been undeservedly neglected in Qumran studies to date. As we saw until very recently only the mediaeval text and the small amount of fragments from Qumran Caves 5 and 6 had been published. What is more, of the available material scholars tended to devote their attention chiefly to the Admonition. With the publication of the Cave 4 fragments of the document which contain a considerable number of further laws it has become clear that the work as a whole is primarily a legal work.¹²

1.2 THE DAMASCUS DOCUMENT AND THE ORIGINS AND HISTORY OF THE QUMRAN COMMUNITY

Ever since the discovery of fragments of the Damascus Document at Qumran this work has played a key role in attempts to reconstruct the origins and history of the Qumran community. Such vigorous attention to CD was sparked off by the presence of a number of pas-

---

⁸ Cf. J.M. Baumgarten, 'The 4Q Zadokite Fragments on Skin Disease', *JJS* 41 (1990) 153-65; *idem*, 'The Disqualifications of Priests in 4Q Fragments of the "Damascus Document", a Specimen of the Recovery of pre-Rabbinic Halakha' in *The Madrid Qumran Congress. Proceedings of the International Congress on the Dead Sea Scrolls Madrid 18 -21 March 1991* eds. J. Trebolle Barrera and L. Vegas Montaner, Leiden: E.J. Brill, 1992, II, pp. 503-13; *idem*, 'A "Scriptural" Citation in 4Q Fragments of the Damascus Document', *JJS* 43 (1992) 95-98; *idem*, 'The Cave 4 Versions of the Qumran Penal Code', *JJS* 43 (1992) 268-76.

⁹ See 'The Laws of the Damascus Document in Current Research', in *The Damascus Document Reconsidered* ed. M. Broshi, Jerusalem: Israel Exploration Society, 1992, pp. 51-62 and *The Dead Sea Scrolls. Hebrew, Aramaic, and Greek Texts with English Translations* ed. J.H. Charlesworth, Tübingen: J.C.B. Mohr (Paul Siebeck)/ Louisville: John Knox Press, 1995, II, pp. 59-75.

¹⁰ *Qumran Cave 4. XIII*, pp. 3-5.

¹¹ E. Qimron, 'The Text of CDC' in *The Damascus Document Reconsidered* ed. M. Broshi, Jerusalem: Israel Exploration Society, 1992, pp. 9-49.

¹² Cf. Baumgarten, 'Laws of the *Damascus Document* in Current Research', p. 55.

sages in the Admonition that seem to describe the origin and early history of the community behind the document. The Laws, by contrast, played only a minor role in this debate. P.R. Davies' study of the Admonition constitutes a recent contribution along these lines.[13] There is no need to repeat here the results of years of investigation into the Admonition. A comprehensive review of scholarship can be found in the introduction to Davies' study.[14] Rather I would like to focus on a recent hypothesis on Qumran origins and early history and its methodological application to this study of the legal part of the Damascus Document, i.e. the Groningen Hypothesis. This hypothesis goes back to F. García Martínez and was recently reiterated in collaboration with A. S. van der Woude.[15] I will restrict myself to a discussion of those elements of the hypothesis that are relevant in the present context.

García Martínez emphasizes that the origins of the Essene movement and the origins of the Qumran community were two distinct developments. According to García Martínez the Essene movement emerged in the Palestinian apocalyptic tradition prior to the Antiochene crisis. The Qumran community, on the other hand, emerged after a split within the Essene movement and resulted in the withdrawal of a group loyal to the Teacher of Righteousness to Qumran. Furthermore, García Martínez highlights the importance of the 'formative period' in which the differences between the Teacher of Righteousness and the Essene movement at large developed. These differences were mainly of a halakhic nature and based on the Teacher's unique self-consciousness of having received the only true interpretation of the law.

Of particular concern for the present study are the corollaries of the Groningen Hypothesis for our perception of the nature of the Qumran library. García Martínez urges us to distinguish within the non-biblical literature found at Qumran between works that reflect the Qumran sect and those that go back to the Essene parent movement of that community.[16] What is more, he emphasizes the composite character of major non-biblical writings from Qumran—a re-

---

[13] *Damascus Covenant*.

[14] *Damascus Covenant*, pp. 1-47. See also J.G. Campbell's recent study of the Admonition *The Use of Scripture in the Damascus Document 1-8, 19-20*, Berlin: De Gruyter, 1995.

[15] F. García Martínez, 'Qumran Origins and Early History: A Groningen Hypothesis', *Folia Orientalia* 25 (1988) 113-36; F. García Martínez and A.S. van der Woude, 'A "Groningen" Hypothesis of Qumran Origins and Early History', *RQ* 56 (1990) 521-41.

[16] 'Qumran Origins and Early History', p. 116.

alization which constitutes an important methodological achievement in recent Qumran studies.[17] As García Martínez has argued, we need to be aware that the different strata of composite works may go back to different communities or stages in the life of one and the same community.

Although I think that the methodological observations of García-Martínez in the 'Groningen Hypothesis' and subsequent publications are very helpful, I have a number of reservations about some aspects of this hypothesis.

a. The literature of the formative period

It seems doubtful to me whether it is practically possible to distinguish between works or parts of composite works from the 'formative period' and works reflecting Essene thought. What is more, in practice I would be inclined to associate works like the Temple Scroll (11QT) and *Miqsat Ma'aseh ha-Torah* (4QMMT), Jubilees, and the bulk of the Laws of the Damascus Document with the pre-Qumranic Essene movement rather than the 'formative period' of the Qumran community as suggested by García Martínez. In a more recent publication García Martínez comments again on the 'formative period' and notes that the Qumran library contains,

> works from the formative period, which present a vision not yet clearly distinct from the Essenism from which they derive.[18]

It seems to me that this description of the literature that emerged from the formative period makes any attempt at distinguishing such literature impossible.

b. The evidence of the classical sources

I am not convinced that it is correct to claim, as does García Martínez, that the classical sources (i.e. chiefly Josephus, Philo, and Pliny the Elder) describe exclusively the Essene movement.[19] By con-

---

[17] To be sure, the fact that major non-biblical writings from Qumran are composite works is reflected in a number of important studies which predate García Martínez' 'Groningen Hypothesis'. I am focusing on his methodological considerations because he succinctly outlines in theory those important methodological advances in Qumran research which are also reflected in the work of J. Muphy-O'Connor and P.R. Davies to name but two, cf. nn. 29-31 below.

[18] F. García Martínez and J. Trebolle Barrera, *The People of the Dead Sea Scrolls. Their Writings, Beliefs and Practices*, Leiden: E.J. Brill, 1995, p. 85.

[19] Cf. 'Qumran Origins and Early History', pp. 116, 118, and esp. the following remarks on p. 126, "Unfortunately the available historical sources from outside Qumran itself totally ignore the activities of this tiny group of desert exiles, so that our knowledge of the history of the community depends entirely on such information as we can extract from the Qumran MSS themselves." See also G. Stemberger,

trast, it seems to me that they include in their description aspects of the life of the wider Essene movement as well as of the Qumran community without distinguishing the two. Thus, Josephus' description of the entry into the community, for example, corresponds more closely to 1QS than to the Laws of D and probably describes the community reflected in one of the later stages of the composition of 1QS. What is more, Pliny the Elder refers to the Qumran site near the Dead Sea in his Natural History 5.17,4(73).[20] It seems doubtful, therefore, that he was referring to the wider Essene movement.

The now challenged consensus view which identified the Qumran community with the Essenes and distinguished between a stricter, celibate type of Essenes that occupied Qumran and a different type of Essenes found in the towns and villages of Palestine produced a picture of the Essenes that corresponded, on the whole, fairly well to the information from the classical sources. Since this consensus view is being increasingly challenged in recent years, it seems to me that the statements about the Essenes in the classical sources will need to be re-evaluated in the light of new hypotheses. It needs to be borne in mind, however, that the reason why the consensus view tallied so well with the evidence from the classical sources is precisely because it was largely based on the information from the classical authors. This procedure failed to take the primary sources as a starting point, and used the evidence of the scrolls only after a framework for interpretation was built on the basis of the classical sources. Such a procedure is methodologically questionable, and it is preferable to evaluate each body of evidence independently before arriving at a synthesis.[21] For the purposes of this study I would like to focus on the internal evidence from the Qumran writings themselves in order to shed light on the relationship between the Qumran community and its parent movement. Once the study of the Dead Sea Scrolls,

---

Jewish Contemporaries of Jesus: Pharisees, Sadducees, Essenes, Minneapolis: Fortress, 1995, p. 132 who argues along similar lines, "In his description of the Essenes, Josephus has [in mind?] the members who were dispersed throughout the country and not those who were living in Qumran."

[20] Cf. G. Vermes and M.D. Goodman, *The Essenes. According to the Classical Sources*, Sheffield: JSOT Press, 1989, p. 33.

[21] For a detailed comparative examination of the evidence of Josephus and the DSS see T.S. Beall, *Josephus' Description of the Essenes Illustrated by the Dead Sea Scrolls*, Cambridge: CUP, 1988. See also R. Bergmeier, *Die Essenerberichte des Flavius Josephus. Quellenstudien zu den Essenertexten im Werk des Jüdischen Historiographen*, Kampen: Kok Pharos, 1993 and Tessa Rajak, 'Ciò Che Flavio Guiseppe Vide: Josephus and the Essenes' in *Josephus and the History of the Greco-Roman Period. Essays in Memory of Morton Smith* ed. F. Parente and J. Sievers, Leiden: E.J. Brill, 1994, pp. 141-60.

with the help of a more sophisticated methodology as well as the publication of new texts, has produced its first substantial results, the evidence from the classical sources will need to be examined anew in the light of these results.

c. The issue of the calendar

Since the publication of the Groningen Hypothesis García Martínez has suggested that the issue of the calendar, i.e. the promotion of a 364 solar calendar, was one of the reasons for the Qumran community's split from the Essene parent movement.[22] By contrast, it seems to me that the promotion of the solar calendar is one of the beliefs held in common by the parent movement and the off-shoot community since it is reflected in works such as Jubilees that clearly do not go back to the off-shoot community.[23]

Recent years have seen a renewed debate on the overall Essene provenance of the Qumran library. This debate is based on and largely inspired by the recently published 4QMMT (*Miqsat Ma'aseh ha-Torah*).[24] This document has led L.H. Schiffman to propose a Saducean background to the Qumran library.[25] In the light of this recent challenge to the Essene provenance of the scrolls a number of scholars have responded by restating the case for an Essene background to the scrolls.[26] In view of the impressive parallels between the Qumran scrolls and the information of the classical writers on the Essenes—which need not be repeated here—I am inclined to favour the Essene hypothesis.

Both associations—be it Essene or Saducean—rely, however, on external evidence. The Essene hypothesis is based on the evidence of the classical sources whereas the Saducean hypothesis draws on the views attributed to the Sadducees in rabbinic literature.[27] In this

---

[22] *People of the Dead Sea Scrolls*, p. 93.
[23] See M.A. Knibb, 'Jubilees and the Origins of the Qumran Community' (An Inaugural Lecture), London: King's College, 1989, esp. pp. 13-14.
[24] E. Qimron and J. Strugnell, *Qumran Cave 4. V. MIQSAT MA'ASE HATORAH* (DJD X), Oxford: Clarendon Press, 1994.
[25] Cf. L.H. Schiffman, '4QMMT—Basic Sectarian Text' in *Qumran Cave Four. Special Report* ed. Z. J. Kapera, Krakow: Enigma Press, 1991, pp. 81-83.
[26] J.M. Baumgarten, 'Disqualifications of Priests', esp. pp. 504-505; O. Betz and R. Riesner, *Jesus, Qumran and the Vatican. Clarifications*, London: SCM, 1994, esp. pp. 36-49; H. Stegemann, 'The Qumran Essenes—Local Members of the Main Jewish Union in Late Second Temple Times', *Madrid Qumran Congress*, I, pp. 83-166. Stegemann provides an extremely thorough re-examination and re-affirmation of the Essene hypothesis. Furthermore, he includes a discussion of a number of challenges to the Essene hypothesis that have been put forward in recent years.
[27] Cf. S. Talmon, 'Qumran Studies: Past, Present, and Future', *JQR* 85 (1994) 1-31, esp. pp. 30-31 for a similar position. Such an approach is also epitomised in the

study I will focus exclusively on the internal evidence of the scrolls themselves. Cross references to external evidence and 'cross thinking' of this kind are important although it seems preferable and methodologically more reliable first to analyse each corpus of literature in their own right. Beyond having clarified my own position in this debate it need not, therefore, detain us since my arguments are independent of any particular view of the scrolls' relationship to other bodies of literature.[28]

1.3 Source Criticism and the Damascus Document

1.3.1 *The Admonition*

A number of scholars have devoted their attention to the literary critical study of the Damascus Document. J. Murphy-O'Connor offered a literary critical analysis of the Admonition in a series of articles that appeared between 1970 and 1972[29] and returned to the document again in 1985 to review some of his earlier conclusions.[30] P.R. Davies' study of the Damascus Document offers a detailed literary critical analysis of the Admonition.[31] Finally, most recently M. Boyce has taken up again the literary critical study of the Admonition in an as yet unpublished dissertation.[32] The occasional reference to the Laws aside each of these three scholars focused exclusively on the Admonition.

1.3.2 *The Laws*

In contrast to the Admonition much less detailed attention has been devoted to the literary critical study of the Laws. This is surprising since several scholars have put forward the view that the Laws are a

---

title of Talmon's collected essays *The World of Qumran From Within. Collected Studies*, Jerusalem: Magnes Press, 1989.

[28] M.D. Goodman's reminder that our knowledge of the spectrum of groupings in the Second Temple period is scarce and that we should allow for the possibility that the scrolls emanate from a hitherto unknown group is, however, well taken, and the possibility he raises is a real one, cf. 'A Note on the Qumran Sectarians, the Essenes and Josephus', *JJS* 46 (1995) 161-66.

[29] 'An Essene Missionary Document? CD II,14-VI,1', *RB* 77 (1970) 201-29; 'A Literary Analysis of Damascus Document VI,2-VIII,3', *RB* 78 (1971) 210-32; 'The Original Text of CD 7:9-8:2 = 19:5-14', *HTR* 64 (1971) 379-86; 'The Critique of the Princes of Judah (CD VIII,3-19)', *RB* 79 (1972) 200-16; 'A Literary Analysis of Damascus Document XIX,33-XX,34', *RB* 79 (1972) 544-64.

[30] 'The Damascus Document Revisited', *RB* 92 (1985) 223-246.

[31] *Damascus Covenant*.

[32] *The Poetry of the Damascus Document*, Edinburgh: Dissertation, 1988.

composite work. Thus already in 1910 Schechter observed the lack of congruity in the Laws when he spoke of,

> the impression that we are dealing with extracts from a larger work, put together, however, in a haphazard way, with little regard to completeness or order. This is particularly discernible in the legal part.[33]

It seems unlikely that Schechter's impression was entirely due to the original position assigned to CD 15-16 which are now placed differently.[34] More recently, Baumgarten and Schiffman have expressed the view that the Laws are composite without, however, going into any detail.[35]

An important exception constitutes an article by A. Rubinstein entitled 'Urban Halakhah and Camp Rules in the "Cairo Fragments of a Damascene Covenant"' in which he examines the composite nature of the Laws of the Damascus Document.[36] The importance of Rubinstein's work lies in his recognition of the composite nature of the Laws as well as providing a first analysis of the diverse components of this collection. Rubinstein begins his study by dividing the Laws of CD into 'Camp Rules' and 'Halakhah Proper', and he in turn subdivides the latter material into 'urban halakhah' and 'general halakhah'. In effect most of his discussion focuses, however, on the distinction between 'urban halakhah' and 'camp rules', a fact that is already reflected in the title of the article. The part of the CD Laws that Rubinstein assigns to the sub-section 'general halakhah' seems to consist of CD 16,6-15.[37] Rubinstein had great difficulty attributing this material to any of his strata since he wrote his study prior to Milik's announcement that inaugurated a reversal of the order of pages 15 and 16 which should precede page 9 in the Laws of CD.[38]

Rubinstein, therefore, assigns the following material to the diverse components of the Laws distinguished by him.

a. CD 9,1-10,10

This block of material poses a number of problems for Rubinstein. He points out that this material is out of place in its present context.

---

[33] Fragments of a Zadokite Work, p. x.
[34] Cf. the announcement by J.T. Milik in *Ten Years of Discovery in the Wilderness of Judaea*, London: SCM, 1959, pp. 151-52. A placement of pages CD 15-16 immediately preceding CD 9 is clearly indicated by 4QD^a 8 i-ii and 4QD^e 6 i- iii.
[35] Cf. J.M. Baumgarten, 'Laws of the *Damascus Document* in Current Research', p. 57 and L.H. Schiffman, *Sectarian Law in the Dead Sea Scrolls. Courts, Testimony and the Penal Code*, Chico: Scholars Press, 1983, p. 9.
[36] *Sefarad* 12 (1952) 283-96.
[37] Cf. 'Urban Halakhah', p. 289.
[38] See note 34 above.

In his discussion of this section Rubinstein very acutely feels the problems posed by Schechter's original ordering of the sheets of CD 9-16. One gains the impression that Rubinstein is on the verge of foreseeing the reversal of the order of the pages that was later suggested by Milik on the basis of 4QD.

b. CD 10,10-12,18 Urban Halakhah
Rubinstein identifies this section as 'urban halakhah' and emphasizes the frequent occurrence of so-called 'urbanisms' such as עיר (city) and בית (house) in this material.

c. CD 12,19-23 Epitome
Rubinstein believes there are two possible explanations for the provenance of this epitome.
    i. The epitome was originally a part of the urban halakhah and served to conclude it.
    ii. The epitome goes back to a later editor and was "occasioned by the conflation of what may be termed the 'camp source' and the 'urban source'...."[39]

d. CD 13,1-16,5 Camp Rules
According to Rubinstein this section consists of camp rules which show a number of affinities with the Community Rule (1QS).

e. CD 16,6-15 General Halakhah
This final part of the CD Laws is a later addition of general halakhah that shows affinities to CD 9,1-10,10 and is out of place in its present context.

Having thus outlined the diverse components in the CD Laws Rubinstein proceeds by spelling out the implications of his hypothesis on the literary development of CD as a whole. He envisages this development in three stages.

a. CD 1-8 The Admonition
Rubinstein argues that with the exception of CD 7,6-8 the Admonition is the earliest part of CD. According to Rubinstein it is the function of the Admonition to explain the reasons for the breakaway of the Jewish sect behind the document from Judaea to Damascus in Syria.

---

[39] 'Urban Halakhah', p. 289.

b. CD 7,6-8 and the Camp Rules
The short note on the life in camps (CD 7,6-8) as well as the camp rules (CD 13,1-16,5) were added to the Admonition and constitute the second layer in the growth of the document.

c. CD 10,10-12,18 Urban Halakhah
The urban section was the last addition to CD. Concerning the chronological relationship between 'camps' and 'cities' Rubinstein suggests two possibilities. Either earlier camp settlements were replaced by cities or camps never actually existed and "their inclusion in the document was of the nature of an act of homage to tradition."[40]

Rubinstein's literary critical approach to the CD Laws constitutes a significant and to a degree isolated endeavour for its time. His results have been generally accepted by Boyce[41] and others[42]. Many of Rubinstein's results differ from the ones reached in my own analysis of this material. Some of our divergences are due to the fact that Rubinstein had completed his work prior to Milik's announcement of the reversed order of pages, i.e. that CD 15 and 16 should precede CD 9. However, a more fundamental difference between Rubinstein's approach and the one that will be followed in my own analysis concerns questions of method, especially the choice of criteria for distinguishing the diverse components of the Laws. The most important distinction emphasized by Rubinstein is the distinction between the so-called urban halakhah and the camp rules. In particular, Rubinstein's identification of 'urbanisms' such as 'town' (עיר) and 'house' (בית) as pointers to an urban background and, more importantly, as a criterion for literary critical judgments does not withstand close scrutiny.[43] Rubinstein himself is rather careful when he evaluates the significance of these urbanisms.[44] In practice, however, the distinction between urban halakhah and camp rules is central to his case. It needs to be borne in mind that the use of עיר and בית in Rubinstein's urban halakhah section is frequently derived from scripture.

---

[40] 'Urban Halakhah', p. 293.
[41] *Poetry of the Damascus Document*, pp. 339-40.
[42] Cf., for example, M. Wise, M. Abegg Jr., and E. Cook, *The Dead Sea Scrolls. A New Translation*, London: Harper Collins, 1996, p. 50 where Cook advocates the major division 'camp rules' and 'city rules' for the Laws of CD in the introduction to his translation of the Damascus Document.
[43] 'Urban Halakhah', pp. 288-89.
[44] Cf. 'Urban Halakhah', pp. 288-89.

CHAPTER ONE

Cf. Jer. 17,22 and CD 11,7b-8a (Sabbath Code)

ולא־חוציאו משא מבתיכם ביום השבת   אל יוציא איש מן הבית לחוץ ומן החוץ אל בית

And do not carry a burden out of your houses on the sabbath.[45] No one shall bring anything out of the house or into the house.

Furthermore, Num. 35,2-5 prescribes the boundaries for the levitical cities, and this passage forms the background to CD 10,21.[46] In particular the urban terminology of CD 10,21 seems to be derived from Num. 35. One suspects that Rubinstein was inspired to isolate a portion of urban halakhah by the presence of the epitome in CD 12,19-23.[47] My own approach to the various headings and concluding statements in the Laws of D is, as will be seen, rather cautious. It is often difficult to relate some of the rubrics in the Laws to the material they serve to introduce or conclude. The procedure in my own analysis, therefore, always avoided reading a block of material in the light of its heading or concluding statement. Rather, I tried to examine the material in its own right before turning to the framework.

A few years later T.H. Gaster's translation of the scrolls divided the Laws of the Damascus Document into three main sections without, however, stating his criteria for such a division:

CD 9,1-12,22	Code for Urban Communities
CD 12,22-14,2	Code for Camp Communities
CD 14,3-16,20	A Supplementary Code.[48]

Like Rubinstein's analysis Gaster's division also goes back to the time prior to Milik's announcement of the reversed order of pages 15-16.

Finally, in the late 1980ies and early 1990ies Pat Tiller and Robert Davis worked on the Laws of the Damascus Document at Harvard under the supervision of John Strugnell. Both produced valuable studies that are unpublished which came to my attention when my own work was nearing completion.

Tiller[49] divides the Laws into four main parts:

---

[45] This translation is taken from the NRSV.

[46] Cf. L.H. Schiffman, *The Halakhah at Qumran*, Leiden: E.J. Brill, 1975, p. 91.

[47] Admittedly Rubinstein does allow for the possibility that the epitome has been added at a later stage, cf. 'Urban Halakhah', p. 289. Nevertheless, his conclusions appear to be influenced by the presentation of CD 10,10-12,18 as 'urban rules' according to CD 12,19-23.

[48] T.H. Gaster, *The Scriptures of the Dead Sea Sect in English Translation*, London: Secker & Warburg, 1957, esp. pp. 83-94.

[49] 'The Laws of the Damascus Document and Qumran', *HNTSP* 1987.

a. Legal Code (4Q material preceding the CD Laws, CD 15-12,22)
b. Community Rules (CD 12,22-14,19)
c. The Penal Code (CD 14,20-22; 4QD)
d. Liturgy for the Feast of the Renewal of the Covenant (4QD)

Tiller relies heavily on the blocks of material in their final form and appears reluctant to break up the apparent structure of the material. As will become clear in the course of this study, one of the areas where my results differ most from earlier commentators is my lack of confidence in the present rather superficial structure of the Laws. Once we look closely at some of the rubrics it becomes clear that the Laws are much less clearly presented than at first appears and that many rubrics provide no more than a superficial sense of coherence for the material. Tiller is aware, however, that the material in CD 15,5-16,6 (admission by swearing the oath of the covenant) and CD 10,4-10 (the judges of the congregation) which he includes in the legal code in his outline is at odds with the bulk of the material found in the legal code, a recognition borne out by my own analysis. Finally, I see no need for distinguishing the penal code from the rest of the communal legislation as Tiller does.

Davis' contribution to the field is a dissertation entitled *The History of the Composition of the Damascus Document Statutes (CD 9-16 + 4QD)*[50] where he distinguishes four stages in the compositional history of the Laws:

a. a pre-Qumranic legal code (4QD^a skin disease material; 6Q15; CD 15,1-5; 16,6-9.10; 9, 10-16; 10,10-12,20)
b.-c. sectarian rules that apply to communities outside of Qumran (CD 10,4-10; 12,22-13,7; 14,3-10.12-15 and the end of D as attested in 4QD^a)
d. a Qumranic redaction (CD 15,5-16,6; 9,16-10,3; 12,20-22; 13,5-20; 13,22-14,2; and 14,10-12).

In broad terms Davis' conclusions are similar to a number of conclusions reached in the course of my own analysis. Thus, it emerges very clearly both from Davis' dissertation and from my analysis of the Laws that they reflect very complex literary developments. It is not surprising in the face of the complexity of the evidence that our conclusions differ in many questions of detail and in our judgment on a number of specific passages. Finally, I was able to include more comprehensively the evidence of 4QD which was still unpublished when Davis produced his dissertation. Davis' work includes much

---

[50] Harvard: Dissertation, 1992.

helpful and perceptive discussion of the evidence and deserves to be read more widely.[51]

1.4 The Present Study

The aim of this study is to provide a first detailed analysis of the Laws of the Damascus Document as attested both in one of the mediaeval MSS as well as the eight ancient MSS of the document from Qumran Cave 4.

As emerged from the outline of scholarship above it is becoming increasingly clear that the Laws are a composite collection. What follows is an analysis of the Laws that argues for the distinction of various strata as well as identifying a considerable amount of redactional activity. This redactional activity is particularly extensive in the material that I have assigned to the communal legislation almost to the exclusion of other sections that comprise legal material of a much more general application.

---

[51] Further outlines of the contents of the Laws of D are found in J.A. Fitzmyer, *The Dead Sea Scrolls. Major Publications and Tools for Study*, Atlanta: Scholars Press, 1990, pp. 132-33 where the whole of the Laws are presented as dealing with a particular community; and J. Trebolle Barrera in F. García Martínez and J. Trebolle Barrera, *People of the Dead Sea Scrolls*, p. 52.

CHAPTER TWO

IDENTIFYING SOURCES AND REDACTIONAL ACTIVITY
IN THE LAWS OF THE DAMASCUS DOCUMENT

In what follows I shall present a source critical analysis of the Laws of the Damascus Document as they have come down to us in the mediaeval Cairo text as well as in the ancient Qumran MSS. As emerged from the outline of scholarship on the Damascus Document in the Introduction a detailed study of the Laws of D along these lines is greatly overdue in Qumran studies.

In order to distinguish various literary strata I have applied four criteria: frame of reference, vocabulary, form, and polemical/ideological stance. Based on the different characteristics of each group of texts certain criteria can be more fruitfully applied to one group of texts than others. Even though a particular criterion might yield more positive results when applied to some texts in contrast to others, each criterion nevertheless contributes something to the process of distinguishing literary strata. Thus, for example, the stratum entitled halakhah displays a large degree of formal coherence whereas a great proportion of the Laws does not. Although a formal analysis yields more numerous results in the case of texts that belong to the halakhah category, the lack of formal coherence of much of the body of communal rules confirms the distinct nature of both groups of texts.

2.1 Frame of Reference

The various parts of the collection of Laws in D can be clearly distinguished in terms of their frame of reference. Whereas a considerable amount of rules deals with matters of communal organization substantial parts of the Laws are more general in character. I have grouped sections together that belong to the former category as communal organization or communal legislation. The material assigned to this literary stratum contains regulations on the organization of a particular community. Furthermore, the organizational structure reflected in this stratum shows important differences from the organizational structure reflected in the Community Rule (1QS and 4QS), and I will note a number of particular examples in the course of my discussion of the 'communal organization' material in the Laws of D.

The second major block of material in the Laws of D, by contrast, contains halakhic exposition that is not associated with a particular community. Rather, one gains the impression that this material is intended—at least in theory—to be of general application. I have gathered the material assigned to this category under the heading halakhah.

2.2 Vocabulary

The distinction between different groups of texts on the basis of vocabulary provides a further criterion. The terms of reference used in each literary stratum of the Laws are often quite distinct. It is instructive to pay particular attention to the terms used in different parts of the Laws to refer to the group addressed or depicted in the texts. For example, the absence of key terms used to designate the community in some parts of the Laws from other sections constitutes an important distinguishing mark.

It is often the case that the distinctive terminology that prevails in parts of the Laws is inseparably linked to other criteria. For example, the criterion of polemical/ideological stance may in practice be closely linked to the criterion of vocabulary. Thus, a passage that is very polemical is often—though not always—couched in terms that are similar to other polemical passages in the same document.

2.3 Form

A third criterion that aids the classification of the divergent elements of the Laws of D is a discussion of their formal structure. I began by firstly examining which parts of the Laws show a considerably degree of formal cohesion and to distinguish them from those that do not. Furthermore, once a formal pattern has been recognized it is possible to group together a number of texts into one stratum on the basis of their form. The formal criterion proved especially instructive in the case of the halakhah.

An important formal feature in the Laws of the Damascus Document are the numerous headings and concluding statements found in that collection. From my analysis of the Laws it emerges that the headings and concluding statements fall into two main categories.

A. *Headings and concluding statements which have been skilfully connected to the surrounding material*
In this category I would include, for example, all the headings of the form 'על plus x', cf. CD 16,10a.13a (par. 4QD^f 4 ii 12-13); 9,8b;

10,10b (par. 4QD⁽ᶜ⁾ 6 iv 20) and 10,14a. Baumgarten plausibly suggests a further possible heading of this type in 4Q D⁽ᵃ⁾ 6 iii 3-4[1], and I would like to suggest 4QD⁽ᵉ⁾ 2 ii 1 as a further possible instance of such a heading occurring in 4QD.[2] Whether or not this first category of headings and concluding statements goes back to a skilful compiler, or whether they were formulated at the same time as the material they announce is a moot point. What is important for the present argument is that these rubrics are integrated into their present context, and that they can be clearly distinguished from a second category of rubrics.

B. *Headings and concluding statements that are more loosely related to the surrounding material*

The identification of headings and concluding statements that belong to this category forms an important part of my source critical examination of the Laws, particularly the identification of redactional material that links the divergent components of the Laws. This redactional material serves not only to present the various parts of the Laws as part of an apparently coherent whole but also frequently provides connections between the Admonition and the Laws. This redactor was at work at a late stage in the growth of the Damascus Document as a whole and because s/he strived to present the whole of the Damascus Document as a unified composition I have chosen the term 'Damascus redactor' and 'Damascus redaction' as a shorthand.

In order to identify such a piece of redactional material I have used a number of criteria, e.g. terminology, ideological stance, attitude towards Israel at large. A further important consideration is the relationship of the rubric to the material that follows or precedes. Does the rubric's announcement correspond to the material that follows? Does the concluding statement constitute a reasonable conclusion to what precedes? These are the kinds of questions I have been

---

[1] Baumgarten, *Qumran Cave 4. XIII*, p. 58. There Baumgarten notes in his comments to lines 4-5, "The possible restoration of הלקט at the beginning of line 4 would yield the rubric [הלקט] ועללות הכרם [על]." The way in which Baumgarten quotes the preposition here in the comments as partially preserved at the beginning of line 4 is not quite in accord with his transcription where the preposition appears as the last word of the previous line that has, however, been deleted by means of drawing a line through it, cf. Plate VIII. Thus, we may have to restore the preposition entirely at the beginning of line 4 and perhaps assume that the scribe first started the new rubric at the end of line 3 and then moved to the beginning of line 4.

[2] Cf. Baumgarten, *Qumran Cave 4. XIII*, p. 144 where Baumgarten reads the beginning of line 1 קד[ ]על. The material that follows, especially lines 5-9, deals with priestly shares. It seems at least conceivable that line 1 preserves the remains of the rubric על קד[ושׁים] introducing this material.

asking. The exegesis of each passage will ultimately decide to which category a heading belongs.

I have come to view the Laws of D as made up of a variety of sources and hope to show that their divergent components have been linked by the work of a redactor. This redactional material is intended to convey the impression that the Damascus Document forms a coherent whole. A detailed reading of the Laws reveals, however, that an initial impression of the Laws as an organized and structured composition is rather superficial and does not stand up to closer scrutiny. It is argued in the present study that this Damascus redaction has been superimposed—often rather clumsily—at a late stage onto a diverse and heterogeneous collection.

2.4 Polemical/Ideological Stance

Finally, a small number of texts can be isolated from the remainder of the Laws because of a particular polemical or ideological stance reflected in them. It is true, as has been pointed out by several scholars, that the Laws of the Damascus Document lack, on the whole, the polemical attitude towards outsiders that dominates the Admonition of the same document.[3] Yet, I will argue, there are passages in the Laws that stand out from the remainder of the collection because of their polemical tone. It seems to me that these exceptional passages in the Laws can be isolated—often as interpolations—and that their presence in the collection of Laws is often overlooked. Thus, although it is right to emphasize the unpolemical, matter of fact style of the bulk of the Laws, the presence of passages that are distinctly polemical needs to be noted as well.

In a recent methodological study Carol Newsom discusses the problem of arriving at an adequate definition of what constitutes a 'sectarian text' in the library of Qumran.[4] The first two definitions dis-

---

[3] On the unpolemical tone of the Laws over against the Admonition, cf. Schechter, Fragments of a Zadokite Work, p. 18 who points out that the Damascus Document "...in its Hagada, is largely polemical, whilst its Halacha affords little else than mere statements."; and J.M. Baumgarten, 'The Laws of the Damascus Document in Current Research', pp. 55-56 who points out on p. 56 that "...the bulk of the CD laws, including the largest topical collection on the Sabbath, is not formulated in polemical fashion.'; see also most recently M.A. Knibb, 'The Place of the Damascus Document', in Methods of Investigation of the Dead Sea Scrolls and the Khirbet Qumran Site. Present Realities and Future Prospects ed. M.O. Wise et al., New York: New York Academy of Sciences, 1994, pp. 149-62, esp. p. 153.

[4] Carol A. Newsom, '"Sectually Explicit" Literature from Qumran', in The Hebrew Bible and Its Interpreters ed. W.H. Propp, B. Halpern and D.N. Freedman, Winona Lake: Eisenbrauns, 1990, pp. 167-87. See also Esther G. Chazon, 'Is Divreh Ha-Me'orot a Sectarian Prayer?', in The Dead Sea Scrolls. Forty Years of Research ed.

cussed by Newsom are 'Use and Readership of Texts' and 'Authorship of Texts'. Newsom argues that although both of these questions are important and should be considered when dealing with texts from Qumran, the Qumran material provides few answers to such questions, and both of these definitions are, therefore, of limited value.

The third definition examined by Newsom is what she calls 'Rhetorical Function of Texts'. Much of Newsom's third definition corresponds to my fourth criterion of polemical/ideological stance. Newsom argues that only texts that can be seen to share a rhetorical function as outlined by her should be called sectarian. On this basis Newsom defines sectarian texts as follows,

> A sectarian text would be one that calls upon its readers to understand themselves as set apart within the larger religious community of Israel and as preserving the true values of Israel against the failures of the larger community. A text may do this in a variety of ways. There may be overtly polemical rhetoric of an "us vs. them" sort. Or there may be references to the community's history, or teaching about the institutional structure of the community.[5]

I agree widely with Newsom's definition of sectarian texts. However, I would like to emphasize the importance of a further methodological dimension that needs to be introduced into this debate. This additional dimension is the composite nature of many key documents from Qumran. It seems to me a dangerous undertaking to make categorical statements about whole documents, such as 'The Damascus Document is a sectarian work'. The view that the Damascus Document is a sectarian work is held by the great majority of scholars among them Newsom herself.[6]

Apart from disagreeing with Newsom's overall judgment of the Damascus Document as a sectarian work, one aspect of her definition of sectarian texts seems questionable to me. Although I subscribe to the first part of her definition cited above, the last example given there of the way in which a text may express its rhetorical function is more problematic.

As far as the Laws of the Damascus Document are concerned it is firstly important to examine this collection in its own right rather

---

Devorah Dimant and U. Rappaport, Leiden: E.J. Brill, 1992, pp. 3-17 and *eadem*, 'Prayers from Qumran and Their Historical Implications', *DSD* 1 (1994) 265-84, esp. pp. 271-72.

[5] '"Sectually Explicit" Literature', pp. 178-79.

[6] '"Sectually Explicit" Literature', p. 169; see also the contribution by Devorah Dimant, 'Qumran Sectarian Literature', in *Jewish Writings of the Second Temple Period. Apocrypha, Pseudepigrapha, Qumran Sectarian Writings, Philo, Josephus* ed. M.E. Stone, Philadelphia: Fortress Press / Assen: Van Gorcum, 1984, pp. 483-550.

than from an angle that focuses on the Admonition. Often one's view of the Laws is overshadowed by a strong impression of the polemical and sectarian character of the Admonition. It is almost certainly the purpose of the Admonition to create such a state of affairs and to guide the readers as to the way in which one should read these Laws. Once one studies the Laws in their own right it quickly becomes apparent that they differ considerably from the Admonition in terms of their 'rhetorical function'. Or, in my own words, they largely lack the polemical stance reflected in the Admonition. It seems to me, therefore, that the Laws are, on the whole, not a sectarian composition. It is questionable, furthermore, whether 'teaching about the institutional structure of the community'[7] is necessarily always a form of *sectarian* self expression. In the Laws of D, for example, a considerable part of the regulations on the organizational structure of the community are formulated in an unpolemical and unrhetorical style.

In sum, I would like to qualify Newsom's definition of sectarian texts by stressing the composite nature of many key documents from the Qumran library. Not all the components of works that are sectarian in their final form should be defined as sectarian themselves. Furthermore, only the organizational structure of *sectarian* communities is a form of expressing the sectarian character of that community. Whether or not a piece of communal legislation is sectarian or not will have to be established carefully in each case by examining their attitude to Jewish society outside the community. In other words, on the basis of Newsom's own definition of sectarian texts, teaching about the organizational structure of a community may be sectarian or not depending on the rhetorical function of these texts. On the basis of the four criteria outlined above I distinguish the following literary strata in the Laws of D. A distinction between the first two strata has sometimes been acknowledged[8] but no detailed study has been undertaken to date.

---

[7] '"Sectually Explicit" Literature', p. 179.

[8] L. Ginzberg already remarked concerning the Laws of the Damascus Document, "The section 12,22-16,6 treats of this [communal organization] exclusively; the laws proper are given in 9,1-12,18.", *An Unknown Jewish Sect*, New York City: Jewish Theological Seminary of America, 1976, p. 108 n. 8. Baumgarten describes the Damascus Document in the following terms, "The Admonition which repeatedly calls for adherence to the proper interpretation of the Law, is thus to be viewed as essentially an introduction to *a corpus of Torah interpretation and sectarian rulings* [emphasis mine]...", 'Laws of the *Damascus Document* in Current Research', p. 55. On the same page Baumgarten states that including the Cave 4 additions two thirds of the Damascus Document consist of 'laws and communal rules'. See also Baumgarten's comments in Charlesworth ed., *The Dead Sea Scrolls*, II, p. 53 n. 191.

1. Halakhah
2. Community Organization
3. Miscellaneous Halakhah
4. Miscellaneous Traditions and Redactional Material

A question that needs to be addressed in this context is whether it is possible legitimately to speak of redactional activity having shaped the Laws of the Damascus Document. Since the mediaeval Cairo text of the Laws is considerably shorter than the versions of the Laws known from Qumran, is it possible to think of a fixed text of the Laws of D? I think it is. It seems that where CD and 4QD overlap only relatively minor divergences occur. Thus, although the Laws of CD lack a considerable amount of legal material that is found in 4QD, the text that they do preserve seems to be reasonably close to 4QD where they overlap. Baumgarten recently commented on the relationship of the mediaeval manuscripts to the ancient manuscripts of D as follows,

> However, it is now clear that the Genizah manuscripts "omit" large sections from the beginning and the ending as well as middle portions of the Qumran versions of the *Damascus Document*. This apparent editorial process merits further study.[9]

Much depends on Baumgarten's choice of the term 'omit' which he placed in inverted commas. The following statement makes it clear, however, that he thinks of a deliberate process of redactional activity. Moreover, Baumgarten's edition of the Cave 4 MSS of D frequently employs terms such as 'omit'[10] and 'abbreviate.'[11] Such language is value laden, and purely descriptive formulations such as 'lacks' or 'has a longer/shorter text' would have been more objective.

In contrast to this Schechter already commented on MS A,

> The MS. is possibly defective at the beginning and is certainly so at the end.[12]

Schiffman has noted that "the Laws—the legal section forming the second part of the *Zadokite Fragments*—frequently turns, without even a pause, from mention of laws applicable to all Jews to mention of regulations bearing exclusively on the organization and conduct of sectarian life.", *Reclaiming the Dead Sea Scrolls. The History of Judaism, the Background of Christianity, the Lost Library of Qumran* with a Foreword by Chaim Potok, Philadelphia and Jerusalem: Jewish Publication Society, 1994, p. 273.

[9] Baumgarten in Charlesworth ed., *Dead Sea Scrolls*, II, p. 58. See also the comments by G. Vermes, *The Dead Sea Scrolls. Qumran in Perspective*, Rev. Ed., London 1994, p. 44 where he similarly describes the shorter mediaeval version of the Damascus Document as resulting from a process of omissions.

[10] Cf. *Qumran Cave 4. XIII*, p. 45.
[11] Cf. *Qumran Cave 4. XIII*, p. 75.
[12] Fragments of a Zadokite Work, p. ix.

Most recently Baumgarten himself appears slightly more tentative in his assessment of the relationship between the mediaeval and the ancient copies of the Damascus Document,

> Schechter was right about the lack of completeness and proper order in Text A, but the question whether this was haphazard or perhaps due to some selectivity on the part of the presumably Karaite copyists in omitting portions of their Vorlage will have to be further investigated.[13]

A good starting point seems to me to look at those places in the mediaeval copies of the Damascus Document where the missing material would have been expected to occur. CD 1,1 begins with an indentation. The beginning of a new section at the equivalent to CD 1,1 is clearly marked with a *vacat* in 4QD^a 2 i 6 and 4QD^c 1,8-9. There are, moreover, indentations also at the beginning of pages 3 and 9 of CD. Thus, it is not at all clear to me that CD 1 necessarily constitutes the first page of the mediaeval MS. In other words, it is not immediately obvious that what is now CD 1,1 ever constituted the beginning of the mediaeval MS.

As far as the end of the text in the mediaeval MSS is concerned, CD 14 breaks off abruptly, and the end of the page is damaged. Since CD 14 contains the beginning of the penal code it seems likely that the mediaeval MS A continued beyond CD 14. We, therefore, simply do not know how the mediaeval text ended, and it may well have preserved the end of the document as it has survived in 4QD^a 11 and 4QD^e 7 ii.

Finally, the situation is similarly uncertain as far as the missing portion between the Admonition and the Laws in CD is concerned. The legal part in CD begins with CD 15,1 clearly in the middle of a passage. Thus, it is again clear that the mediaeval text did include material preceding CD 15 that is now lost.

We may also observe that every single one of the eight 4QD MSS contains additional material not in CD, i.e. no ancient copy corresponds to the shorter text of CD. In all, it seems most likely to me that CD's shorter text is due to accidental loss rather than deliberate omission although it is impossible to say so with certainty.

Another point that is worth making here is that in what follows the analysis offered here is more detailed when it comes to the communal legislation than it is for the halakhic parts of the Laws. There are two main reasons for this slight asymmetry of this study.

---

[13] *Qumran Cave 4. XIII*, pp. 6-7.

1. The communal legislation displays more signs of redactional activity and up-dating than the halakhic portions of the Laws. This difference is to a large degree determined by the nature of the material. Communal legislation by its very nature needs to be up to date if it is to fulfil its purpose. If a new person takes over the leadership of a group one of the first tasks of the new regime must be the up-dating of the legislation that stipulates who is in charge. If an offence is committed for the first time and it is deemed unacceptable, legislation seeking to abolish or at least reduce such behaviour needs to be included in the regulations.
2. I am not an expert in halakhah. Others steeped in the Jewish legal tradition are infinitely more qualified than myself to elucidate the halakhic issues that are raised by this material, and Profs. Baumgarten, Schiffman and others continue to do so with great proficiency and erudition. My own approach to the halakhic material is based on my interest in the diversity of the Laws of D and my attempts to distinguish a number of strata as well as my related interest in the question of the identity of the social groups behind the various types of material found in the Laws. In short, I hope that my analysis is able to contribute some insight into our appreciation of the halakhic portions despite my shortcomings.

As far as the additional legal material from the Cave 4 MSS is concerned, I offer translations and comments on all of its substantial portions since these fragments have hardly been discussed in the scholarly literature to date with the notable exception of the ongoing stream of publications by their editor.

CHAPTER THREE

HALAKHAH

I have chosen to retain the now customary term halakhah with reference to legal material found in the scrolls.[1] I am well aware of the reservations expressed by some against employing terminology derived from rabbinical literature and scholarship with reference to Qumran law.[2] I have retained the standard terminology after some consideration mainly because of my dissatisfaction with alternatives that I considered. I use the term halakhah in this study chiefly to distinguish a considerable body of material in the Laws of D, as well as elsewhere in the scrolls, that contains legislation that is general in its formulation and application and which does not refer to a particular organized community. The other sizeable block of material in the Laws of D aside from the halakhah contains regulations for a particular community. My own usage of the term halakhah is, therefore, more limited than the usage by some. Y. Sussman, for example, refers to the legal part of the Damascus Document from Cairo as 'halakhic' in its entirety.[3] I prefer to use the term halakhah with reference to the Laws of D in the limited sense described above because it enables me to distinguish two, in my view rather disparate, blocks of material in the Laws.[4]

---

[1] This terminology is used very frequently in the secondary literature on the scrolls. Thus, it occurs, for example, in the title of L.H. Schiffman's influential study, *Halakhah at Qumran*, and it is used also both in the main text of E. Qimron and J. Strugnell, *Qumran Cave 4. V* as well as in Y. Sussman's classic exposition dealing with the question of halakhah and the DSS in Appendix 1 of the same volume, cf. pp. 179-200.

[2] Cf. J. Strugnell, 'MMT: Second Thoughts on a Forthcoming Edition' in *The Community of the Renewed Covenant. The Notre Dame Symposium on the Dead Sea Scrolls* ed. E. Ulrich and J.C. VanderKam, Notre Dame: Notre Dame University Press, 1994, pp. 57-73, esp. pp. 65-6; also *idem*, 'More on Wives and Marriage in the Dead Sea Scrolls: (*4Q416* 2 ii [Cf. *1 Thess* 4:4] And *4QMMT* §B)', *RQ* 17 (1996) 537-47, esp. p. 541 n. 7. Prof. Shemaryahu Talmon has also expressed similar reservations in a discussion at the Hebrew University's Orion Centre in April 1996.

[3] Cf. the follwoing statement by Sussman, "The entire second part of this document [that is, CD] deals with matters of a halakhic nature...", Appendix 1 in Qimron and Strugnell, *Qumran Cave 4. V*, p. 179. Sussman also describes the Community Rule as a 'halakhic composition' (p. 184) whereas those texts (1QS and 4QS) would not fall within the category of halakhah as the term is used in this study.

[4] Philip Davies employs the term halakhah in a limited sense not dissimilar from my own usage, cf. P.R. Davies, 'Halakhah at Qumran', in *A Tribute to Geza Vermes*

The material in the Laws of the Damascus Document that I have assigned to the stratum halakhah has been distinguished from the remainder of the Laws on the basis of the criteria outlined above.[5] In contrast to the communal legislation in the Laws this group of texts contains no legislation that is associated with a particular organized group within the larger community of Israel. Inevitably, like every text, it goes back to (a) particular group(s) in the society in which the author(s) were at home. Yet, unlike the material assigned to the communal legislation, these texts lack explicit references to a particular organized community.

A sizeable proportion of the material that belongs to the halakhah stratum corresponds to a formal pattern not found in the communal legislation of the Laws. The halakhah stratum as a whole has a strong scriptural basis about which more will be said in the discussion below. This basis in scripture is frequently explicit. However, a number of formally cohesive passages lack such an explicit scriptural framework. In what follows I distinguish material that explicitly refers to the Hebrew Bible in the course of its halakhic exposition from material that lacks an explicit scriptural basis.

The formal structure to which a sizeable portion of the halakhah stratum conforms consists of three elements. At times only one or two of the three formal elements are found in a text. The three formal elements around which the halakhah is structured are:

A. *Heading of the 'על plus x'-type*
Individual units in the halakhah stratum are often, though not always, introduced by a heading of the type 'על plus x', i.e. 'Concerning X' cf. 4QD^a 6 iii 3-4[6]; CD 16,10a.13a (par. 4QD^f 4 ii 12-13); 9,8b; 10,10b (par. 4QD^e 6 iv 20); 10,14a, and perhaps also 4QD^e 2 ii 1. As has been pointed out by Baumgarten a heading of this type is also used in 4Q159 (Ordinances).[7] What is more, similar headings are found in 4QMMT, compare 4QMMT B 8, 13, 21, 24, 52, 55 to name but a few examples. By contrast, headings introduced with...וזה סרך ('And this is the rule...') are common in the communal legislation of the Laws (cf. CD 10,4; 12,22-23; 13,7; 14,12)[8] as well as the Community Rule (cf. 1QS 5,1 and 6,8).

---

ed. P.R. Davies and R.T. White, Sheffield: JSOT Press, 1990, pp. 37-50; reprinted in *idem, Sects and Scrolls. Essays on Qumran and Related Topics*, Atlanta: Scholars Press, 1996, pp. 113-26.
  [5] See pp. 15-23 above.
  [6] See p. 17 n. 1 above.
  [7] 'Laws of the *Damascus Document* in Current Research', p. 56 and *Qumran Cave 4. XIII*, pp. 14-15.
  [8] Cf. the observation by C. Milikowsky, "It is my impression that the more legal

B. Scriptural Citation, Paraphrase, or Explicit Reference

A number of scholars have devoted their attention to an examination of the use of scriptural citations in the Dead Sea Scrolls.[9] As far as our present purposes are concerned the discussion of scriptural citations is touched upon only in as far as these citations and references constitute one of the formal elements frequently found in the halakhah stratum of the Laws. Not all the references to scripture follow the biblical text closely enough to be called citations, hence my threefold designation for this formal element. Numerous inherently complex issues such as what text(s) of the Hebrew Bible did the authors of the DSS use, and what was their attitude towards it (them), are closely related to the important question of the status of the Bible at Qumran. However, even to touch upon these problems would go beyond the scope of this work.

All the explicit references to scripture that occur in the halakhah stratum of the Laws are introduced by an introductory formula.[10] These introductory formulae are then followed by a scriptural citation, paraphrase, or explicit reference. Occasionally, as we shall see, an explicit appeal to scripture can be found twice or even three times in one formal unit.

C. Halakhic Exposition

This formal element can be of considerable length as, for example, in the Sabbath Code in CD 10,14-11,18b, or rather brief as in CD 10,10b-13. Most of the halakhic exposition found in the Laws of D employs the basic form of apodictic law, i.e. אל plus jussive plus איש.

In his discussion of the Sabbath Code in CD Schiffman has commented on the form of this material.[11] Both Schiffman's outline of

---

sections [...] are generally not titled *serekh*." ('Law at Qumran. A Critical Reaction to Lawrence H. Schiffman, *Sectarian Law in the Dead Sea Scrolls: Courts, Testimony, and the Penal Code*', *RQ* 12 (1986) 237-249, p. 241).

[9] For a detailed survey and discussion of isolated explicit citations of the Old Testament in the scrolls see J.A. Fitzmyer, 'The Use of Explicit Old Testament Quotations in Qumran Literature and in the New Testament', in *idem, Essays on the Semitic Background of the New Testament*, London: Geoffrey Chapman, 1971, pp. 3-58; further G. Vermes, 'Biblical Proof-Texts in Qumran Literature', *JSS* 34 (1989) 493-508 and M. Fishbane, 'Use, Authority and Interpretation of Mikra at Qumran', in *Mikra. Text, Translation, Reading and Interpretation of the Hebrew Bible in Ancient Judaism and Early Christianity* ed. M.J. Mulder, Assen/Maastricht: Van Gorcum/Philadelphia: Fortress, 1988, pp. 339-77.

[10] Cf. Fitzmyer, 'Use of Explicit Old Testament Quotations', pp. 7-16 for a comprehensive discussion of the different types of introductory formulae used in the DSS and the New Testament.

[11] Cf. esp. *Halakhah at Qumran*, pp. 80-83. See also Baumgarten, *Qumran Cave 4. XIII*, p. 13.

the formal structure of the material in general as well as his description of the structure of its individual components show close affinities with my formal analysis. Thus, for example, Schiffman points out that the individual components of the Sabbath Code are mostly formulated with אל plus jussive plus איש.[12] I would like to emphasize that these formal characteristics are not restricted to the Sabbath Code but are found in a much larger literary stratum of the Laws of D. In other words, my own analysis stresses the presence of a formal pattern in several places in the Laws of D and integrates the results of this formal analysis into a wider source critical study of the Laws. Moreover, Schiffman recognizes the presence of headings in the Laws of D as a whole and in the introduction to the Sabbath Code in particular. He fails to recognize, however, that the same type of heading as is used to introduce the Sabbath Code occurs elsewhere in the Laws of D to introduce passages that have affinities with the Sabbath Code and that conform to the same formal pattern.[13]

In response to Schiffman's discussion of the Sabbath Code, T. Zahavy has published a short note in which he argues that the Sabbath Code is a composite rather than a unitary text.[14] Zahavy introduces further formal elements into the analysis of the individual components of the Sabbath Code, i.e. expressions such as השבת or ביום השבת. Another important aspect of Zahavy's argument is his suggestion of an alternative interpretation for all those rules that are part of the Sabbath Code but lack explicit reference to the sabbath. Thus Zahavy suggests that—with the exception of CD 11,7-9—the rules that are not explicitly associated with the sabbath may be of more general application.

This alternative interpretation suggested by Zahavy certainly constitutes a possibility. Yet, it is exceedingly difficult to arrive at any certain conclusions in these cases as Zahavy himself seems to be aware. He, therefore, reserves definitive judgment on the general or specific application of the eleven rules which lack explicit reference to the sabbath. What is important for our present purposes is that he isolates these eleven rules on the basis of formal criteria, i.e. the ab-

---

[12] *Halakhah at Qumran*, p. 81.
[13] Cf. for example, the following comments by Schiffman on headings in the CD Laws, "The first law [of the Sabbath Code] is preceded by a heading: *'al ha-shabbat*, [...] Such headings are found throughout the *Zadokite Fragments*, often beginning with the term *serekh*." *Halakhah at Qumran*, p. 82. Schiffman does not distinguish between the headings in the Laws of D that introduce halakhah (על plus x') and those that introduce communal legislation or constitute redactional material (וזה סרך).
[14] 'The Sabbath Code of Damascus Document X,14-XI,18: Form Analytical and Redaction Critical Observations', *RQ* 10 (1979-81) 589-91.

sence of the formal element השבת or ביום השבת. I am not convinced, however, that this so-called formal element occurs often enough to qualify as such. It is absent in eleven out of twenty six rules. Moreover, in the fifteen individual rules that do incorporate such an element four different expression are used, i.e. השבת, ביום השבת, בשבת, and ביום השישי. It is difficult to be sure whether these four expressions have been employed at several instances in the Sabbath Code in a rather haphazard fashion, or whether they should be treated as a distinct formal element on the basis of which literary critical conclusions can be made. On balance the former seems more probable to me.

In what follows I will set out the material that I have assigned to the halakhah stratum. I have divided my presentation of the material into the following sub-categories:

3.1 Halakhah in the Legal Material of D that is Represented by CD and Parallels in 4QD
3.1.1 Halakhic Exposition of Scripture
3.1.2 Halakhic Exposition Lacking an Explicit Reference to Scripture
3.1.3 Discussion

3.2 Halakhah in the Additional Legal Material from 4QD
3.2.1 *Torot*: Halakhic Exposition Dealing with Issues of Particular Concern to the Priesthood
3.2.2 Various Agricultural Laws
3.2.3 Various Laws Dealing with Ritual Defilement and Purification
3.2.4 The Wife Suspected of Adultery and the Betrothed Slave Woman
3.2.5 The Jubilee Year, a Prohibition of Transvestism, Ethical Standards in Business, and the Arrangement of Marriages

Although the halakhah stratum is not entirely homogenous it is important to note that the various categories share a great deal more with each other than any of this material has in common with the communal legislation. I will spell out more comprehensively the most important characteristics of the material assigned to the halakhah stratum as a whole in the course of this chapter. I have provided all the texts for the halakhic material drawn from the recently published additional legal material from 4QD. For the halakhic material that is represented by CD and parallels from 4QD I have confined myself to setting out in detail the formal structure of the material.

3.1 HALAKHAH IN THE LEGAL MATERIAL OF D THAT IS REPRESENTED BY CD AND PARALLELS IN 4QD

3.1.1 *Halakhic Exposition of Scripture*

The passages assigned to this sub-category of halakhah conform closely to the formal pattern outlined above and all include an explicit reference to scripture.

CD 16,6b-9 The Binding Oath[15]
  B. *16,6b-7a Scriptural citation, paraphrase, or explicit reference*
  a) Introductory formula
  b) Citation of Dt. 23,24
  C. *16,7b-9 Halakhic exposition*
  Basic form: כל...אשר + imperfect + איש + אל + jussive

CD 16,10-12 On Women's Oaths[16]
  A. *16,10a Heading*
  B. *16,10b Scriptural citation, paraphrase, or explicit reference*
  a) Introductory formula
  b) Paraphrase[17] of Num. 30,7-9, esp. v. 9 (Hebrew)
  C. *16,10c-12 Halakhic exposition*[18]
  Basic form: אל + jussive + איש

---

[15] For a comparative analysis of the material on oaths in CD 16 and 11QT cf. L.H. Schiffman, 'The Law of Vows and Oaths (*Num.* 30,3-16) in the *Zadokite Fragments* and the *Temple Scroll*', *RQ* 15 (1991) 199-214.

[16] Cf. Vermes, 'Biblical Proof-Texts', p. 499.

[17] Cf. Fitzmyer, 'Explicit Old Textament Quotations', pp. 14-15.

[18] The instruction for the husband to annul oaths that constitute a transgression of the covenant (ברית) in CD 16,12a, also attested in 4QD^f 4 ii 12, is interesting. What covenant is meant here? The community's covenant as in passages like CD 15,5.6.8.9 or the biblical covenant between God and his people? Intriguingly the expression used in the preceding section is unambiguous, i.e. the law (התורה). There are a number of possible interpretations. Firstly, the term covenant could be used here in a general sense to refer to the law as appears to be Schiffman's understanding ('Law of Vows and Oaths', p. 205). Secondly, it is conceivable that the reference is to the community's covenant in which case CD 16,12a would constitute a secondary elaboration of a halakhic passage. Finally, and least likely is the possibility that the term covenant is here used to refer to marriage, as it might in the material on the arrangement of marriages in 4QD^d 9,4 [4QD^e 5,17] if Baumgarten's partial reconstruction is accepted. In view of the emphasis on ensuring that vows are within the law in CD 16,6b-9 it is likely that the present passage has the same concern in mind with reference to women's oaths, and I am therefore inclined to follow Schiffman's suggestion.

CD 16,13-17a[19]; 9,1 par. 4QD ͣ 8 ii 8-9 and 4QD ͤ 6 iii 15-16
Freewill Offerings

  A. *16,13a Heading*
  C. *16,13b-15a Halakhic exposition*[20]
  Basic form: אל + jussive + איש
  B. *16,15b Scriptural citation, paraphrase, or explicit reference*
  a) Introductory formula
  b) Citation of Mic. 7,2 [21]
  C. *16,15c-17a Halakhic exposition*
  Basic form: אל + jussive + איש
  B. *CD 9,1; 4QD ͤ 8 ii 8-9; 4QD 6 iii 15-16*
  Scriptural Citation, paraphrase, or explicit reference
  a) Introductory formula
  b) Citation of Lev. 27,29 followed by a reference to Lev. 20,23[22]

The introductory formula and explicit reference to scripture in CD 9,1 (4QD ͣ 8 ii 8-9 [4QD ͤ 6 iii 15-16]) clearly forms part of the halakhah stratum of the Laws on formal grounds.[23] It seems likely to

---

[19] The end of CD 16 is very fragmentary and it is difficult to determine whether CD 16,17b-20 and the fragmentary remains of this material as preserved in 4QD ͣ 8 ii 1-7 (cf. Baumgarten, *Qumran Cave 4. XIII*, pp. 65-66) and 4QD ͤ 6 iii 13-15 (cf. *Qumran Cave 4. XIII*, pp. 157-58) should be included into the halakhah stratum in the Laws. Because of its fragmentary state any comments on this material are inevitably tentative. The occurrence of the verb יענש, familiar from the penal code in D, S, and 4Q265, at the end of CD 16,17 as well as the frequent occurrence of the root שפט would indicate that some of the lost material contained penal legislation. On the other hand, it is possible to make a tentative case for regarding this material as part of the halakhah stratum and an integral part of the section that runs from CD 16,13-9,1. Baumgarten suggests that 4QD ͣ 8 ii 2 might be referring to the punishment for denying under oath the misappropriation of someone else's property and refers to Lev. 5,24 as a possible scriptural basis (*Qumran Cave 4. XIII*, pp. 65-66). This possible scriptural foundation, and Baumgarten provides a list of other passages from the Bible that may form the background to this passage, as well as the occurrence of the participle העודר in CD 16,18 (cf. CD 16,13 where the same root נדר is used) might suggest an association of this material with the halakhah stratum of the Laws. Because of the fragmentary nature of this material it is not possible, at this stage, to come to any firm conclusions.
[20] 4QD ͦ 4 ii 13-14 reads אל יקחו מיד ישראל where CD 16,14 reads אל יקחו מאת ישראל, cf. Baumgarten, *Qumran Cave 4. XIII*, p. 178. The difference in meaning between both readings is negligible.
[21] Cf. Fitzmyer's discussion in 'Explicit Old Testament Quotations', pp. 42-43. The citation (איש את רעיהו יצודו חרם) differs slightly from MT which reads איש את־אחיהו יצודו חרם.
[22] Cf. I. Rabinowitz, 'The Meaning and Date of "Damascus" Document IX,1', *RQ* 6 (1967-9) 433-5, esp. p. 433; and more recently Baumgarten in Charlesworth ed., *Dead Sea Scrolls*, II, p. 43 n. 139.
[23] Cf. Y. Yadin's interpretation of CD 9,1 in *The Temple Scroll*, 3 Vols., Jerusalem: Israel Exploration Society, 1983, I, p. 382. Yadin argues that CD 9,1 should be read with II Kings 17,8 and 17,17 in mind. Rather than dealing with the problem of gentile courts, as some have thought, Yadin suggests this passage deals with the

me that CD 9,1 (4QD^a 8 ii 8-9; [4QD^e 6 iii 15-16]) contains a second scriptural citation that follows on from and belongs to the section CD 16,13-17a. As is the case in the following section CD 9,2-8a which also includes two citations, the citation in CD 9,1 shares with the citation in CD 16,15b the root חרם which appears to be the catchword that links both citations. In CD 9,2-8a the verbs נטר and נקם provide a comparable link between the citations in 9,2 and 9,5.[24] By contrast, P. Winter has argued that CD 9,1 should be read in the context of the following rules in CD 9,2-8a prohibiting vengeance and grudges.[25] Winter stresses the importance of paying attention to the context in which CD 9,1 occurs. Although Winter's suggestion of taking CD 9,1 with what follows constitutes a possibility, I hope to have shown with my own analysis that a connection with what precedes is more likely. A definitive conclusion is difficult to reach, however, because of the fragmentary state of the mediaeval as well as the ancient manuscripts at this point. However, whether one takes CD 9,1 with what follows or with what precedes it is clearly part of the halakhah stratum in the Laws of D.

CD 9,2-8a The Requirement of Reproof[26]
 B. *9,2a Scriptural Citation, paraphrase, or explicit reference*
 a) Introductory formula

---

problem of human sacrifice according to the statutes of the gentiles which is punishable by death according to CD 9,1.
 [24] For a different view see, B.Z. Wacholder, 'Rules of Testimony in Qumranic Jurisprudence: CD 9 and 11QTorah 64', *JJS* 40 (1989) 163-74. Wacholder argues that CD 9,1 should be taken with what follows. Furthermore, Wacholder claims that CD 9,1-8 is only properly understood if one perceives it as an exegesis of 11QT 64, and that the connection between CD 9,1 and 9,2-8 is provided by 11QT 64,6-11. Both CD 9,2-8 and 11QT 64 are based on Lev. 19,17. In my view it is more likely that both texts deal with Lev. 19,17 and that this shared scriptural basis suffices to explain the connection between the two texts. Wacholder's argument can be illustrated with his interpretation of CD 9,16-10,3 which he presents as follows, "The objective of 9.16-10.3 is to define more accurately the ambiguous על פי שנים עדים ועל פי שלושה עדים of 11Q Torah 64.8-9.", 'Rules of Testimony', p. 169. The ambiguous Hebrew phrase quoted by Wacholder is of course taken directly from the book of Deuteronomy, cf. Dt. 17,6 and 19,15, and not at all peculiar to 11QT 64. Thus, Wacholder's case is not convincing and the links between CD and 11QT discussed are best explained as caused by both texts drawing on the same passages from scripture. For alternative interpretations of the expression בחוקי הגוים see also Z.W. Falk, '"BEHUQEY HAGOYIM" in Damascus Document IX,1', *RQ* 6 (1967-9) 569 and J.D.M. Derrett, '"BEHUQEY HAGOYIM": Damascus Document IX,1 Again', *RQ* 11 (1982-84) 409-15.
 [25] 'Sadoqite Fragments IX,1', *RQ* 6 (1967-9) 131-6.
 [26] The subject of rebuke is dealt with in both the halakhah stratum of the Laws as well as the communal legislation, cf. CD 9,16b-10,3 and my discussion in section 5.2 below. Furthermore, reproof is the subject of 4QD^a 7 i. In his synoptic description of the contents of D Baumgarten includes 4QD^a 7 i-iii under the heading

b) Citation of Lev. 19,18
C. *9,2b-4 Halakhic exposition*
Basic form: כל איש...אשר
B. *9,5 Scriptural Citation, paraphrase, or explicit reference*
a) Introductory formula
b) Citation of Nah. 1,2[27]
C. *9,6-7a Halakhic exposition*[28]
Basic form: אם-clause continuing the basic form כל איש...אשר
B. *9,7b-8a Scriptural Citation, paraphrase, or explicit reference*
a) Introductory formula
b) Citation of Lev. 19,17[29]

CD 9,8b-10a Oaths
  A. *9,8b Heading*
  B. *9,8c-9a Scriptural Citation, paraphrase, or explicit reference*
  a) Introductory formula
  b) Explicit reference to 1 Sam. 25,26.31[30]
  C. *9,9b-10a Halakhic exposition*
  Basic form: איש אשר

CD 10,14-11,18b The Sabbath Code[31]
  A. *10,14a Heading*
  C. *10,14b-16a Halakhic exposition*
  Basic form: אל + jussive + איש

'Overseer of Camp' and aligns this material immediately preceding CD 15 (*Qumran Cave 4. XIII*, pp. 4-5). I have assigned the fragmentary remains of 4QD^a 7 ii-iii par. to the communal legislation of the Laws, see p. 149 n.1 below. 4QD^a 7 i, on the other hand, is closer to the halakhah stratum of the Laws, particularly CD 9,2-8a. Thus, 4QD^a 7 i 3 is based on Lev. 19,18, a passage that is quoted also in CD 9,2 par. 4QD^e 6 iii 17. Note further the use of אל plus jussive plus איש in 4QD^a 7 i 3.

[27] The citation uses the substitute הוא where MT has the divine name as the subject, cf. Baumgarten, 'A New Qumran Substitute for the Divine Name and Mishnah Sukkah 4.5', *JQR* 83 (1992)1-5, esp. p. 2.

[28] Whereas CD 9,6 reads ובחרון אפו 'in his fierce anger', 4QD^e 6 iii 19 reads ובחר[ו]ן אפו 'when his anger flares up', cf. Baumgarten, *Qumran Cave 4. XIII*, p. 158. Furthermore, 4QD^b 9 i reads the additional words מחודש לחודש['and from month to month' not found in CD 9,6, cf. Baumgarten, *Qumran Cave 4. XIII*, p. 105. For two different translations of the expression ענה בו cf. G. Vermes, *The Complete Dead Sea Scrolls in English*, London: Allen Lane, 1997, p. 138 and I. Robinson, 'A Note on Damascus Document IX,7', *RQ* 9 (1977) 237-40. See also Baumgarten, *Qumran Cave 4. XIII*, p. 158.

[29] MT reads עמיתך whereas CD's citation uses רעיך.

[30] Cf. Fitzmyer, 'Explicit Old Testament Quotations', pp. 14-15 and J.M. Baumgarten, 'A "Scriptural" Citation in 4Q Fragments of the Damascus Document', *JJS* 43 (1992) 95-98, esp. p. 97.

[31] Cf. Schiffman, *Halakha at Qumran*, pp. 77-133 for a discussion of this material; see also *idem*, *Reclaiming the Dead Sea Scrolls*, pp. 275-82; Fishbane, 'Mikra at Qumran', p. 370 and S.T. Kimbrough Jr., 'The Concept of Sabbath at Qumran', *RQ* 5 (1964-66) 483-502. On the form of the Sabbath Code see my comments above. The still unpublished text 4Q265 inlcudes a fragment containing Sabbath

B. 10,16b-17a Scriptural Citation, paraphrase, or explicit reference
a) Introductory formula
b) Citation of Dt. 5,12
C. 10,17b-11,18a Halakhic exposition[32]
Basic form: אל + jussive + איש
The catchword על which occurs in CD 11,17a and
11,17b links 11,17b-18a to what precedes.[33]
B. 11,18b Scriptural Citation, paraphrase, or explicit reference
a) Introductory formula
b) Citation of Lev. 23,38[34]

CD 11,18c-21a Preserving the Purity of the Altar
C. 11,18c-20a Halakhic exposition
Basic form: אל + jussive + איש
This statement is linked to the preceding material by the
catchwords מזבח and עולה that occur in CD 11,17b-18a and 11,19.
B. 11,20b-21a Scriptural Citation, paraphrase, or explicit reference
a) Introductory formula
b) Adapted citation of Prov. 15,8[35]

3.1.2 *Halakhic Exposition Lacking an Explicit Reference to Scripture*

The passages assigned to this second sub-category of halakhah conform to the same formal pattern as found in the previous category. Unlike the previous section these passages lack an explicit basis in

---

legislation, cf. F. García Martínez, *The Dead Sea Scrolls Translated. The Qumran Texts in English*, Leiden: E.J. Brill, 1994, p. 72, J. Maier, *Die Qumran-Essener: Die Texte vom Toten Meer*, 2 Volumes, München: Reinhardt, 1995, II, p. 215, and Vermes, *Complete Dead Sea Scrolls*, p. 155.

[32] Cf. H. Bietenhardt, 'Sabbatvorschriften von Qumran im Lichte des rabbinischen Rechts und der Evangelien', in *Qumran Probleme. Vorträge des Leipziger Symposiums über Qumran-Probleme vom 9. bis 14. Oktober 1961* ed. H. Bardtke, Berlin: Akademie, 1963, pp. 53-74. The version of the Sabbath Code as preserved in 4QD^r 6 v contains two significant variants: 4QD^r 6 v 17 lacks the reference to the hired labourer (שוכרו) of CD 11,12 and 4QD^r 6 v 18 lacks the prohibition to spend the sabbath in the vicinity of gentiles that is found in both CD 11,14-15 and 4QD^r 5 i 9.

[33] This has been noted by Baumgarten in Charlesworth ed., *Dead Sea Scrolls*, II, p. 49 n. 176.

[34] Cf. Fitzmyer, 'Explicit Old Testament Quotations', pp. 41-42. The same phrase from Lev. 23,38 is taken up in the fragmentary halakhic composition 4Q513, cf. M. Baillet, *Qumran Cave 4. III (4Q482-4Q520)*, (DJD VII), Oxford: Clarendon Press, 1982, pp. 287-95 and J.M. Baumgarten, 'Halakhic Polemics in New Fragments from Qumran Cave 4' in *Biblical Archeology Today: Proceedings of the International Congress on Biblical Archeology, Jerusalem, April 1984* ed. Janet Amitai, Jerusalem: Israel Exploration Society, 1985, pp. 390-99, esp. pp. 395-99.

[35] CD 11,20-21 reads זבח רשעים תועבה ותפלת צדקם כמנחת רצון, and the MT of Prov. 15,8 reads זבח רשעים תועבה יהוה ותפלת ישרים רצונו, cf. Fitzmyer, 'Explicit Old Testament Quotations', p. 42. See also Baumgarten, 'A "Scriptural" Citation', p. 97. Baumgarten argues that the present passage is intended to promote "...the equivalence of prayer to sacrifice." I will return to this question in my discussion below.

scripture. In common with the material presented above these passages lack references to a particular organized community.

CD 10,10b-13 Purification with Water
This section is linked to the preceding theological explanation of the upper age limit for judges in CD 10,7b-10a through the catchword מעט.
    A. *10,10b Heading*
    C. *10,10c-12a Halakhic exposition*[36]
    Basic form: אל + jussive + איש
    C. *10,12b-13 A Further Halakhic Statement*
This statement is linked to the preceding material by the catchword מרעיל that occurs in CD 10,11 and 10,13.

CD 12,6b-11a Relations with Gentiles—Some Restrictions[37]
    C. *12,6b-11a Halakhic exposition*[38]
    Basic form: אל + jussive + איש

3.1.3 *Discussion*

As noted in the introduction to this chapter the material identified as belonging to the halakhah stratum has been distinguished from the communal legislation on the basis of a number of criteria. A substantial body of halakhic traditions in the Laws of D as represented in CD and parallels in the ancient MSS do not refer to a particular organized community. I will comment on this material before presenting a number of non-community specific halakhic texts from the additional legal material in 4QD each accompanied by brief comments. We will see that although their present context in the Damascus Document as a whole indicates that these halakhic traditions have been taken on board by a particular community it is instructive to interpret this material without presuppositions drawn from the communal legislation in the Laws.

a. Society at Large as Frame of Reference
A key feature that unites the material assigned to the halakhah stratum in the Laws, as well as distinguishing it from the communal

---

[36] CD 10,12 reads אל יטהר במה כלי, whereas 4QD⁵ 6 iv 21 reads אל יטהר בם כל כלי, cf. Baumgarten, *Qumran Cave 4. XIII*, p. 159.

[37] For a comparative analysis see L.H. Schiffman, 'Legislation Concerning Relations with Non-Jews in the *Zadokite Fragments* and in Tannaitic Literature', *RQ* 11 (1989) 379-89.

[38] According to L. Ginzberg, *Unknown Jewish Sect*, p. 77 what is at issue at CD 12,9-10 is produce of grain and grapes that has been harvested but not yet tithed. Ginzberg is followed by L.H. Schiffman, 'Legislation Concerning Relations with Non-Jews', p. 387.

legislation, is its lack of references to the organization of a particular community.[39] Rather, the basic frame of reference in this material is society at large, cf., for example, the references to the gentiles in CD 9,1; 11,15; 12,6.9; 4QD[a] 5 ii 5; 4QD[d] 8 ii 2; and the foreigner in CD 11,2.

b. Strong Scriptural Orientation

Another very important characteristic of the material that makes up the halakhah stratum is its strong scriptural orientation.[40] This scriptural orientation is, as we saw, at times explicit but sometimes less so. Schiffman has pointed out with reference to the Sabbath Code that the formulation of halakhic exposition in the style 'אל plus jussive plus שיא' is itself reminiscent of the style of parts of the Hebrew Bible, esp. Lev.[41] His observation applies to a much larger portion of the Laws.

Because of the strong biblical orientation of the halakhah stratum caution is required when drawing conclusions from statements in this material on the background of a particular community. It seems clear that the communities reflected in the communal legislation of the Laws cherished the standpoints expressed in the halakhah, but we have to exercise caution in attempts to use the material from the halakhah stratum as a window into the life of the community in as much as particular practices or terms may be derived from scripture

---

[39] The designation 'camp' (מחנה) occurs only in CD 10,23 in the halakhah stratum of the Laws of D where it may well be a secondary addition. This reference to the camp occurs in a second rule concerning the consumption and preparation of food on the sabbath that follows somewhat unexpectedly and repetitively after the preceding one. In the communal rules the camp is the principal form of organization, cf. CD 15,14; 9,11; 13,4.5.7.13.16.20; 14,3.9; 4QD[a] 11,17; 4QD[e] 7 ii 14. In the Sabbath Code, by contrast, the city is the primary frame of reference, cf., for example, CD 10,21 and 11,5. If the camp community were indeed the frame of reference for the Sabbath Code we would expect passages like CD 10,21 and 11,5 to have been applied to the camp. Schiffman's suggestion that camp here denotes 'the settled area' (*Reclaiming the Dead Sea Scrolls*, p. 282) begs the question why this passage employs a different term to refer to the settled area from CD 10,21 and 11,5. The phrase 'the association of Israel' (חבור ישראל) that occurs in CD 12,8 is comparable to an expression found on Hasmonean coins and does not seem to refer to a particular community within Israel, cf. C. Rabin, *The Zadokite Documents. I. The Admonition II. The Laws*, Oxford: Clarendon, 1954, p. 61 n. 8.

[40] Talmon has drawn attention to "the characteristically biblical wording of their [the community's] law codes, which sets them apart from the quite distinct formulations of rabbinic legal copora.", 'Qumran Studies', p. 14. I would want to add to this observation that the strong scriptural orientation sets apart the halakhic material in the scrolls not only from rabbinic halakhah but also from communal legislation in the Qumran scrolls.

[41] *Halakhah at Qumran*, p. 82.

rather than express present-day realities.[42] Let me discuss three issues in particular that may display scriptural influence.

i. The presence of women
Both the halakhic material in the Laws and the communal legislation include numerous references to women and children.[43] However, a number of references to women that occur in the halakhah stratum of the Laws derive from its scriptural frame of reference. Thus, great caution is required when inferring present-day realities from the references to women in the halakhic exposition of Num. 30,7-9 in CD 16,10-12 dealing with women's oaths.

ii. The attitude to the temple
A further practice that is taken for granted in the material under discussion is the participation in the official sacrificial cult, cf. CD 16,13-17a. The adapted citation of Prov. 15,8 in CD 11,20-21 may at first sight be taken to reflect a critical attitude towards the sacrificial cult, and this is the interpretation frequently adopted by scholars. Once we take into account the whole context of the citation, i.e. CD 11,18c-21a, it becomes apparent, however, that it is the purity of sacrifices that is at issue here. It seems to me that the emphasis of the halakhic exposition of Prov. 15,8 in CD 11,18c-20a is placed not on opposition to sacrifices *per se* but rather on opposition to sacrifices being brought by the wrong people.[44] Again, we need to be careful not to draw conclusions from this evidence without being aware which features are firmly rooted in scripture.[45] Thus, participation in the cult is taken for granted in the Hebrew Bible, and even a passage such as CD 11,20-21 with its warning against the wrong kind of

---

[42] See my critique of Rubinstein's so-called urbanisms in the Laws of the Damascus Document pp. 11-12 above.

[43] For a discussion of the evidence on women in D and 1QSa in contrast to S, cf. C. Hempel, 'The Earthly Essenc Nucleus of 1QSa', *DSD* 3 (1996) 253-69 esp. pp. 262-66.

[44] As noted by J.M. Baumgarten, *Studies in Qumran Law*, Leiden: E.J. Brill, 1977, p. 43.

[45] In a comparative study of the topic of purity García Martínez has discussed 11QT, 4QMMT, CD and 1QS. In his introduction to the section dealing with CD 9-12,20 he argues that CD contains halakhot of a later period which "show us which were the important problems for the community, once the bonds which joined it to Jerusalem and the Temple were broken.", (*People of the Dead Sea Scrolls*, p. 149). It seems to me that those parts of CD singled out by García Martínez may well be closer in time and place to 4QMMT than he is prepared to allow for, and it is not clear to me on what basis he assumes that these halakhot presuppose a separation from the temple and from Jerusalem. In fact, passages like CD 9,13-14 and 11,17-21 in the section commented on by García Martínez would speak against such a view.

sacrifice is reminiscent of ideas expressed in passages like Isa. 1,10-17 where the term תועבה used in Prov. 15,8 recurs in 1,13.

Baumgarten has suggested that the references to the sacrificial cult in the Damascus Document may go back either to a period before the sect severed its involvement with the cult or a time when some members had begun taking up cultic participation again after a rift.[46] A comparable view is espoused by Schiffman who suggests that the sect continued to legislate on the subject of temple worship after its separation from the temple because they expected to be able to establish proper worship sometime in the future.[47] These suggestions share the assumption that the material in question describes the state of affairs in the sectarian community. By contrast, I hope to have shown that the halakhic traditions incorporated in the Laws of D do not refer to a particular community and are heavily dependent on scripture.

iii. Private property
Private property is referred to both in the halakhah stratum of the Laws, cf. CD 10,18 and 10,12 as well as the communal legislation, cf., for example, CD 14,12b-17a. Again, it seems advisable to exercise caution in interpreting the references to private property in the halakhic material.[48]

Thus, a strong scriptural orientation as well as a national frame of reference characterize the halakhah stratum as represented in the Laws of CD and their parallels in 4QD. These characteristics are also evident in a sizeable portion of the additional legal material from 4QD to which I will now turn.

3.2 Halakhah in the Additional Legal Material from 4QD

3.2.1 *Torot: Halakhic Exposition Dealing with Issues of Particular Concern to the Priesthood*

Two sections preserved in 4QD but not in CD contain halakhic traditions that deal with concerns and reflect interests that apply particularly to the priesthood. They share with the halakhah stratum of the Laws, to which they have been assigned as a sub-category, a

---

[46] *Studies in Qumran Law*, pp. 43-46.
[47] *Reclaiming the Dead Sea Scrolls*, p. 282.
[48] In contrast to the approach advocated here Schiffman draws on the disparate parts of the Laws of the Damascus Document to describe the practice of 'the sect' in his discussion of the issue of the ownership of property, cf. *Reclaiming the Dead Sea Scrolls*, pp. 106-107.

lack of reference to a particular community. I have adopted the term *torot* from Milgrom's analysis of Lev. 1-16 where he describes *torot* as constituting 'the special lore of the priesthood'.[49]

3.2.1.1 *The Disqualification of Various Categories of Priests*

One fairly well preserved and extensive block of material from the Cave 4 additions to the Laws of the Damascus Document contains regulations on the disqualification of priests. Relevant fragments are preserved in three 4QD MSS, and I have produced a composite text from the material preserved on this topic in 4QD[a, b and h].

A. *Composite Text*[50]
(4QD[a] 5 ii 1-16 ; 4QD[b] 5 iii 1-8; 4QD[h] 2, 1-2; 4 i 5-11[51])

[	וכ]ול א[שר	1
[	] וכול כהה [עיני]ם או[וכול אשר אי]נו	2
[	ממהר לה[ב]ין וכול אשר נקל בל[שונו או בקול] טרוד	3
[	דבר לו [ו]לא פצל דברו להשמיע [קולו איש מאלה] לא יקרא בס[ופר	4
[	התו[רה] למה ישוג בדבר מות [ ] [עדה וח]	5
[	] אחו הכהנים בעבודה ואל [	6
[	[איש] מבני אהרון אשר ישבה לנואים]	7
[	לחללה בטמאתם אל ינש לעבודת] הקודש	8
[	מבית לפרוכת *vacat* ואל י"כל את קודש ה[קודשים	9
[	איש מבני אהרון אשר ינדד לעבו]ד את הנואים	10
[איש מבני	להורית עמו בישוד עם ונם לבנו<ד> " " מ " "]	11
[הלך (?)	אהרון אשר ה[פיל שמו מן האמ'ת ו]	12
[	בשרירות לבו לאכול מן הקודש]	13
[	מישראל את עצת בני אהרון הם "]	14
[	את האוכל וחב בדם]	15
[	ביחשם *vacat* וזה סרך מושב] ערי ישראל	16
[	[אנשי] הקוד[ש במ[חניהם ו[עריהם בכ]ול	17
[	מו[שב א]	18

---

[49] J. Milgrom, *Leviticus 1-16. A New Translation with Introduction and Commentary*, New York: Doubleday, 1991, p. 2.

[50] The line numbers of the composite text do not correspond to the line numbers of any of its constituent components. Unless otherwise indicated text and restorations from 4QD here as well as throughout this book are taken from Baumgarten, *Qumran Cave 4. XIII*.

[51] The composite text does not include the three isolated and partially preserved words in 4QD[h] 4 i 9-11, cf. *Qumran Cave 4. XIII*, p. 196.

B. Translation

1 [and any]one w[ho   ]
2 [   ] and anyone with dim [eye]s or [and anyone who is not]
3 quick-wi[tt]ed and anyone who speaks hurriedly⁵² [or with an] unsteady [voice]
4 [and] does not pronounce his words distinctly to make [his voice] heard. No[ne of these] shall read from the bo[ok]
5 of the la[w] lest he mislead in a capital matter [ ] congregation and [   ]
6 [   ] his brothers the priests in the service. And not [   ]
7 [one] of the sons of Aaron who is taken captive by the nations [   ]
8 to defile it (or: him) with their uncleanness. He shall not approach the [holy] service [   ]
9 within the curtain. *Vacat.* And he shall not eat from the sacred [food   ]
10 one of the sons of Aaron who departs to ser[ve the nations   ]
11 to instruct his people in the foundation of the people and also to betray [and one of the sons of]
12 Aaron who caused his name to fall from the truth and [walked]
13 in the stubbornness of his heart to eat from the sacred [   ]
14 from Israel the advice (or: council) of the sons of Aaron [   ]
15 the food (or: the one who eats) and he shall be guilty on account of the blood [   ]
16 according to their genealogy. *Vacat.* And this is the rule for the meeting of [the cities of Israel   ]
17 [the men of] holine[ss in] their [c]amps [and] their cities according to a[ll   ]
18 [mee]ting [   ]

C. Textual Notes

6 The spelling of third masculine plural suffix in אחו 'his brothers' is one of the orthographic features of 4QDᵃ attested also more widely in the DSS.⁵³

8 Another orthographic feature of 4QDᵃ is the spelling of the third person maculine singular suffix in לחללה 'to defile it (or: him)'.⁵⁴

11 The reading <רד>לבנו suggested by Baumgarten for 4QDᵃ 5 ii 9 seems likely.⁵⁵

---

⁵² Baumgarten translates this word as 'speaking too softly' ('Disqualifications of Priests', p. 506) or 'whose [speech] is too soft (?)' (*Qumran Cave 4. XIII*, p. 102). In each case Baumgarten's translation is followed by a question mark. The exact meaning of this word is uncertain. I take it to be a *niphal* of קלל. Whatever the exact meaning of this term may be it seems quite clear that it denotes some kind of defective pronounciation of scripture on the part of priests.

⁵³ Cf. Baumgarten, *Qumran Cave 4. XIII*, p. 30. See also Qimron, *The Hebrew of the Dead Sea Scrolls*, Atlanta: Scholars Press, 1986, pp. 33-35.

⁵⁴ Cf. Baumgarten, *Qumran Cave 4. XIII*, p. 30.

⁵⁵ Cf. the comments in the textual notes in Baumgarten, 'Disqualifications of Priests', p. 507 and *Qumran Cave 4. XIII*, p. 50.

D. Commentary

Although the beginning of this section is missing it seems quite clear that it deals with the disqualification of priests from certain aspects of their office. The material may be divided into two main sections:[56]

a. Ll. 1-5: Disqualification of Priests from Reading the Torah

Even though the text of these lines is rather fragmentary it seems clear what is at issue. Priests who in one way or another have difficulties pronouncing scripture correctly must be disqualified from reading the Torah in the service lest they mispronounce and cause error in a capital case. Too little is preserved of l. 6 to make out precisely what is at issue.

b. Ll. 7-16a: Disqualification of Priests from the Holy Service and Eating Sacrificial Food

Again the text of these lines is rather fragmentary. Yet the common subject matter that runs through this whole section seems to be the exclusion of certain priests from eating the sacrificial offerings. Three types of offences are spelled out:

i. Ll. 7-9 deal with priests who have been taken captive by a foreign nation. Such priests are in a state of uncleanness (l. 8a), are disqualified from approaching the service (8b) and from eating the sacrificial food (9b). Baumgarten has commented that the expression 'within the curtain' (מבית לפרוכת) in l. 9 indicates that we have here remnants of a rule that referred to the high priest who alone had access to the holy of holies on the Day of Atonement (Lev. 16).[57] A lost reference to the high priest is indeed a possibility. It seems also conceivable that the inner sanctum was mentioned here in a context other than the annual entry of the high priest.

ii. L. 10 refers to priests who depart to serve elsewhere. On the basis of Hos. 9,17 Baumgarten proposes that the use of the verb נדד probably implies a departure to the nations.[58] This suggestion seems plausible. However, rather than taking this offence with what fol-

---

[56] Baumgarten has suggested a tripartite division of this material,
"A. Priestly Torah readers were required to have distinct pronunciation.
B. Priests who were in foreign captivity could not minister in the sanctuary nor partake of the offerings.
C. Priests who migrated into pagan lands as well as apostates were regarded as no longer belonging to the «council of the people» and were thus likewise excluded from partaking of the offerings.", 'Disqualifications of Priests', p. 509.
[57] *Qumran Cave 4. XIII*, p. 51.
[58] 'Disqualifications of Priests', p. 508.

lows, as Baumgarten does,[59] it is equally possible that l. 10 should go with what precedes.

iii. Ll. 11-16a seem to deal with the case of apostate priests.
Ll. 16b-18 preserve fragments of a concluding statement or a heading to a new section. It seems more probable that we have here an introduction to what follows because the links with what precedes are feeble indeed. This is also the option favoured by Baumgarten.[60] Unfortunately the immediately following section from 4QD has not been preserved. We may estimate on the basis of an average of twenty-four to twenty-five lines per column in 4QD^a that approximately eight lines of text have been lost between the end of this text in 4QD^a 5 ii 16 and the material on skin disease in 4QD^a 6 i 1.

The main interest of this collection of regulations for our present purposes is the place of this material in the Laws of the Damascus Document. This section shares with the halakhah stratum of the Laws of D a lack reference to a particular organized community within Israel. It is distinct from the bulk of the halakhah in D in that it is less firmly anchored in scripture. One may assume that this text goes back to a priestly *milieu* as is indicated by the concerns echoed in these laws. The non-community specific character of this piece of halakhah was noted by Baumgarten who has argued that this text, "...represents the common traditional law of the Second Temple period".[61] I agree widely with Baumgarten's evaluation. There is one statement in Baumgarten's conclusion, however, which seems problematic to me. Baumgarten comments,

> It may be that on this matter[i.e. the disqualification of priests], as on other questions of purity, the *Qumran Zadokites* [my emphasis] adopted a more stringent position. But their position was not outside the parameters of customary law.[62]

This association of our text with the 'Qumran Zadokites' does not seem justified. Ever since the preliminary publication of 4QS^d 1,1-3 by G. Vermes[63] it has become clear that *Qumran Zadokites* is a difficult term to use with reference to the Qumran community let alone the Qumran library as a whole. It seems especially inappropriate with reference to this particular text since the priests are exclusively referred to as 'the sons of Aaron' here.

---

[59] 'Disqualifications of Priests', p. 509.
[60] 'Disqualifications of Priests', p. 509.
[61] 'Disqualifications of Priests', p. 513.
[62] 'Disqualifications of Priests', p. 513.
[63] 'Preliminary Remarks on Unpublished Fragments of the Community Rule from Qumran Cave 4', *JJS* 42 (1991) 250-55.

HALAKHAH

Of all the material that makes up the collection of Laws in D this section has most in common with the sections on skin disease, flux, and childbirth to which I will now turn.

3.2.1.2 *Skin Disease, Fluxes, and Childbirth*

Fragments dealing with the subject of skin disease, fluxes, and childbirth are preserved in four MSS of the Damascus Document from Cave 4 (4QD^a, 4QD^d, 4QD^g, and 4QD^{h}).[64] MS D^a contains the largest amount of text of the four. I have produced a comprehensive composite text.[65] It seems appropriate to treat this long section together since the various topics treated are based on Lev. 12-15 which forms the scriptural background to this material.

A. *Composite Text*[66]
(4QD^a 6 i-iii; 4QD^d 7; 4QD^g 1 i-ii; 4QD^h 4 ii)

```
1   [ שאת א]ו ספחת או ב]הרת        [ היא והספחת מכתעץ
2   [ו]אבן וכול מכה בבוא הרו]ח וא[חזה בניד ו]ש[ב הדם
3   למ[עלה ולמטה והניד [ ]       [ אחר הדם ]           [
4   וראה הכוהן את עור הבשר [ ] החי ואת המת [ אם לוא ישפל   [
5   המת מן [ החי          ב[שבעת [ הימי]ם [             [
6   [עד אשר י]שוב הדם לניד [   ואח]ר ישוה [ב]ו [ כאשר [ אמר
7   והסג[י]רו הכוהן [ שבעת ימים עד [ אשר יצמח הבשר וראה הכוהן
8   ב[י]ום השביעי [ והנה רו]ח החיים עולה ויורדת והבשר צמח
9   נרפא מן [ הנגע? טהורה? ה]ספחת לוא יראנה הכוהן לעור הבשר
10              ]  ואם שפל השת או השפחת בשפה [           [
11  [ מן העור ]       הכ]הן וראה הכוהן אותו כמראי הבשר החי [
```

---

[64] A number of studies have dealt with this material prior to the appearance of the official edition of 4QD, cf. especially J.M. Baumgarten, 'Skin Disease'; *idem* in Charlesworth ed. *Dead Sea Scrolls*, II, pp. 59-75; J.T. Milik, 'Fragment d'une source du Psautier (4QPs 89) et fragments des Jubilés, du Document de Damas, d'un Phylactère dans la Grotte 4 de Qumran', *RB* 73 (1966) 94-106, esp. pp. 105-106 and Planche III; and E. Qimron, 'Notes on the 4Q Zadokite Fragments on Skin Disease', *JJS* 42 (1991) 256-59.

[65] Baumgarten has published a less comprehensive composite text comprising exclusively the material dealing with skin disease, cf. Baumgarten, 'Skin Disease', pp. 158-59 and Baumgarten in Charlesworth ed. *Dead Sea Scrolls*, II, pp. 64-69.

[66] The line numbers of this composite text do not correspond to the line numbers of any of its constituent fragments. The group of small fragments 4QD^a 6 i a-e which appear to deal with the subject of skin disease (cf. Baumgarten, *Qumran Cave 4. XIII*, pp. 54-55) have not been included in the composite text. Nor did I include the remains of the small fragment 4QD^a 6 ii a which possibly deals with purification after childbirth, cf. Baumgarten, *Qumran Cave 4. XIII*, p. 57.

CHAPTER THREE

12 [ ] צרעה [היאה האוחזה בעור החי וכמשפט הזה] [
13 [ ] וראה הכוהן ביום השביעי והנה נוסף מן החי אל [
14 [ ] המת   צ[ר]עת ממארת היא vacat ומשפט נתק הרוש והז[קן]
15 [ ] ו[ר]אה הכוהן והנה באה הרוח ברוש או בזקן באאוחזה [
16 בניד ופר[ח הנגע] מתחת השער והפך מראה לדק צוהב כי כעשב [
17 הוא אשר י[ש הרחש תחתו vacat ויקיץ שורשו ויבש פרחו vacat ואשר [
18 אמר וצוה הכוהן ונלחו את הרוש ואת הנתק לא ינלחו למען אשר [
19 יספור הכוהן את השערות המיתות והחיות וראה אם יוסף מן [
20 החי אל המת בשבעת הימים טמא הואה ואם לו ליוסף מן החיות [
21 אל המיתות והגיד נמלא דם ורוח החיים עולה ויורדת בו [נרפא]
22 הנגע זה משפט [תור]ה[ ] הצרעת לבני אהרון להבדיל [ ]
23 vacat   ומ[שפט הזב את זובו כול איש א[שר זו]ב זו[וב]
24 מבש[רו   א]ו א[שר] יעלה [ע]ל[ו] מחשבת זמה או אשר [ ]
25 [ ]מנעו כמנע [ ]
26 [ ] וכבס בנ[ד]יו [ ] ורחץ במים [
27 [ ]ו[משפט] הזבה כול אשה   בו הנוגע בו ור[חץ]
28 [ ] ת[שב א]ת   הזבה דם שב[עת ימים תהיה כנד[תה ב]
29 [ ] הנדה וכ[ול]   שבעת הימים [ ]
30 [ ]הנו[ג]ע בה]
31 [ ]
32 [ ] חקוץ [
33 [ ] המים [
34 [ ]
35 [ ] וכמי הנדה   המים [
36 [ ] החיי[ם] שני [
37 [ ] ידה [
38 [ ]
39 [ ] האש[ ]ה   אשר י[קרב]
40 [ ] אליה ע[ו]ן נדה עלו ואם ראתה [ע]ו[ד והיאה לו [בעת
41 [ ] נדתה [שבעת ימים והיאה אל תוכל קודש ואל ת[בו]
42 אל המקדש עד בו השמש ביום השמיני vacat
43 [ ] ואשה אשר [תזרי]ע וילדה זכר [וטמאה א]ת שבעת [הימים
44 [ ] כ]י[מ]י [נדת [ראותה וביום השמיני ימול בשר [ערלתו]ו
45 [ ] ושלושה ושלושים יום תשב בדם טוהרה ואם נקבה תלד
46 [ ] וטמאה שבועים כנדה   ד[אותה ו]ששה וששים יום תשב בדם
47 [ ] טוהרה והיאה [קודש] לוא תוכל ולא תבו אל המקדש
48 [ ] כי מ[שפט מות הו]אה   תתן את
49 [ ] הי]לד למנקת בטוה[רה
50 [ ] ו[אם לוא השינה יד]ה[די שה ולקחה בן יונה או תר לעולה
51 [ ] ו[המירה   א]ת ה[שה
52 [ ]
53 [ ] את מי הנדה]
54 אל vacat]

B. Translation

1. [an eruption o]r a scab or a bri[ght spot   ] it and the scab (resulted from) a blow with wood
2. [or] stone or any blow. When the spir[it] enters [and tak]es possession of the artery, and the blood [re]sumes
3. [to fl]ow up and down, and the artery [   ] after the blood [   ]
4. [And the priest shall examine the] living and the dead [skin of the flesh. If the]
5. dead skin [is not lower than the living   over a period of] seven [day]s
6. [until] the blood returns to the artery [and afterwar]ds he shall compare [i]t [as] he has said,
7. the priest shall lo[c]k him up [for seven days un]til the flesh grows. And the priest shall examine
8. on the seventh [d]ay [and if (lit.:behold) the spi]rit of life is flowing up and down, and the flesh has grown,
9. then he is healed from [the disease (?) Pure (?) is the] scab. The priest shall not examine the skin of the flesh
10. [   ] But if the eruption or the scab is lower when it is rubbed [ ]
11. [than the skin   the prie]st. And (when) the priest examines it, it has the appearance of living flesh [ ]
12. [*sara'at*] has taken possession of the living skin. And thus shall be the rule [ ]
13. [   ] and the priest shall examine (it) on the seventh day: if something has been added from the living to
14. [the dead   ] then it is malignant [*sa*]*ra'at*. And the rule for an eruption on the head and the be[ard]
15. [and] the priest shall examine (it) and if the spirit has entered the head or the beard taking possession
16. of the artery, and [the disease] progress[es] from under the hair and turns its appearance into soft yellow, for it is like a plant
17. which [h]as a worm under it *vacat* gnawing off its root and causing its blossom to wither. And as to what
18. he said, 'And the priest shall command for them to shave the head but not to shave the eruption.' This is so that
19. the priest may count the dead and the living hair and examine whether anything has been added from
20. the living to the dead during the seven days. (If so) then he is unclean. But if nothing has been added from the living
21. to the dead, and the artery is filled with blood, and the spirit of life rises and sinks in it, the disease
22. [is healed]. This is the rule for the [la]w of *sara'at* for the sons of Aaron to separate [ ]
23. *Vacat*. And the rule for those suffering from flux. Anyone w[ho suf]fers from fl[u]x
24. from [his] flesh [o]r w[ho] brings up[on] himself licentious thoughts or who [ ]

25 [   ] his (or: its) touch is like the touch of [   ]
26 and he shall wash his cl[oth]es [and bathe in water]
27 him (or: it) and he who touches him (or: it) shall wa[sh   And] the rule for [a woman with a discharge. Every]
28 menstruating [woman shall be in] her [impu]rity for sev[en days   she shall] stay [ ]
29 seven days [   ] the impurity and eve[ry]
30 [and he who tou]ches her [ ]
31 [ ]
32 she loathes [   ]
33 the water [   ]
34 [ ]
35 with the waters of purification
36 the livin[g water] two
37 her hand [ ]
38 [ ]
39 [   ] the woma[n   he who dr]aws near [ ]
40 [towards her the s]in of impurity (is) upon him. And if she [ag]ain saw (her blood, cf. CD 5,7) and she is not [in the time of]
41 [her impurity] (which lasts) seven days, she shall not eat anything holy and she shall not en[ter]
42 the sanctuary until sundown on the eighth day. *Vacat.*
43 And a woman who [con]ceives and gives birth to a male child [she shall be unclean fo]r seven [days]
44 [according to] the da[ys of her menstrual] uncleanness. [And on the eighth day the flesh of his] foreskin [shall be circumcised].
45 [And for thirty three days she shall remain in the blood of her purification. And if she gives birth to a female child]
46 [she shall be unclean for two weeks according to] her menstru[al uncleanness.] And [for sixty six days she shall remain in the blood]
47 [of her purification. And she] shall not eat [anything holy and she shall not enter the sanctuary]
48 [for] th[is is pun]ishable by death. [She shall give the]
49 [chi]ld to a wet nurse during [her] purifica[tion   ]
50 [And] if [her] means are not sufficient [to afford a sheep then she shall take a dove or a turtle dove as a burnt offering]
51 [and] it may be substituted for the [sheep   ]
52 [   ]
53 [ ] the water of sprinkling [   ]
54 God. *Vacat.* [ ]

C. Textual Notes

4 The reconstruction of the last three words of this line is taken from Baumgarten.[67]

5-6 The words בְּ[שבעת הימ]ים at the end of l. 5 are taken from 4QD^d 7,5. The phrase [עד אשר ישוב הדם לניד] ואח[ר ישוה has been inserted superlinearly in 4QD^g 1 i 6a.[68] The exact placement of the last two words in l. 5 in relation to this superlinear text from 4QD^g is uncertain.

6-7 I have here followed the text of 4QD^d 7,6-7. In his reconstruction of the equivalent passage in 4QD^g 1 i 6 Baumgarten appears to presuppose a shorter text.[69] An intercolumnar addition in 4QD^g 1 i provides some additional text that results in a text for 4QD^g that is somewhat closer to that of 4QD^d.[70]

9 The reconstructions in this line have been tentatively suggested by Baumgarten for 4QD^g 1 i 8.[71]

10 For שפל, the reading found in 4QD^g 1 i 9, 4QD^h 4 ii 5 reads the imperfect ישפל.

12 Qimron suggests reconstructing רוח for the first word in this line since רוח is the subject of the verb אחז in ll. 2 and 15.[72]

14 The *vacat* in this line is found in 4QD^g 1 i 13 but not in 4QD^a 6 i 5 nor in 4QD^h 4 ii 10. A deleted marginal addition in 4QD^a 6 i reads, 'an erupt[ion] on the bald forehead' ([ש]פח[ת] נבחת תיחבה). Baumgarten suggests locating it in the context of 4QD^a 6 i 5 (i.e. l. 14 of the Composite Text dealing with the diseased head and beard) on the basis of the occurrence of the term 'bald forehead' (נבחת). Milik had tentatively proposed placing it after 4QD^a 6 i 2.[73]

17 The first *vacat* in this line is found in 4QD^a 6 i 8. The second *vacat* is found in 4QD^g 1 i 17 but not in 4QD^a 6 i 8.

19 The reading השערות goes back to a suggestion by E. Qimron.[74]

20 At the beginning of 4QD^a 6 i 11 the letter *kaph* has been deleted by placing a dot above it.

21 4QD^a 6 i 12 reads the preposition על rather than אל at the beginning of this line. אל is the reading in 4QD^g 1 i 20. It also occurs in an equivalent phrase in 4QD^a 6 i 11.

26-38 The text of these lines, the beginning of the legislation dealing with women with a discharge, is based on 4QD^g 1 ii 6-18. There does not ap-

---

[67] Cf. 'Skin Disease', p. 159 and Baumgarten in Charlesworth ed., *Dead Sea Scrolls*, II, p. 64.

[68] On this reading cf. E. Qimron, 'Notes on the 4Q Zadokite Fragments', p. 256. Baumgarten had originally read ישׁב ('Skin Disease', p. 159) but subsequently adopted Qimron's suggestion (*Qumran Cave 4. XIII*, p. 188).

[69] Cf. *Qumran Cave 4. XIII*, p. 188.

[70] On the intercolumnar addition cf. Baumgarten, *Qumran Cave 4. XIII*, pp. 188-89 and *idem* in Charlesworth ed. *Dead Sea Scrolls*, II, p. 72 n. 3.

[71] *Qumran Cave 4. XIII*, p. 188.

[72] 'Notes on 4Q Zadokite Fragments', p. 257.

[73] Cf. Baumgarten, *Qumran Cave 4. XIII*, p. 53.

[74] 'Notes on 4Q Zadokite Fragments', p. 258.

pear to be any overlap with 4QD^a 6 ii. 4QD^a 6 i breaks off with line 16 and based on an average of twenty four to twenty five lines per column in 4QD^a we may assume that the great bulk of 4QD^g 1 ii 6-18 preserves material lost at the end of 4QD^a 6 i.[75]

54 The end of the material on the purity of women after childbirth is followed by a rubric introducing halakhah dealing with the harvest, cf. 4QD^a 6 iii 3b ff. par. 4QD^e 3 ii 12.

D. *Commentary*

This piece of halakhah is based on Lev. 12-15. Parts of this section follow Lev. in the sequence of topics treated, i.e. flux is dealt with after skin disease, cf. Lev. 14-15.[76] The order of Lev. has been changed, however, with regard to purification after childbirth which is dealt with after the topic of flux in D.

The section is structured as follows,

a. Ll 1-22 The Law of Disease[77]
   i. Ll. 1-14a Diseased Skin
   ii. Ll. 14b-22a Diseased Head or Beard[78]
   iii. L. 22b Rubric concluding the Law of Disease
b. Ll. 23-42 The Law of Fluxes[79]

---

[75] Maier has adopted a similar arrangement, cf. *Qumran-Essener*, 1995, II, pp. 220-21.

[76] This has been noted by Baumgarten, cf. J.M. Baumgarten, 'Zab Impurity in Qumran and Rabbinic Law', *JJS* 45 (1994) 273-77, p. 274.

[77] As has been pointed out by Baumgarten it seems probable that the present piece of legislation forms the background to CD 13,4b-7a (Baumgarten, 'Skin Disease', p. 162). I will argue below in my discussion of CD 13,2b-7a that these lines seem to have undergone development. It seems likely that CD 13,4b-7a was inserted into the section dealing with the authority in the camp in the light of Lev. 13-14 and perhaps also of the halakhic traditions contained in the present passage from 4QD. Moreover, as has been noted by Baumgarten ('Zab Impurity', p. 275; also *Qumran Cave 4. XIII*, p. 54), the catalogue of transgressions preserved in 4QD^e 2 i-ii includes a reference to skin disease and flux, cf. chapter nine below.

[78] L. 18 contains an adapted citation of Lev. 13,33. As noted by Baumgarten the citation varies from MT and LXX, and the difference results in an enhanced position of authority for the priests (*Qumran Cave 4. XIII*, p. 54). The formula used to introduce this adapted citation resembles the formulae used in the halakhah elsewhere in the Laws of D.

[79] The topic of flux is dealt with in a number of texts from Qumran such as 4Q274 Tohora^a (cf. Baumgarten, 'Zab Impurity'; idem, 'The Laws About Fluxes in 4QTohora^a (4Q274)', in *Time to Prepare the Way in the Wilderness. Papers on the Qumran Scrolls by Fellows of the Institute for Advanced Studies of the Hebrew University, Jerusalem, 1989-1990* ed. D. Dimant and L.H. Schiffman, Leiden: E.J. Brill, 1995, pp. 1-8; also J. Milgrom, '4QTohora^a: An Unpublished Qumran Text on Purities', in *Time to Prepare the Way in the Wilderness* ed. Dimant and Schiffman, pp. 59-68), 4QOrd^c (cf. M. Baillet, *Qumran Grotte 4. III*, pp. 295-98; and J. Milgrom, 'First Day Ablutions in Qumran', in *Madrid Qumran Congress* ed. Trebolle Barrera and Vegas Montaner, II, pp. 561-70), 11QT^a 45,15-17 (cf. Yadin, *Temple Scroll*, II, p. 194), and 11QT^b fg. 17 (cf. F. García Martínez, '11Q Temple^b. A Preliminary Publication' in *Madrid*

i. Ll. 23-27a Men with a Discharge
   ii. Ll. 27b-42 Women with a Discharge[80]
c. Ll. 43-51 Purification After Childbirth[81]
   i. Ll. 43-45a Purification After the Birth of a Male Child
   ii. Ll. 45b-48a Purification After the Birth of a Female Child
   iii. Ll. 48b-49 Prohibition of Nursing the Child During Purification[82]
   iv. Ll. 50-51 Sacrificial Animals Acceptable for Offerings

Only four words remain of ll. 52-54, and it is not possible to say much about these lines except to note that they appear to deal with the subject of purification.[83]

This material does not seem to conform to a formal structure. Rather it constitutes a halakhic narrative that is very similar in style to Lev. 12-15 itself. This piece of halakhic exegesis is quite unlike anything else found in the Laws of the Damascus Document. Most other halakhic sections in the Laws are formulated as a series of prohibitions. Although we have encountered an extended halakhic exposition on a unified theme in the form of the Sabbath Code in CD 10,14-11,18 both sets of rules are distinct in that the Sabbath Code displays a degree of formal consistency that is absent from this material.

However, the material on skin disease, flux, and childbirth shares with the halakhic material elsewhere in D a strong scriptural orientation. It is closest in character to the material on the disqualification of priests. Both texts overwhelmingly reflect priestly concerns and seem to be addressed to a priestly readership. Both texts refer to the priesthood as 'the sons of Aaron' (בני אהרון), cf. 4QD^a 6 i 13 par. (l. 22 of the Composite Text above) and frequently in the material on priestly disqualifications, cf. 4QD^a 5 ii 4-5.8.9-10. The most frequent designation for individual priests differs slightly in both texts however. Whereas the section on priestly disqualifications displays a preference for the phrase 'one of the sons of Aaron' (איש מבני אהרון), the

---

Qumran Congress ed. Trebolle Barrera and Vegas Montaner, II, pp. 363-91, esp. p. 390).

[80] Cf. L.H. Schiffman, 'Pharisaic and Sadducean Halakhah in the Light of the Dead Sea Scrolls', *DSD* 1 (1994) 285-99, esp. pp. 296-98.

[81] As noted by Baumgarten this topic is also dealt with in 4Q265 Serekh Damascus and the book of Jubilees, cf. *Qumran Cave 4. XIII*, p. 56. See also, *idem*, 'Purification after Childbirth and the Sacred Garden in 4Q265 and Jubilees', in *New Qumran Texts and Studies. Proceedings of the First Meeting of the International Organization for Qumran Studies, Paris 1992* ed. G.J. Brooke with F. García Martínez, Leiden: E.J. Brill, 1994, pp. 3-10.

[82] On this prohibition which goes beyond the requirements of Lev. and rabbinic halakhah cf. Baumgarten, *Qumran Cave 4. XIII*, p. 57.

[83] Cf. Baumgarten, *Qumran Cave 4. XIII*, p. 58.

bulk of the present passage prefers to talk of 'the priest' (הכוהן, cf. 4QD^a 6 i 2.4.[6].9.10) which is the terminology in the bulk of Lev. 12-15, cf. however Lev. 13,2. Another characteristic that this material has in common with the material on priestly disqualifications is the priestly terminology for food: holy offerings (קודש, cf. 4QD^a 5 ii 11; 4QD^a 6 ii 3, [9]) and most holy offerings (קודש ה[ק]ודשים, cf. 4QD^a 5 ii 7).[84]

In sum, both sections from 4QD that deal with priestly concerns show no evidence of an association with a particular community and clearly belong to the halakhah stratum of the Laws.

3.2.2 *Various Agricultural Laws*

A sizeable portion of the additional legal material preserved in 4QD comprises legislation dealing with agricultural matters, especially legal obligations to be honoured at harvest time. I will set out and briefly discuss each text in turn before giving reasons why these agricultural laws have been assigned to the halakhah stratum of the Laws.

3.2.2.1 *Two Fragments Introducing Agricultural Halakhah, Gleanings, and Bread offerings*

The fragmentary remains of two fragments belonging to MSS A and E respectively (4QD^a 6 iii a and 4QD^e 3 i) contain material that deals with agricultural matters but precedes the subsequent rubric introducing the topic of gleanings in 4QD^a 6 iii 3-4 par. 4QD^e 3 ii 12. According to Baumgarten 4QD^a

> [f]rg. 6 iii a belongs before the text extant in frg. 6 iii as an introduction to the harvest (קציר) laws; cf. the rubric written in red ink before the parallel harvest laws in 4Q270.[85]

The rubric in red ink referred to here is found in 4QD^e 3 i 19. Thus, Baumgarten has already suggested an approximate relationship between the two fragments grouped together here. No overlapping text seems to be preserved in the modest remains of both fragments. The noun 'harvest' (קציר) does occur in both fragments but in different forms, i.e. undetermined in 4QD^e 3 i 20 and accompanied by the conjunction and the article in 4QD^a 6 iii a 2. The rubric written in red ink in 4QD^e 3 i 19 constitutes the only example of red ink in the extant 4QD MSS. The use of red ink is also attested in a number of other scrolls from Qumran, but it is a relatively rare phenom-

---

[84] Note the expression 'sacred food' (טהרה הקודש) used in 4QMMT B64-72, a section dealing with lepers (צרועים) alongside the term 'holy offerings' (קודשים).
[85] *Qumran Cave 4. XIII*, p. 57.

enon.[86] The writing in 4QD[c] 3 i 19 proves difficult to decipher, and Baumgarten suggests the following reading and reconstruction for the faintly visible remains of l. 19 [על] ארצות [חו]קי 'Concerning the laws of the lands' which he takes to be a heading introducing agricultural laws following a suggestion by H. Stegemann.[87]

The first substantial portion of agricultural halakhah deals with gleanings and bread offerings.

A. *Composite Text*[88]
(4QD[a] 6 iii ; 4QD[b] 6; and 4QD[c] 3 ii)

1 {על} [הלקט] ועללות הכרם עד עשרה נרנרים העוללת
2 וכול הלקט עד סאה לבית הסאה והיא אשר זרעה
3 אין בה תרומה [ו]פרט [אין בה] ובעוללה עד
4 עשרה נ[רנרים] ובנקוף הזית [ופר]י תבואותו אם
5 שלמה היא נקפה אחד משלושים vacat וכול [ ]
6 [ ] ואם רפוס השדה או קדה בשרף ונפרס מסאה
7 לבית סאה מעשרה בה ואם תלקוט נפש אחת [סאה]
8 אחת ממנו ביום אחד תרומה בה עשרון [אחד]
9 [על שה־] חלות התרומה לכל בתי ישראל אוכלי לחם
10 [הארץ] ל[ה]רים אחת בשנה עשרון אחד תהיה האחת
11 [לפני] השלמו לישראל אל [י]רם איש

B. *Translation*

1 {Concerning} [the grain-gleanings] and the grape-gleanings of the vineyard: up to ten berries of the grape-gleanings.
2 And all the grain-gleanings: up to a *seah* per *bath seah*. And that which does not have its seed
3 in it [does not incur] a holy offering [nor] fallen berries nor grape-gleanings up to
4 ten b[erries.] And of the olive-gleanings [and the frui]t of its yield: if it
5 is complete the olive-gleanings: one out of thirty. *Vacat.* And all [ ]
6 [ ] And if the field is trampled down or damaged by fire, and it is divided (with part of the field yielding) more than a *seah*
7 per *bath seah* it shall be tithed. And if one person picks one
8 [*seah*] from it in one day its holy offering shall be [one] tenth. [ ]
9 [Concerning the two] cakes for the holy offering: it is for all the houses of Israel when they are eating the bread of
10 [the land to] set aside one (holy offering) per year. Each shall be one (tenth).

---

[86] See Y. Nir-El and M. Broshi, 'The Red Ink of the Dead Sea Scrolls', *Archaeometry* 38 (1996) 97-102.
[87] Cf. *Qumran Cave 4. XIII*, p. 147.
[88] The composite text arranged here begins where substantial amounts of text have survived. The line numbers do not correspond to the line numbers of any of the underlying fragments.

11 [before] it has been completed for Israel no one [shall] lift up [ ]

C. Textual Notes

3 4QD^a 6 iii 7 reads ובעוללתו 'and of its grape-gleanings' whereas 4QD^c 3 ii 14 reads ובעוללה which is the reading I adopted for the composite text. The difference in meaning is slight.

4 As noted by Baumgarten 4QD^b 6,4 includes a *vacat* before the rubric introducing the olive-gleanings.[89]

5 Here I follow the reading of 4QD^b 6,5. 4QD^a 6 iii 9 lacks the *vacat* and proceeds with the letter *s(h)in* after which it breaks off.

D. Commentary

As Baumgarten has shown, this passage deals with two distinct topics, gleanings and bread offerings. I will divide what follows accordingly.[90]

a. Ll. 1-8 Gleanings

The scriptural legislation on gleanings is found in Lev. 19,9; 23,22 and Dt. 24,19-21. However, the Bible does not specify an upper limit for gleanings. Our text and the Mishnah have developed more specific guidelines, cf. especially *mPeah*.

In his comments on 4QD^a 6 iii 2 Baumgarten[91] notes that agricultural legislation is introduced by a rubric and set off with a *vacat*. The rubric in question is the heading contained in line 1 of the Composite Text above. The fragmentary lines that precede this rubric include a reference to 'the waters of sprinkling' (4QD^a 6 iii 2). The material described by Baumgarten as preceding 4QD^a 6 iii in 4QD^a 6 iii a already dealt with agricultural matters, however. Moreover, Baumgarten suggests a possible connection between rites of purification, which seem to lie behind the reference to the waters of sprinkling, with the harvest as indicated by 4QTohorot A and 4QTohorot G (4Q274 and 4Q284a).[92] When we combine Baumgarten's observations on 4QD^a 6 iii 2 par. with his comments on 4QD^a 6 iii a and 4QD^c 3 i the following overall picture emerges. The *vacat* and the rubric in 4QD^a 6 iii 2 par. introduce a new subject matter. The topic being introduced is not that of agricultural ha-

---

[89] Cf. *Qumran Cave 4. XIII*, p. 103.
[90] Cf. J.M. Baumgarten, 'A Qumran Text with Agrarian Halakhah', *JQR* 86 (1995) 1-8 and *Qumran Cave 4. XIII*, esp. pp. 148-50.
[91] *Qumran Cave 4. XIII*, p. 58.
[92] See J.M. Baumgarten, 'Liquids and the Susceptibility to Defilement in New 4Q Texts', *JQR* 85 (1994) 91-101. 4Q284a and 4Q274 both deal with the impurity conveyed by the fruit juices of ripe fruit at harvest time. The subject of the harvest seems to be merely incidental to the chief concern of the texts which is the preservation of purity.

lakhah, as Baumgarten proposes, since the latter was apparently introduced previously in 4QD^a 6 iii a and 4QD^r 3 i. Rather, the new rubric in 4QD^a 6 iii 2 par. introduces the topic of gleanings within a larger section on the harvest.

Baumgarten refers to Isa. 17,6 and tentatively suggests that the limit of ten berries mentioned repeatedly in this text may have been derived from the sum of the numbers mentioned in that verse.[93] This suggestion may receive some support from the use of a comparable exegetical technique in the legislation on witnesses in CD 9,16-20. This passage is based on Dt. 17,6 and 19,15. As Schiffman has shown CD 9,16-20 attaches a distinct significance to each number mentioned in the biblical text.[94] The treatment of Dt. 17,6;19,15 in CD 9,16-20 is comparable to the treatment of Isa 17,6 in the present passage on Baumgarten's interpretation in that both D passages display a dislike for the vague use of numbers in scripture and arrive at a much more specific regulation that nevertheless incorporates all the elements of the passage(s) from scripture. However, the exegetical process underlying CD 9,16-20 differs in that it attaches a distinct significance to each number in the biblical text as Schiffman was able to show.

b. Ll. 9-11 The holy offering from the bread

As noted by Baumgarten this passage draws on Num. 15,20 and Lev. 23,17. Our text differs from the rabbinic position according to which the holy offering was taken from the dough whereas here it is taken from the bread. Baumgarten suggests that this difference may be explained as a result of a harmonization of both biblical passages by our author.[95]

L. 10 specifies that the holy offering from the bread is required only once a year. Baumgarten proposes the term ראשית in Num. 15,20 as a possible basis for the reasoning of legist here.[96] We may add that the other verse on which this regulation is based, i.e. Lev. 23,17, also refers to the bread offering as 'first-fruits' (בכורים). As Baumgarten has noted, this requirement for an annual holy offering from the bread differs markedly from rabbinic requirements according to which the holy offering is to be set aside every time dough was kneaded to make bread.[97] The requirement to offer bread only once

---

[93] *Qumran Cave 4. XIII*, p. 148.
[94] *Sectarian Law*, pp. 74-78. See also pp. 95-96 above.
[95] 'Agrarian Halakhah', p. 7.
[96] 'Agrarian Halakhah', p. 6.
[97] As noted by Baumgarten the annual requirement for the holy offering from the bread is comparable to the position vis-à-vis the half shekel payment to the temple which according to 4Q159 1 ii 6-8 is required only once during a person's life time, cf. 'Agrarian Halakhah', pp. 7-8.

54 CHAPTER THREE

a year links the section on the bread offering to the preceding material since all of the topics are related to the harvest which inevitably only occurs once a year for the various crops.

3.2.2.2 *More Agricultural Halakhah*
4QD^a 6 iv contains further agricultural halakhah.

A. *Text*
(4QD^a 6 iv)

1 [ ]ם[ ] ○ [ ]　כול הלולי[
2 [יהיו]ל[הם]וכל עצי המ[אכל { עצי הפרי }]וכול נטעי הכר[ם
3 [ימכו]רו ואחר מנורים ובארץ הקודש באדמ[ה]כמשפטם
4 יוכ[ל] לו הרב[יע]ית בשנה אי]ש ונ[טע [○○ ם]ו[○ מהם לקנ[ות]
5 [ ] ○ [ ]　הזאת בש[נ]ה קדשו [כי]
6 [ ] ונ[ממנחה (?)
7 [ ] ○]ת[ ]ל[ ]
8 [ ] ת[בואתו לו [לחו]סיף
9 [ ]]○ הא[שה]

B. *Translation*
1 [　　　　all the praise offerings of]
2 the plants of the vineyar[d and] all the fru[it] trees [shall be for] them
3 according to their rule [in the lan]d of holiness and in the land of sojourn. And afterwards they may sel[l]
4 from them [　one may p]lant in the fourth year but not [ea]t
5 [for] they are holy in [this] y[ear　　　　]
6 from the gift offering (?) and [　　　]
7 [　　　　　　　　　　　]
8 [to in]crease for him [its] y[ield　]
9 [　　　　　]

C. *Textual Notes*
1 The editor's restoration is based on 11QT^a 60,3-4.[98]
4 *Waw* and *nun* are not reconstructed in Baumgarten's transcription, but his translation clearly presupposes a reconstruction along these lines.

D. *Commentary*
According to Lev. 19,23-25 the fourth year produce from the fruit trees is to be offered to the Lord. A number of Qumran texts as well

---

[98] Cf. *Qumran Cave 4. XIII*, p. 60.

as Jub. 7,35-37 stipulate that the fourth year produce of the fruit trees belongs to the priests on the basis of this passage, cf. 4QMMT B 62-63;[99] 11QT[a] 60,3-4; and 1QapGen 12,13-15. The evidence has been examined at some length by Baumgarten.[100] Our text may now be added to this list, and the third person masculine plural suffix in line 2 (להם) most probably refers to the priests.[101]

Baumgarten notes that the expression 'land of sojourn' (ארץ מגורים) in l. 3 refers to the exile in Ez. 20,38. The earlier expression '[groun]d of holiness' (אדמ[ה הקודש) which is partly restored, presumably on the basis of a comparable phrase from Zech. 2,16 (Hebrew), refers to Palestine. We may further note that a similar expression 'land of Israel' (אדמת ישראל) is found alongside the expression 'the land of their sojourn' (ארץ מגוריהם) in Ez. 20,38, thus giving additional support to Baumgarten's proposed restoration. In Zech. 2 the expression land of holiness clearly refers to Palestine as the references to Judah and Jerusalem in the same verse indicate. Baumgarten's overall interpretation of 4QD[a] 6 iv 3 as stipulating that the rules apply to both Palestine and the diaspora is plausible although it does rely on a restoration. Baumgarten considers whether the present passage may shed light on the identification of 'Damascus' in the Admonition. He ends on a cautious note,

> We should, however, caution that this sectarian formulation of the law [4QDa 6 iv 3] may be academic rather than based on the sect's own history.[102]

I have reservations about describing the present material as 'sectarian' and would prefer to see it as halakhic traditions that were cherished by a much broader spectrum of society and not necessarily exclusive to a particular sect. Apart from this qualification I concur with this warning.

Baumgarten also draws attention to the comparable expression מגוריהם in 1QS 6,2. The latter passage does not seem to refer to the exile but rather to the dwelling places of community members as

---

[99] Cf. Qimron and Strugnell, *Qumran Cave 4. V*, pp. 164-65. As the editors of MMT have shown the passage in question is clearly based on the fruits of the fourth year legislation in Lev. 19 even though it mentions neither fruit nor the fourth year explicitly.

[100] 'The Laws of ʿOrlah and First Fruits in the Light of Jubilees, the Qumran Writings, and Targum Ps. Jonathan', *JJS* 38 (1987) 195-202. See also M. Kister, 'Some Aspects of Qumranic Halakhah', in *The Madrid Qumran Congress* ed. Trebolle Barrera and Vegas Montaner, II, pp. 571-88, esp. pp. 575-88.

[101] Cf. Baumgarten, *Qumran Cave 4. XIII*, p. 60.

[102] *Qumran Cave 4. XIII*, p. 9.

suggested by Knibb.[103] The chief difference between the present passage and 1QS 6,2 is their frame of reference. 1QS 6,2 contains a piece of communal legislation dealing with a particular community whereas the present passage contains halakhic traditions that are formulated in a style that addresses all Israel. It seems to me, therefore, that the expression that is found in 1QS 6,2 is of limited value for our understanding of the present passage.

3.2.2.3 *Various Prescriptions on Tithing*

The first part of 4QD^f 2 par. deals with the subject of tithing. In Baumgarten's synoptic outline of the contents of D 4QD^f 2 is included twice. First under the heading 'Measures and tithes', which is the present passage, and again under the second heading 'Impurity of idolaters' metals; corpse impurity; sprinkling'. In his synopsis Baumgarten does not refer to any parallels in the other 4QD MSS for the topic of tithes. 4QD^e 3 iii does, however, include fragmentary remains of this section. I will discuss here the first part of 4QD^f 2 which deals with an aspect of agricultural halakhah.

A. *Composite Text*[104]
(4QD^f 2,1-6; 4QD^e 3 iii 13-15)

1 [   ] מנורן יורד את העשרון מן הח[ו]מר היא הא[י]פה
2 [הבת כא[שר הק]ים אל?] האיפה והבת {ב} תכון אחד שניהן ומן [החטים ש]שית
3 [האיפה לחמר ומעשר הבת לפ]רי העץ אל יבדל איש להרים לשה [אח]ד מן המאה
4 [אל] יאכל איש]   מן הגורן] ומן הגנה טרם ישלחו [הכוה]נים את ידם
5 [לבר]ך לריאשונה]   [בית לאיש יסכור ובחסנ] [ח ואז ינקה
6 [ק]ן [[ואת הי]   [שדה המעורב

B. *Translation*

1 [   ] from the threshing floor he shall bring down a tenth per h[omer which is an e]phah

2 [and a *bath*, a]s [God] has ord[ained,] the *ephah* and the *bath* shall have the same value. And from [the wheat a s]ixth

3 [of an *ephah* per *homer*. And a tenth of a *bath* for the fr]uit of the trees. No one shall differ by setting aside from the shee[p on]e out of a hundred.

4 [No] one shall eat [from the threshing floor] and from the garden before [the pries]ts stretch out their hand

---

[103] See M.A. Knibb, *The Qumran Community*, Cambridge: CUP, 1987, p. 115.
[104] The line numbers correspond to the line numbers of 4QD^f 2 which preserves most of the text with only a few additional letters taken from 4QD^e 3 iii. For a different translation cf. Baumgarten, *Qumran Cave 4. XIII*, p. 174.

5 [to bles]s first [   ] house to a man he may sell and [   ] and then he shall be exempt from obligation
6 [   ] and the [   ] the mortgaged field[105]

C. *Commentary*

The last section of agricultural halakhah deals with the subject of tithing. This passage is characterized by the frequent use of the form אל + jussive + איש familiar from other halakhic portions of the Laws. In particular this section deals with the topic of the standardization of measures (l. 2). The biblical law prescribing such a standardization is found in Ez. 45,11. This issue is further addressed in 4Q159 Ord^a 1 ii 13-14 and 4Q513 Ord^b 1-2 i.[106]

L. 4 prohibits the consumption of the now tithed food before a priestly blessing. As noted by Baumgarten the same phrase occurs in 1QS 6,5 with reference to the communal meal.[107] In its present context 1QS 6,5 refers to the communal meals of a particular community in contrast to the present passage which addresses Israel at large. It is noteworthy, however, that 1QS 6,5 employs harvest terminology: 'new wine' (תירוש) and 'the first fruits of the bread' (ראשית הלחם). To this we may add the description of the messianic banquet in 1QSa 2,17b-21a where the same terminology recurs for the priestly blessing as well as the 'harvest terminology'. The occurrence of the same prohibition of eating prior to the priestly blessing in our halakhic text on tithing may account for the 'harvest terminology' employed in 1QS and 1QSa with regard to communal meals. It seems likely that 1QS 6,5 and 1QSa 2,17b-21a constitute communal legislation that has developed out of halakhic traditions associated with the harvest.

L. 5 is rather fragmentary and it is uncertain what was legislated in the second part of this line. Baumgarten suggests that it deals with circumstances in which one may be exempt from the obligation to tithe which seems plausible.[108]

---

[105] Here I have adopted the translation suggested by García Martínez, cf. *Dead Sea Scrolls Translated*, p. 59. Note that this fragment appears there as 4QD^c 1 ii.

[106] Cf. Baumgarten, *Qumran Cave 4. XIII*, p. 174. For editions of 4Q513 and 4Q159 see J.M. Allegro with the collaboration of A.A. Anderson, *Qumran Cave 4. I (4Q158-4Q186)* (DJD V), Oxford: Clarendon Press, 1968, pp. 6-9; Baillet, *Qumrân Grotte 4. III*, pp. 287-98, and Schiffman in Charlesworth ed., *Dead Sea Scrolls*, I, pp. 145-75.

[107] *Qumran Cave 4. XIII*, p. 174.

[108] Cf. Baumgarten, *Qumran Cave 4. XIII*, p. 174.

3.2.2.4 *Overall Assessment of the Agricultural Halakhah*

The various agricultural laws discussed above[109] have been assigned to the halakhah stratum in my analysis for the following reasons.

a. Non-Community Specificity

These agricultural laws lack references to a defined community but reflect instead a national, all-Israel perspective.[110] None of the extant fragments refer to a communal office such as the overseer (מבקר) nor are any of the self-designations mentioned that we frequently encounter in the communal legislation of D such as camp (מחנה) or congregation (עדה). This is not entirely an argument from silence since substantial amounts of text are preserved in a number of cases, and, more significantly, since these texts use a national frame of reference, cf. 4QD^e 3 ii 19 (כול בתי ישראל), 21 (ישראל). Moreover, if we accept Baumgarten's analysis of 4QD^a 6 iv 3 as referring to the diaspora as well as Palestine this constitutes another example of a national perspective, i.e. the homeland (אדמ[ת הקודש]) and the place of exile (ארץ מגורים).

b. Formal Characteristics

The agricultural legislation seems to include a heading of the type 'על plus x' characteristic of the halakhah stratum of the Laws, in 4QD^a 6 iii 3-4. Baumgarten suggests reconstructing two further headings of this type in 4QD^e 3 ii 19 and as part of the heading in red ink in 4Q^e 3 i 19 which are mentioned here only for the sake of completeness.

A number of texts discussed above are too fragmentary for a detailed stylistic analysis. I will briefly comment only on two sections. The section dealing with gleanings in 4QD^e 3 ii par. seems rather distinctive stylistically in the Laws since it is written in a 'staccato style' with large parts of it listing quantities of measures. The material on tithing in 4QD^f 2,1-5 par., on the other hand, employs the formulation אל plus איש plus jussive in 4QD^f 2,3 and 4.

c. Scriptural Basis

A chief characteristic of the halakhah stratum of the Laws as defined in this study is its firm basis in scripture. The agricultural halakhot

---

[109] Two further small fragments that appear to deal with agricultural matters have not been included here, i.e. 4QD^a 6 iii b (cf. *Qumran Cave 4. XIII*, p. 59) and 4QD^e 3 ii a (cf. *Qumran Cave 4. XIII*, p. 150).

[110] Baumgarten has noted the non-sectarian character of the section on gleanings in 4QD^e 3 ii, cf. 'Agrarian Halakhah', p. 5.

outlined above share this characteristic to a large extent. Thus, the legislation on gleanings is based on Lev. 19,9; 23,22 and Dt. 24,19-21, the material dealing with the holy offering of the bread is based on Num. 15,20 and Lev. 23,17, the fourth year produce is legislated upon in Lev. 19,23-25, and, finally, the standardization of *ephah* and *bath* is based on Ez. 45,11.

In sum, I hope to have shown that a strong case can be made for assigning the diverse agricultural laws in 4QD to the halakhah stratum of the Laws of D.

3.2.3 *Various Laws Dealing with Ritual Defilement and Purification*

Among the additional legal material from Cave 4 the laws relating to the agricultural sphere are followed by a section of laws dealing with ritual defilement from various sources and purification.

A. *Composite Text*[111]
(4QD^d 8 i 3; 8 ii 1-6; 4QD^e 3 iii 19-21; and 4QD^f 2,7-13)

1 ממשפטי היחד שלוש פעמים אל יבא איש את [   ] בדם זבחם [   ] ו[כסות
2 בטהרתו ומכול הזהב והכסף והנחושת [וה]בדיל והעו[פרת א]שר עשו הגואים פסל
3 אל יבא איש אל טהרת[ו כיא אם] מן החדש הבא מן הכור [   ] אל יבא איש
4 כול עור ובגד ומן כול הכל[י] אשר יעשה מ[לאכה בהם אשר יטמאו לנפש אדם
5 כיא אם הוזו כמשפט [הטהרה במי] הנדה בקץ הרשע איש טה[ור מ]כול
6 טומאתו אשר יעריב א[ת השמש וכול נער אשר לו]א מלאו ימיו לעבור על
7 הפ[קודים א[ל]יזה]

B. *Translation*
  1 from the ordinances of the community three times. No one shall bring [   ] with the blood of their sacrifices [and] clothes
  2 among his pure stuff. And from all the gold, silver, copper, [t]in, and le[ad with w]hich the gentiles have made idols
  3 no one shall bring any of it to [his] pure stuff [unless] it is from the new (metal) coming (straight) from the furnace [   ] No one shall bring
  4 any hides or garments or any of the [wor]king tools which are defiled with corpse impurity
  5 unless they have been sprinkled according to the law of [purification with the waters of] sprinkling in the time of wickedness by a man puri[fied from] all

---

[111] The line numbers of this composite text do not correspond to the line numbers of any of the underlying fragments.

6 his uncleanness who waits for [sun]down. [And any young boy who has no]t reached the age to pass over to
7 the mu[stered shall no]t [sprinkle]

C. *Textual Notes*

3 All three MSS are slightly at variance with one another here. I have largely followed 4QD^f. 4QD^d 8 ii 3 apparently lacks sufficient space for reconstructing the words אל טהרת[ו] which are clearly attested in 4QD^e 3 iii 21 and 4QD^f 2,10. However, an examination of the photograph on Plate XXIV reveals that the preserved text of 4QD^d 8 ii is imprecisely aligned in the transcription. The first preserved letters of l. 3 ought to begin just to the left of the first preserved letters of l. 2. Moreover, Baumgarten's reconstruction of יביאיהו in 4QD^d 8 ii 3 follows the reading of 4QD^f 2,9 whereas 4QD^d's reading may equally have corresponded to 4QD^e 3 iii 21 which preserves a shorter form of the verb without the suffix (יבא). On the basis of these observations it seems less certain that 4QD^d lacks sufficient space for the additional words אל טהרת[ו]. The second minor variant is the verb without the suffix (יבא) in 4QD^e 3 iii 21 as opposed to the suffixed form (יביאיהו) in 4QD^f 2,9.

D. *Commentary*

The material contained in this passage is held together both by a noticeable thematic coherence as well as a considerable amount of formal coherence. With the exception of l. 1a this section deals with the subject of sources for ritual defilement and purification. It is impossible to establish the relationship of l. 1a to the remainder of the material because we are devoid of its proper context. All that may be noted is the rather distinctive use the self-designation *yaḥad* which relates uneasily to the halakhic material that follows since the latter displays no signs of applying to a particular community. Another expression that is noticeably at odds in its present context is the reference to 'the time of wickedness' (קץ הרשע) in l. 5. I will argue below that the preoccupation with periods of time that make up salvation history is in general absent from the legal part of the Damascus Document.[112] On the few occasions when such references are found interspersed in the Laws they are best assigned to the work of the Damascus redactor. The present example is an instructive case since the reference to the time of wickedness in this section is out of place in two respects. Firstly, it is clearly at odds with the general character of the halakhic exposition that they should apply to a limited period. By contrast, it is the implied intent of halakhic stipulations like those laid down here to be adhered to, at least in theory, indefinite-

---

[112] See pp. 80-81 below.

ly. Secondly, the reference to the time of wickedness in this passage is very difficult syntactically. This seems evident even though there may be some text missing in l. 5. It is very difficult syntactically to have such a general statement on the applicability right in the middle of a halakhic statement rather than at the end or at the beginning of a piece of legislation. In the light of these considerations I attribute this reference to the time of wickedness to the work of the Damascus redactor.[113] Thus, with the exception of l. 1a and the secondary reference to the time of wickedness in l. 5 this section contains a halakhic exposition on sources of defilement and purification.

Apart from this noticeable thematic coherence this material further displays a certain amount of formal coherence with other halakhic sections in the Laws of D, cf. the use of אל + jussive + איש in ll. 1 and 3 (twice). In fact, the phrase 'no one shall bring' (אל יבא איש) runs through this passage almost like a refrain. This catch phrase may have been used for instruction and/or collating of halakhic traditions. Another 'catchword' that appears to link the now largely lost prohibition in ll. 1b-2a to the prohibition involving metals used by pagans in ll. 2b-3a is טהרה.

The formal and thematic coherence of this piece of halakhah is evident in the following outline:
a. pagan cultic practices as a source of defilement (1b-3b)
  i. objects defiled through contact with pagan sacrifices (1b-2a)
  ii. metals defiled through use in pagan idolatry (2b-3a)
b. defilement may be avoided by using only metals straight from the furnace (3b)
a. objects defiled through corpse impurity (3c-4)
b. defilement may be dealt with through the ritual of purification and rules on the correct performance of the ritual[114] (*tebul yom* and the age of the sprinkler) (5-7)

To conclude, the bulk of this text (ll. 1b-7) has been assigned to the halakhah stratum of the Laws. It lacks references to a particular community and displays a considerable degree of formal coherence.

---

[113] *Pace* Baumgarten (*Qumran Cave 4. XIII*, pp. 131, 174-75). According to Baumgarten the expression time of wickedness is 'characteristic of the style of CD'. Although the expression occurs in both the Admonition and the Laws of D, as noted by Baumgarten, I would argue it is characteristic of the concerns of the Admonition but alien to the concerns of the legal part, cf. pp. 80-81 below.

[114] This topic is also dealt with in 4QMMT B14-16 and the still unpublished 4Q276 1 and 4Q277 1. For a discussion and preliminary editions of 4Q276 1 and 4Q277 1 see J.M. Baumgarten, 'The Red Cow Purification Rites in Qumran Texts', *JJS* 46 (1995) 112-119.

We lack the context of l. 1a which makes it very difficult to interpret except to say that it is difficult to relate the self-designation יחד to what follows. More generally, it is difficult to relate l. 1a to the rest of the Laws since this occurrence of the self-designation יחד is the only occurrence in D in contrast to the Community Rule where it occurs scores of times. היחיד is frequently emended to היחד in CD 20,1.14.32. As Davies has shown, these passages form part of a supplement to the Admonition that goes back to the community behind the Community Rule.[115] This survey indicates that the terminology found in l. 1a is alien far beyond its immediate context. Finally, the reference to the time of wickedness was ascribed to the work of the Damascus redactor.

3.2.4 *The Wife Suspected of Adultery and the Betrothed Slave Woman*

In this section I include the group of fragments from 4QD^e that make up 4QD^e 4 as well as 4QD^a 12.[116]

A. *Composite Text*
(4QD^e 4; 4QD^a 12)[117]

[יבא איש אשה להאלותה	]	1
[הרואה אם יראה אשת	]	2
אם [אמרה אנוסה היתי	רעהו]	3
לא יב]ראה כי אם דמה יצוא	]	4
יביאה לפני אי]ש [מן] הכוהנים ופרע	לא יצא]	5
הכהן את ראשה והשביע את [האשה והשקה את	]	6

---

[115] Cf. *Damascus Covenant*, pp. 173-97.
[116] Here I largely follow the arrangement suggested by Baumgarten, *Qumran Cave 4. XIII*, pp. 4-5. According to Baumgarten's comments (*Qumran Cave 4. XIII*, p. 79) Milik suggested that the fragmentary remains of 4QD^a 13 also pertained to the ordeal of *sotah*. Although 4QD^a 13 does not appear to preserve material that parallels 4QD^e 4,1-8 Milik's suggestion that both pertain to the ordeal of *sotah* seems reasonable if difficult to verify with certainty. 4QD^a 13 is too fragmentary for any detailed analysis and is mentioned here for the sake of completeness. Baumgarten further refers to 4QD^h 5, a very poorly preserved papyrus fragment. Because of its poor state of preservation and a number of fairly uncertain readings I did not include that fragement in my discussion. For Baumgarten's edition of 4QD^h 5 cf. *Qumran Cave 4. XIII*, p. 197 where he notes in his comments, "The poor condition of this papyrus manuscript limits the transcription of the fragment [...] to a tentative status." The termionology יקח איש את האש[ה] in l. 4 corresponds to the terminology used in the laws on the arrangment of marriages. Possibly this fragment deals with the same topic.
[117] The line numbers of the composite text correspond to the line numbers of 4QD^e 4 which preserves the most substantial amount of text. I have inserted the fragmentary remains of 4QD^a 12 where appropriate.

HALAKHAH

```
7  [                    ] האשה את מי המרים המאררים [ לא תקח מיד]ו כ[ל
8  [                                                    ] המים [ הקדושים
9  [                                                         ] א[ל יתן איש את
10 [                                           ] לפני [ ע]דים ש[נים   [
11 [                                                                ]ם יש[
12 [                                                              ] המלכים
13 [ ] אל יקרב [   ] אל[ ישכב א]י[ש] עם אשה
14 [                                ] ה[ש]ופחה החרופה ooא
15 [                      ] שבע ש[נים כאשר ] אמר לא ת[
16 [                                       ] י[קחנה את לב]נו [
17 [                                                ]ה את אשר ל[ ]
18 [                                                   ] oooo[
19 [                                             ] מן הקד[ש] לחמו
20 [                      ] הש[מיני ]                  [ ] ישכב עם
21 [                [                 ] עולה [ ]oo
```

B. *Translation*

1 [   ] a man shall bring a woman to place a curse upon her
2 [   ] the one who sees if he sees the wife of
3 [his neighbour   if] she said I was raped[118]
4 [he shall not b]ring her unless her period stays
5 [out he shall bring her before o]ne [of] the priests, and [the priest] shall derange
6 [her head (i.e. the hair on her head) and shall make the] woman [swear] and he shall make h[er] drink
7 [the bitter water of the curse.] She shall not take [any]thing from [his] hand
8 [the] holy [water]
9 [no] one shall give
10 [in front of] t[wo] witnesses [ ]
11 [ ]
12 [   ] the kings
13 [ ] he shall not [ap]proach [no] one shall lie with a woman
14 [the] female slave who is betrothed [ ]
15 [seven y[ears according to that which] he has said, you (or: she) shall not[ ]
16 [he shall t]ake her for [his] so[n]
17 [   ] that which [   ]
18 [   ]
19 [from the holi[ness] his bread
20 [the ei]ghth [   ] he shall lie with
21 [   ] burnt offering [ ]

---

[118] As noted by Baumgarten (*Qumran Cave 4. XIII*, p. 153) our text concords with the understanding of the Hebrew נתפשה in Num. 5,13 reflected in later Jewish exegesis, cf. *Sifre Numbers*, in contrast to modern translations.

C. *Commentary*

Ll. 1-8 deal with the ordeal of *sotah* and are based on Num. 5,11-31. In terms of form the use of לא plus imperfect is close to the biblical style, cf. Num. 5,15, as opposed to the frequent use of אל plus jussive in D, even in lines 9-21 of this Composite Text. L. 2 presupposes witnesses of some sort whereas the biblical legislation prescribes the ordeal of *sotah* for cases without witnesses, cf. Num. 5,13 (ועד אין בה).

Ll. 9-21 contain fragmentary material dealing with sexual relations. Ll. 11-21 of the Composite Text are based on 4QD^a 12 and 4QD^e 4. The placement of the individual fragments that make up 4QD^e 4 is uncertain.[119] Since ll. 9-16 are paralleled by 4QD^a 12 the placement of the fragments containing these lines is to a large extent confirmed.

Despite the fragmentary nature of these lines a number of observations can be made. Firstly, the material in ll. 9-16 displays the same formal characteristics as the halakhic exposition stratum in the Laws of D, i.e. אל plus jussive plus איש, cf. ll. 9 and 13. Moreover, l. 15 seems to preserve remnants of an introductory formula introducing a scriptural citation or reference that has not survived. The reference to the slave woman in l. 14 appears to be based on Lev. 19,20-22 as noted by Baumgarten.[120]

To conclude, the formal cohesion and firm basis in scripture indicate that ll. 9-16 of the Composite Text belong more in the realm of scriptural exposition than communal legislation. The material dealing with the ordeal of *sotah* in ll. 1-8 constitutes a piece of halakhic exposition of scripture. It lacks the formal cohesion that frequently characterizes the halakhic exposition in the Laws of D and which is also present in the subsequent section. I would nevertheless associate the material dealing with the ordeal of *sotah* with the stratum containing halakhic exposition of scripture because it is clearly based on Num. 5. 11-31.

3.2.5 *The Jubilee Year, a Prohibition of Transvestism, Ethical Standards in Business, and the Arrangement of Marriages*

The unifying feature of the bulk of this section is an emphasis on honesty and moral behaviour as captured in the Baumgarten's phrase 'Integrity in commercial dealings and marriage' in his synoptic outline of the contents of D.[121] Ll. 10b-18 demand equally honest

---

[119] Cf. *Qumran Cave 4. XIII*, p. 154 and Plate XXX.
[120] Cf. *Qumran Cave 4. XIII*, p. 79.
[121] *Qumran Cave 4. XIII*, pp. 4-5.

transactions when it comes to the arrangement of marriages as are prescribed for business transactions in ll. 7b-8. As will become apparent in my discussion of this material below, Lev. 25 and Dt. 22 provide a number of links between the diverse issues dealt with in this section.

A. *Composite Text*[122]
(4QD^b 7; 4QD^d 9; 4QD^e 5; 4QD^f 3)

ואהב לו]	1
[ ]	2
וזה פרוש]	3
[בכסף] [	4
[ואם לוא השינה דיו לה[שיב לו] והניש[ה] שנת ה[יובל]	5
[ואדם ואל ישוב ל] עוונתיו אל [י]הי[ו כלי]	6
[נבר על איש ואשה] כאחת כי תועבה היא vacat ואשר אמר כי [ ] המכרו [	7
[ממכר או קנה מיד] עמיתך לוא תונו איש את עמיתו vacat וזה פר[וש]	8
[ ] בכול אשר הוא יודע אשר ימצא [	9
[ ] והוא יודע אשר הוא מועל בו באדם ובהמה ואם	10
את בתו ית[ן] איש לאיש את כול מומיה יספר לו למה יביא עליו את משפט	11
האררה אשר אמר משנה עור בדרך ונם אל יתנה לאשר לוא הוכן לה כי	12
הוא כלאים שור וחמור ולבוש צמר ופשתים יחדיו vacat אל יבא איש	13
אשה בברי]ת הקודש אשר ידעה לעשות מעשה בדבר ואשר ידעה	14
מעשה [בביה] אביה או אלמנה אשר נשכבה מאשר התארמלה וכול	15
אש]ר] עליה שם רע בבתוליה בבית אביה אל יקחה איש כי אם	16
בראות נשים נאמנות וידעות ברורות ממאמר מבקר אשר על	17
מחנ]ה ואחר יקחנה ובלוקחו אותה יעשה כמ[ש]פט [ולוא] יניד עלי[ה]	18

B. *Translation*
1 and he loves him [ ]
2 [ ]
3 And this is the exact statement of [ ]
4 [ ] with money [ ]
5 [ ] and if he cannot afford to bu[y it back], and the [jubilee] year is drawing ne[ar]
6 [ ] and a human being. And he shall not[123] return to [ ] his sins. [Men's clothing sh]al[l] not

---

[122] The line numbers of the composite text do not correspond to the line numbers in any of the constituent fragments.

[123] Here my reading and translation differs markedly from Baumgarten, cf. my textual note to line 6. Baumgarten translates "and God will release (יעזוב)..." and understands the first half of this line in the light of the previous line, i.e. God releases from sin those who grant release to the poor referrring especially to Ps. 41,1 and 11QMelch 2,6 (*Qumran Cave 4. XIII*, p. 176). It seems to me that the first half of this

7 [be shared by a man and a woman] for this is an abomination. *Vacat*. And as to what he said, For [if you sell]
8 [anything to or buy anything from] your fellow you shall not cheat one another. *Vacat*. And this is the exact state[ment]
9 [ ] according to all that he knows that he will find [ ]
10 [ ] and he knows that he is betraying him concerning a human being or concerning an animal. And if
11 a man [giv]es [his daughter] to another (in marriage) he shall report to him all her shortcomings lest he bring upon himself the judgment of
12 the curse as he has said, The one who leads astray the blind from the path. And also he shall not give her to one who is not suitable for her for
13 that is two kinds (like ploughing with) an ox and a donkey, and to wear wool and linen together. *Vacat*. No one shall bring
14 [a woman into the cove]nant of holiness who has had sexual encounters
15 [(while she was living) in the house of] her father, or a widow who has had sexual relations since she has been widowed, or any (woman)
16 [who] had a bad reputation in her youth in her father's house—no one shall take any of these unless
17 on examination by trustworthy women who are knowledgeable and chosen at the word of the overseer who is over
18 [the cam]p. And afterwards he may take her, and when he takes her he shall act according to the l[a]w [and not] report on her

C. *Textual Notes*

6 My transcription of this line differs from Baumgarten's transcription of 4QD^f 3,3. Having examined the photograph of 4QD^f 3,3 on Plate XXXVIII it seems possible to me that the third word of this line in the Composite Text which Baumgarten takes to be יעזוב (*Qumran Cave 4. XIII*, p. 175) could also be read ישב. The phrase in context (ואל ישוב ל[ ] עוונותיו) would then resemble Jer. 11,9-10 which Baumgarten uses as a basis for reconstructing 4QD^b 5 ii 3.[124]

line is best taken as a prohibition consisting of אל plus jussive since the second half of the line contains another prohibition. Moreover Baumgarten's interpretation presupposes a rather rare case of the subject preceding the verb for emphasis whereas לא plus jussive occurs scores of times in D. Finally, the verb usually used in D with reference to the forgiveness of sins is כפר (cf. CD 3,18; 4,10; 14,19), a consideration which though not decisive on its own is noteworthy in conjunction with the preceding observations. Three recent translations of of 4QD^f 3,3 by García Martínez (*Dead Sea Scrolls Translated*, p. 57 where 4Q 271 [D^f] is referred to as 4Q 268 [D^c]), Maier (*Qumran-Essener*, 1995, II, p. 231), and Cook (Wise, Abegg, and Cook, *A New Translation*, p. 63) take אל to be a negation here. The concordance in *Qumran Cave 4. XIII*, p. 203 erroneously lists what should be אל on the editor's reading (4Q271 3,3) under the preposition אל.

[124] Cf. *Qumran Cave 4. XIII*, p. 101.

14 4QD^e 5,17 reads הקו[ה]ש whereas 4QD^d 9,4 lacks the article.
15 4QD^e 5,19 has a *vacat* before אלמנה או whereas D^f 3,12 does not.
18 Baumgarten reads traces of a final *mem* in 4QD^d 9,8 which if adopted would result in reconstructing the first word of this line as רבי]ם providing the expression 'the overseer who is over the many'. An examination of the photograph reproduced on Plate XXIV reveals, however, only minute traces of a letter that may equally be part of a *he*, cf. the *he* in הוה in 4QD^d 8 ii 4 reproduced on the same Plate. If it did constitute the remains of a *he*, which is the possible reading I favour in the transcription above, the overall expression might be 'the overseer who is over the camp'. Such a reconstruction is supported by the fact that the Laws of D most frequently associate the overseer with the camp.[125] The continuous text ends here with the end of 4QD^f 3,15. Only traces of letters are preserved in 4QD^f 3,16 which has not been included here.

D. *Commentary*
Too little remains of ll. 1-4 to permit comment except to say that the heading or concluding statement partially preserved in l. 3 recurs in l. 8.

a. L. 5 The redemption of property
The subject at issue in l. 5 is the redemption of property sold in poverty either through payment or in the jubilee year. As Baumgarten has pointed out this material is based on Lev. 25.[126] Lev. 25,28 is particularly close in terminology to this line, and perhaps closer than Lev. 25,47-55 referred to by Baumgarten.

b. Ll. 6-7a A prohibition of transvestism
The remains of ll. 6-7a preserve two prohibitive clauses only the second of which is reasonably well preserved. Both prohibitives make us of the negation אל followed by the jussive, a style frequently attested in the halakhah stratum of the Laws of D. The second prohibition forbids cross dressing, a subject also prohibited in 4Q159 2-4,7. The latter parallel is used by Baumgarten in reconstructing 4QD^f 3,3-4.[127] The scriptural basis of this prohibition is Dt. 22,5. Both the use of the form of the prohibitive familiar from other halakhic sections in the Laws as well as the scriptural foundation of this prohibition point to an association of this passage with the halakhah stratum of the Laws.

---

[125] For a list of passages that mention the overseer in conjunction with the camp(s) see p. 82 below.
[126] *Qumran Cave 4. XIII*, p. 176.
[127] Cf. *Qumran Cave 4. XIII*, p. 176.

c. Ll. 7b-10a Ethical standards in business

Ll. 7b-10a are concerned with the question of ethical standards in business transactions. I treat these line together although ll. 8b-10a are fragmentary and may have dealt with a different topic. Ll. 8b-10a share with the prohibition quoted from Lev. 25,14 in ll. 7b-8a a concern for openness and honesty. As we saw with reference to l. 5 Lev. 25 deals with redemption of property in the sabbatical year and the jubilee year. In its immediate context in Lev. 25,13-17 verse 14 refers to the appropriate manner in which to redeem property within the framework of the jubilee cycle rather than constituting a general admonition to fair dealing as is the case in the present passage. Thus, both ll. 7b-8a and l. 5 are based on Lev. 25.

d. Ll. 10b-18 The arrangement of marriages

Ll. 10b-18 deal with the arrangement of marriages and make up the most substantial portion of the Composite Text presented above. Baumgarten notes a similar sequence of topics in 4Q159 2-4 where we find a prohibition of transvestism followed by the issue of the defamation of a bride's virginity. This loose correspondence in topics and sequence between 4Q159 and 4QD is based on the fact that both documents are here expounding Dt. 22. The prohibition of cross dressing is found in Dt. 22,5, and the law dealing with defamation of a bride's virginity follows in Dt. 22,13-21. Moreover, Dt. 22,10-11 provides the passage forbidding ploughing with an ox and a donkey or wearing wool and linen appealed to in ll. 10b-18 of the Composite Text above. The prohibition of wearing clothes made of wool and linen (Dt. 22,11) is also appealed to in 4QMMT B75-82 in a passage critical of marriages between priests and Israelites. Dt. 22,11 and perhaps also Dt. 22,10 appear to have been referred to regularly to describe unsuitable unions.[128]

Thus, Lev. 25 and Dt. 22 lie behind a great deal of the material contained in this section. This basis in scripture leads us to the question of the literary place of this passage in the Laws which is the chief concern of the present study. The material presented above shares a number of important characteristics with the halakhah stratum of the Laws, and the bulk of this section can be assigned to the halakhah stratum. The evidence is rather complex, however, when we come to ll. 17b-18a. Let me begin by substantiating my case for assigning the bulk of this section to the halakhah stratum of the Laws. Firstly, we saw that most of the issues dealt with in this section

---

[128] D.J. Harrington has drawn attention to a wisdom text (4Q418 103) that appeals to Dt. 22,10 in an agricultural context, cf. *Wisdom Texts from Qumran*, p. 59.

are based on scripture, particularly Lev. 25 and Dt. 22, and these passages provide something of a red thread that holds these topics together. The fragmented impression of parts of this section is, no doubt, also caused by its fragmentary nature. Secondly, the section shares a number of formal characteristics with the halakhah stratum of the Laws, cf. the prohibitives (אל plus jussive [plus איש]) in ll. 6, 12, 13, and 16 and the references to scripture introduced with the formula (ו)אשר אמר in ll. 7 and 12. Finally, with the exception of ll. 17b-18a, to which I will turn shortly, this section contains halakhah that is not explicitly associated with a particular community.

This picture is radically altered when we turn to ll. 17b-18a which introduce the overseer (מבקר) into the process of selecting experienced women to examine prospective brides whose virginity has been called into question. A comparable process of examination is described in 4Q159 2-4,8-10, a passage for which J.H. Tigay has proposed a restoration that is now dramatically confirmed by 4QD^d 9,7.[129] Tigay surveys evidence of this praxis that spreads over two thousand years and various cultures. What is of central importance for our present purposes is the presence of a law prescribing the examination of prospective brides in both 4QD^d 9 par. and in 4Q159 2-4,8-10 with the important difference that only in 4QD the overseer has been integrated into this procedure. The role of the overseer was apparently the selection of suitable women to conduct the examination. As the example of 4Q159 shows a law prescribing such an examination circulated in halakhic texts in the context of interpreting Dt. 22. It seems to me, therefore, that the Composite Text presented above constitutes another halakhic text dealing with issues raised in Dt. 22 as well as Lev. 25 which has been adapted to become part of the communal legislation governing the community behind the Laws by the addition of ll. 17b-18a.

CD 13,16b-18a preserves a number of regulations that refer to the role of an individual, most probably the overseer, in the context of marriage, divorce, and the disciplining of children.[130] Thus, the overseer seems to play a role when it comes to marriage according to the communal legislation in the Laws. Ll. 17b-18a of the Composite Text above seem to reflect an updating of non-community specific halakhot dealing with the arrangement of marriages in the light of the status quo in the community that transmitted these halakhot.

---

[129] J.H. Tigay, 'Examination of the Accused Bride in 4Q159: Forensic Medicine at Qumran', *JANES* 22 (1993) 129-34.
[130] See p. 126 below.

In sum, the passage dealing with the redemption of property, transvestism, fair trade and marriage arrangement has been assigned to the halakhah stratum of the Laws and draws particularly on Lev. 25 and Dt. 22. The regulations dealing with the arrangement of marriages have been updated for use in the camp community as ll. 17b-18a demonstrate.

3.3 Conclusions

A number of conclusions may now be drawn for the interpretation of the halakhah stratum of the Laws of D.

a. Priestly Background

Priestly concerns predominate especially in the additional legal material from 4QD, cf. the material on the disqualification of priests and skin disease. It seems likely that these traditions originated with priestly groups long before the emergence of the *yahad* and probably also prior to the emergence of the parent movement of the *yahad* whose communal legislation is preserved side by side with the halakhah in the Laws of D. There is no reason to believe, moreover, that the halakhic positions expressed in this stratum of the Laws were not held by other Jews beyond the confines of the communities reflected in the communal legislation of the Laws. Here I am in close agreement with a number of scholars who have argued that the scrolls contain halakhah with a much wider application.[131] I have tried to identify more precisely which portions of the Laws are more likely to have originated outside the confines of a particular community and to have been cherished more widely.

b. The Need to Compare Like with Like

Whereas it is customary to read the Damascus Document and the Community Rule side by side, this procedure sheds less light on the halakhah stratum of the Laws than it does on the Admonition or the

---

[131] Cf. Baumgarten, 'Disqualifications of Priests', p. 513 where he concludes with reference to the material on the disqualification of certain categories of priests, "There is a large body of halakha which apparently was not limited to any of the three groups [Pharisees, Sadducees, and Essenes], but represents the common traditional law of the Second Temple period." S. Talmon has expressed similar views and agreement with Baumgarten's judgment, cf. 'Qumran Studies', p. 17 n. 68. Further, Y. Sussman has noted that, "it is not clear whether the halakha in the other works of the sect [i.e. other than 4QMMT] (as well as in the Apocrypha and elsewhere) was unique to the sect or was unanimously accepted", Appendix 1 in Qimron and Strugnell, *Qumran Cave 4. V*, p. 186. See also Schiffman, *Reclaiming the Dead Sea Scrolls*, p. 274.

communal organization stratum of the Laws. The halakhah stratum is more appropriately read alongside documents or parts of documents such as 4Q159 (Ordinances^a),[132] 4QMMT, and 11QT with which it has a great deal in common. Y. Sussman has commented with reference to 4QMMT, "The halakhah of MMT does not govern the communal life of the sect."[133] Sussman's description of the halakhot in MMT closely resembles my own description of the halakhah stratum in the Laws of D. These similarities are accounted for by the many affinities not between the Laws of D in their entirety and MMT, as is usually argued, but between a particular stratum in the Laws of D and MMT.

c. The Absence of Redactional Activity

In contrast to the communal legislation the halakhah material shows no evidence to speak of of redactional activity and updating.[134] It appears that this material was transmitted much more faithfully without the need being felt for updating it and adjusting it to present-day community realities. We look in vain, for example, for evidence of attempting to bring the halakhah in line with the community reflected in the Community Rule. The reasons for this lack of redactional activity in the halakhah are palpable. The halakhah stratum has a pronounced scriptural orientation. The forms of expression employed and the social relations described are frequently scripturally based rather than reflecting a particular contemporary community. This feature accounts for the more faithful handling of this material as traditions to be handed on. The communal legislation which displays traces of revision and updating, by contrast, was intended to be relied upon in a particular contemporary situation and was therefore clearly in need of constant revision and updating. For example, the non-scriptural title and office of the overseer appears to have developed in the course of the community's existence. Once this title had come into use, it would have been felt necessary to insert references to this figure in the communal legislation, a process perhaps reflected in CD 13,2b-7a.[135] Similarly, if the kind of community that lies behind the Laws of the Damascus Document in their final form referred to itself as 'the many' (הרבים), then this self-designation

---

[132] Similarities between the Laws of D and 4Q159 were noted already by Baumgarten, cf. 'Laws of the *Damascus Document* in Current Research', p. 56.

[133] Appendix 1 in Qimron and Strugnell, *Qumran Cave 4. V*, p. 186.

[134] Exceptions are the reference to the camp in CD 10,23 which I take to be a secondary addition, cf. p. 36 n. 39 above, and the updating of the material on the arrangement of marriages, cf. pp. 68-70 above.

[135] See section 6.2 below.

needed to be integrated into the communal legislation of the Laws alongside earlier self-designations such as 'camp' (מחנה) and 'congregation' (עדה), as was indeed the case on my analysis of the communal legislation in the Laws.

d. The Absence of Polemic

The halakhah stratum is, on the whole, free of overt polemics against opponents. This feature distinguishes this material clearly from the Admonition of the Damascus Document as well as from a small layer of polemical material in the Laws themselves. It lies in the nature of halakhic exposition, of course, that the interpretations arrived at often differ from the halakhic decisions taken in other groups. However, even if the author(s) responsible for the halakhic exposition found in this stratum were at times consciously propounding a view that differed from the position taken by other Jewish groups they certainly never polemicised against those who held a different view from their own.[136]

In sum, the halakhah stratum of the Laws preserves legal traditions that originated independently from the communal legislation. These halakhic traditions have a great deal more in common with works such as 4Q159 Ord[a], 4QMMT, and 11QT than the Community Rule and are best read and studied alongside the former group of text from the corpus of the scrolls. I argued that the halakhah stratum displays a considerable degree of formal cohesion and presupposes a national frame of reference. I noted, furthermore, that the halakhic traditions discussed above show little evidence of redactional activity and up-dating. The communities behind D in its final form cherished these halakhic traditions and incorporated them alongside their communal legislation.

---

[136] For a halakhic text with an explicitly polemical edge cf. the reference to 'the error of blindness' (תעות עורון) in 4Q513 4,4 cf. Baillet, *Qumrân Grotte 4. III*, p. 290, Baumgarten, 'Halakhic Polemics', pp. 395-7, and Schiffman in Charlesworth ed., *Dead Sea Scrolls*, I, pp. 160-61.

CHAPTER FOUR

COMMUNITY ORGANIZATION PART ONE: ADMISSION INTO THE COVENANT COMMUNITY

The material that has been assigned to the stratum community organization of the Laws of D contains regulations that seem to prescribe for the life of a particular organized community within Israel. This basic feature clearly distinguishes these texts from other material within the corpus of the Laws.

Furthermore, a certain set of vocabulary is used predominantly in this material when referring to the community whose organization is being regulated, e.g. 'the camp(s)' מחנה (cf. CD 9,11; 12,23; 13,4.5.7. 13.16.20; 14,3.9; 4QD^a 7 ii 6; 7 iii 3; 11,17; 4QD^e 7 ii 14; 4QD^h 4 i 8)[1] and 'the congregation' עדה (cf. CD 10,4.5.8; 13,10.11.13; 14,10; 4QD^b 5 iii 6; 4QD^e 7 i 14).[2] Detailed attention is devoted in my discussion of these texts below to subtle shifts in terminology in order to distinguish a number of secondary passages that have entered this material in the course of its transmission.

4.1 Admission into the Covenant Community

Here I will deal with the regulations on the admission of new members into the community as laid down in the Damascus Document.

A. *Text*[3]
(CD 15,5b-16,6a; 4QD^a 8 i; 4QD^c 6 i-ii; 4QD^f 4 ii)

15:5b	והבא בברית לכל ישראל לחוק עולם את בניהם אשר יניעו
15:6	לעבור על הפקודים בשבועת הברית יקימו עליהם *vacat* וכן
15:7	המשפט בכל קץ הרשע לכל השב מדרכו הנשחתה ביום דברו

---

[1] This list does not include 4QD passages that parallel either the text of CD or the text of another 4QD MS. On the reference to the camp in CD 10,23, cf. p. 36 n. 39 above.

[2] On the prevalence of the latter self-designation in the Laws of D cf. H. Stegemann, 'Das Gesetzeskorpus der "Damaskusschrift" (CD IX-XVI)', *RQ* 14 (1990) 409-34, p. 420.

[3] Unless otherwise indicated the text and reconstructions of CD here and elsewhere in this book are taken from Qimron, 'Text of CDC'. The reconstructions of the final lines of CD 15 are based on the parallel text of 4QD^a 8 i.

CHAPTER FOUR

15:8	עם המבקר אשר לרבים יפקדוהו בשבועת הברית אשר כרת
15:9	משה עם ישראל את הברית לשׁ[וב] אל תורת משה בכל לב ו[ב]כ[ל]
15:10	נפש אל הנמצא לעשות בכ[ל] קץ ק[י]ׄ[מו ואל יודיעהו איש את
15:11	המשפטים עד עמדו לפני המבקר שמה יתפתה בו בדרשו אתו
15:12	וכאשר יקים אותו עליו לשוב אל תורת משה בכל לב ובכל נפש
15:13	נק[ר]אים הם ממנו אם ימעל vacat וכל אשר נגלה מן התורה לרוב]
15:14	המחנה והוא שנה בו יוד[יעה]וׄ המבקר אותו וצוה עליו ויל[מד]וׄ
15:15	עד שנה תמימה ולפי דעתו קׄרׄבׄ וׄכׄוׄלׄ היותו אויל ומשונע אל יׄבׄוׄ וכל פתׄ[י] ,שׁ[ו]נה
15:16	וכהה עינים לבל[ו]תׄי ראות וחגר או פסח או חרש או נ[ער ז]ׄעטו[ט אל
15:17	יבוא אי[ש מאלה אל תוך העדה כי מלאכי הקודש [○○סלת בם
15:18	[אמׄ[ר להם [○] [○]
15:19	[דור]
15:20	[○○ ול
15:21	
15:22	
15:23	[כרתי]
16:1	עמכם ברית ועם כל ישראל על כן יקום האיש על נפשך לשוב אל
16:2	תורת משה כי בה הכל מדוקדק vacat ופרוש קציהם לעורון
16:3	ישראל מכל אלה הנה הוא מדוקדק על ספר מחלקות העתים
16:4	ליובליהם ובשבועותיהם וביום אשר יקום האיש על נפשו לשוב
16:5	אל תורת משה יסור מלאך המשטמה מאחריו אם יקים את דבריו
16:6a	על כן נימול {ב} אברהם ביום דעתו

B. *Translation*

15,5b And he who enters the covenant for all Israel it shall be an eternal statute, together with their children who reach

   6 the age to pass over to the mustered, they shall bind themselves with the oath of the covenant. <u>And thus</u>

   7 <u>shall be the case during all the time of wickedness for everyone who turns from his corrupt way.</u> On the day on which he speaks

   8 to the overseer <u>over the many</u> they shall muster him with the oath of the covenant which Moses

   9 made with Israel, the covenant to re[turn] to the law of Moses with all one's heart and [with] al[l]

  10 one's soul, to that which is found to do in al[l] the time of his uph[ol]ding the oath. And no one shall make known to him the

  11 ordinances until he stands before the overseer lest he reveal himself to be a simpleton[4] when he examines him.

---

[4] For a translation along these lines cf. Baumgarten's translation in Charlesworth ed., *Dead Sea Scrolls*, II, p. 39. Such a translation of יתפתה seems plausible in the light of what is said in CD 15,15-16 below. Note the recurrence of the noun פתי in l. 15. For a different translation cf. G. Vermes, *Complete Dead Sea Scrolls*, p. 136.

12 Once he swears an oath to return to the law of Moses with all (his) heart and all (his) soul
13 they shall be [free from] responsibility if he acts unfaithfully. And all that has been revealed from the law to the multitude
14 of the camp and (if) he errs in it, the overseer shall instr[uct] him and he shall give orders regarding him and he shall tea[ch] him
15 for a full year, and according to his knowledge _{he shall draw near. An no} fool or imbecile _{shall enter}. And no one who is a simple[ton] _{or} mis[gui]ded,
16 no one with dimmed eyes unable t[o see, no one who limps, is lame or deaf], no y[oun]g boy—none
17 [of these] shall enter [the midst of the congregation for the angels of holiness [ ]
18 [he sai]d to them
19-22 [ ]
23 [I have made]
16,1 with you a covenant and with all Israel. Therefore he shall bind himself to return to
2 the law of Moses for in it everything is laid down in detail. *But the exact statement of their times with regard to the blindness*
3 *of Israel concerning all these, behold they are laid down in detail in the book of the divisions of the times*
4 *into their jubilees and weeks.* And on the day on which he binds himself to return
5 to the law of Moses the angel of Mastema shall depart from following him, if he keeps his word.
6a For this reason Abraham was circumcised on the day he received his knowledge.⁵

C. *Textual Notes*

15,9 Here I am following the reading הברית suggested by Rabin;⁶ Qimron reads דברו.⁷ The most recent edition of the CD Laws by Baumgarten also reads הבר[י]ת.⁸

15,10 The MS is damaged in the centre of this line, and a number of readings for the remains of the word following קץ have been proposed. The reading adopted above follows a suggestion by Nebe.⁹

---

⁵ This translation of ביום דעתו follows a suggestion by Prof. E. Ullendorff.
⁶ *Zadokite Documents*, p. 73.
⁷ Cf. 'Text of CDC', p. 39 and the reproduced photograph p. 38.
⁸ See Baumgarten in Charlesworth ed., *Dead Sea Scrolls*, II, p. 38.
⁹ G.W. Nebe, 'Das Sprachvermögen des Mebaqqer in *Damaskusschrift* XIV,10', *RQ* 16 (1993) 289-91, p. 289 n. 1: "Ich wuerde in XV,10 cher קץ כ[ל]ל בכל[קץ ק]י[מו 'in der ganzen Zeit seines (Eid-) Erfüllens' (vgl. *Ps* 119,106) [...] lescn." For the photograph see Qimron, 'Text of CDC', p. 38. Qimron reads ק]רב['war' (p. 39), and this reading seems to lie behind Schiffman's recent translation 'the period of his drawing near' (*Reclaiming the Dead Sea Scrolls*, p. 100). Baumgarten reads and reconstructs קץ [הרשע (Baumgarten in Charlesworth ed., *Dead Sea Scrolls*, II, p. 38). Traces of a downstroke of the *qoph* seem to be visible in the photograph of the MS which speaks against Baumgarten's reconstruction.

15,11 I have adopted Qimron's reading שמה here.¹⁰ 4QDᵃ 8 i 2 reads למה although only traces of the *lamed* remain.¹¹

15,12 4QDᵃ 8 i 3 reads יקים עלו where CD's text has יקים אותו עליו.

15,14 4QDᵃ 8 i 5 reads ויצוהו עלו where CD's text has וצוה עליו. Traces of the suffix in ויל[מד]ו appear to be visible in the photograph of the MS but the suffix has not been included in Qimron's transcription.¹² Baumgarten reads ויל[מ]ד with *lamed* and *dalet* identified as possible readings, but his translation adds 'him' in parenthesis.¹³ 4QDᵉ 6 ii 7 reads וילמדהו although the suffix is no more than a possible reading.¹⁴ The first three words of this line are only faintly preserved and the readings are no more than probable. I have adopted Qimron's reading שנה.¹⁵ Rabin suggests reading שׁוה and translates 'though he had agreed to it'.¹⁶

15,15 Four additional words as well as the additional *waw* have been included in subscript on the basis of 4QDᵃ 8 i 6-7 which results in a much improved Hebrew text for this line.

15,18 The reconstruction [אמ]ר is taken from Baumgarten.¹⁷ It does not appear to be based on a parallel from 4QD.

15,23 This word is restored with the help of 4QDᶠ 4 ii 3. Since pages CD 9-12 preserve twenty three lines per page it seems reasonable to assume the text restored immediately preceding CD 16,1 would occur in l. 23 of CD 15.¹⁸

16,1 4QDᶠ 4 ii 3 reads עמכה where CD's text has עמכם. For יקום read יקים¹⁹ and for נפשך we should probably read נפשו.²⁰

16,4 As in 16,1 we should read יקים for יקום.

D. *Commentary*

This passage describes the entry into the movement that lies behind the communal legislation of the Laws of the Damascus Document by swearing the oath of the covenant. The admission process that emerges from this passage differs considerably from the more elaborate procedure laid down in 1QS 6,13b-23.²¹

---

¹⁰ Cf. 'Text of CDC', p. 39.
¹¹ Cf. Baumgarten, *Qumran Cave 4. XIII*, p. 63 and Plate X.
¹² Cf. 'Text of CDC', pp. 38-39.
¹³ Baumgarten in Charlesworth, *Dead Sea Scrolls*, II, pp. 38-39.
¹⁴ Cf. Baumgarten, *Qumran Cave 4. XIII*, p. 156 and Plate XXXI.
¹⁵ 'Text of CDC', pp. 38-39. Qimron's reading is preferable in the light of what follows in CD 15,14b-17 where proper instruction is emphasized and misguided candidates are excluded.
¹⁶ *Zadokite Documents*, pp. 74-75.
¹⁷ Cf. Baumgarten in Charlesworth ed., *The Dead Sea Scrolls*, II, p. 38.
¹⁸ Cf. Baumgarten, *Qumran Cave 4. XIII*, p. 178 where he reads and restores the first half of 4QDᶠ 4 ii 3 as follows, לאמור [על] פי הדׄ[ברי]ם האלה כרתי.
¹⁹ Cf. Qimron, 'Text of CDC', p. 41 n. 2.
²⁰ Cf. Qimron, 'Text of CDC', p. 41 n. 3.
²¹ For a discussion of the admission process in D and S see C. Hempel, 'Community Structures in the Dead Sea Scrolls: Admission, Organization, and Disciplinary Procedures', in *The Dead Sea Scrolls Jubilee Collection* ed. P. Flint and J.C.

The tone of this passage is unpolemical towards Israel as a whole. Israel at large is referred to in a neutral and even positive manner at several instances. CD 15,5b and 16,1 speak of the covenant with all Israel, and 15,9 contains a further reference to the covenant that Moses made with Israel. Thus, at least in theory, the movement behind this piece of communal legislation sees itself as representing all Israel.

However, the passage is not entirely homogeneous in this respect, and the different attitude towards Israel at large distinguishes CD 15,6b-7a from the remainder of the passage. CD 15,6b-7a reads: 'And thus shall be the case during all the time of wickedness for everyone who turns from his corrupt way.' Rather than referring to new members as those who enter the covenant, this phrase describes newcomers as 'everyone who turns from his corrupt way.' This formulation stands out from the passage as a whole because of its polemical attitude towards that part of Israel that does not belong to the community. These considerations alerted me to the possibility that CD 15,6b-7a is a redactional phrase that has been added at a secondary stage to this piece of legislation. This suggestion receives further support from two additional observations.

Firstly, according to my translation of CD 15,5b-6a what is said in 15,6b-7a is adding nothing new except a polemical edge to what has been stated already. Why should a separate reference be necessary to 'everyone who turns from his corrupt way', when CD 15,5b speaks of new members—and their older children—in general? On this translation CD 15,6b-7a is superfluous in terms of content, as well as standing out because of its polemical tone.

To be sure, not everyone has translated lines 5b-7a in this way. The translators of this passage fall into two camps. There are those who render את בניהם 'together with their children' (Charles,[22] Cothenet,[23] Maier (1995),[24] and Schechter[25]), and this seems to me the grammatically preferable translation. The great majority of translators take 15,5b-6a to refer to the admission of the children of members, and 15,6b-7a to deal with new members in general (Burrows,[26]

VanderKam, Leiden: E.J. Brill, forthcoming.
 [22] R.H. Charles, *The Apocrypha and Pseudepigrapha of the Old Testament in English with Introductions and Critical and Explanatory Notes to the Several Books*, Oxford: Clarendon Press, 1977, II, p. 833.
 [23] É. Cothenet, 'Le Document de Damas' in *Les Textes de Qumran* ed. J. Carmignac, É. Cothenet et H. Lignée, Paris: Letouzey et Ané, 1963, II, pp. 129-204, esp. p. 182.
 [24] J. Maier, *Qumran-Essener*, 1995, I, p. 30.
 [25] S. Schechter, Fragments of a Zadokite Work, p. lv.
 [26] M. Burrows, *The Dead Sea Scrolls*, London: Secker &Warburg, 1956, p. 363.

Dupont-Sommer,[27] García Martínez,[28] Gaster,[29] Lohse, Maier (1960 and 1992),[30] Rabin,[31] and Vermes). Thus, Vermes translates the passage in question as follows:

> And when the children of all those who have entered the Covenant, granted to all Israel for ever, reach the age of enrolment, they shall swear with the oath of the Covenant. And thus shall it be during all the age of wickedness for every man who repents of his corrupted way.[32]

Along the same lines Lohse renders 15,5b-7a:

> Und für jeden, der in den Bund eingetreten ist, der für ganz Israel bestimmt ist, sei es ewige Satzung: ihren Söhnen, die das Alter erreicht haben, um zu den Gemusterten hinüberzugehen, sollen sie den Eid des Bundes auferlegen. Und so ist die Anordnung in der ganzen Zeit der Gottlosigkeit für jeden, der von seinem verderbten Weg umkehrt.[33]

Both translations try to make sense of an awkward Hebrew text. Lohse renders בשבועת הברית יקימו עליהם 'den Eid des Bundes auferlegen', although it appears from CD 15,12 that the *hiphil* of קום with the preposition על plus suffix means 'to bind oneself by oath'.[34] Vermes's translation takes the verb in the latter sense, but it is difficult to see how one would justify taking את בניהם as the subject of the sentence as his translation does.[35]

---

[27] A. Dupont-Sommer, *The Essene Writings from Qumran*, Oxford: Blackwell, 1961, p. 161.

[28] F. García Martínez, *Dead Sea Scrolls Translated*, p. 39.

[29] T.H. Gaster, *Scriptures of the Dead Sea Sect*, p. 92.

[30] J. Maier, *Die Texte vom Toten Meer*, München: Reinhardt, 1960, I, p. 65; and J. Maier and K. Schubert, *Die Qumran-Essener*, München: Reinhardt, 1992, p. 187.

[31] C. Rabin, *Zadokite Documents*, p.72. Rabin, furthermore, provides the following grammatical explanation of the text as he understands it, "This is a sentence with a double *casus pendens*, i.e. extraposition of both subject and object.", p. 72 n. 3. However, Rabin's translation of יקימו עליהם with 'let their sons...swear' seems unlikely in the light of the use of a comparable phrase in CD 15,12 where it appears to have a reflexive sense such as 'to swear' or 'to take upon oneself (an oath).' Rabin takes יקימו to be a *piel* and refers to Esth. 9,21 as an example.

[32] *The Dead Sea Scrolls in English*, Harmondsworth: Penguin, 1995, p. 106.

[33] *Die Texte aus Qumran*, Darmstadt: Wissenschaftliche Buchgesellschaft, 1986, pp. 97-98.

[34] For a discussion of the latter use cf. Schiffman, *Sectarian Law*, pp. 70-71 n. 80.

[35] Vermes translates this crucial sentence differently in *The Complete Dead Sea Scrolls in English*, p. 136 but still understands CD 15,5b-6a to deal exclusively with children of members. For an understanding of this passage along similar lines cf. also E. Qimron, 'שבועת הבנים in the Damascus Covenant', *JQR* 81 (1990) 115-118 and *idem* 'Further Observations on the Laws of Oaths in the Damascus Document 15', *JQR* 85 (1994) 251-257, especially p. 256.

The recent new translation of this passage by Baumgarten also falls into this category of translations:

> And those who enter the covenant for all of Israel as an eternal statute shall have their sons, who have reached (the age) for passing among those that are mustered, take the oath of the covenant. Similar (is) the precept during the entire time of evil for everyone who repents from his corrupt way.[36]

It seems likely to me that the second group of translators, failing to recognize CD 15,6b-7a as a secondary addition, tried to make sense of the present convoluted text. Once one recognizes, however, that 15,6b-7a is secondary, the translation of 15,5b-6a offered above is grammatically justifiable, meaningful as well as being consistent regarding the use of the *hiphil* of קום in lines 6 and 12 of page 15.

Secondly, the reference to 'all the time of wickedness' is reminiscent of the Admonition of the Damascus Document where the exact phrase occurs in CD 6,10, and a reference to 'the time of wickedness' is found in CD 6,14. In the mediaeval text of the Laws the expression occurs only in CD 12,23 outside the present passage.[37]

CD 12,23b-13,1a forms part of a linking passage in the Laws that introduces legislation on the meeting of the camps and the crucial phrase reads,

המתהלכים באלה בקץ הרשעה עד עמוד משוח אהרן וישראל

> Those who walk in these in the time of wickedness until the Messiah of Aaron and Israel arises...

A good case can be made for assigning this phrase to the work of a redactor who is responsible for a number of redactional passages that serve to present the various components of the Damascus Document as a unity. We will come across the work of this redactor elsewhere in the Laws primarily in linking passages that serve to provide a transition from one section to the next. This redactional material serves to present the various parts of the Laws as part of an apparently coherent whole but also frequently provides connections between the Admonition and the Laws, and I have chosen the term

---

[36] Baumgarten in Charlesworth ed., *Dead Sea Scrolls*, II, p. 39.

[37] Baumgarten's edition of the CD Laws partly reconstructs a third reference to the time of wickedness in CD 15,10 (Charlesworth ed., *Dead Sea Scrolls*, II, p. 38). As noted on p. 75 n. 9 above such a reading is palaeographically unlikely. A further occurrence of 'the time of wickedness' in the Laws is reconstructed by Qimron in CD 14,18-19, cf. 'Text of CDC', p. 37. However, this reconstruction is supported neither by 4QD^a 10 i 12 nor by 4QD^d 11 i. Both MSS preserve some additional text corresponding to the damaged end of CD 14.

'Damascus redactor' and 'Damascus redaction' as a shorthand. The term Damascus redaction was chosen on the basis of the document's modern title Damascus Document which is based on a number of references to Damascus in the Admonition. As far as I am aware no other text from Qumran contains 'Damascus terminology'—not even the text known as Serekh Damascus (4Q265)!—and Damascus redaction is a serviceable shorthand expression to describe the literary activity of a redactor intent on presenting the Damascus Document as a whole as a unified composition.

The concept of a time of wickedness corresponds more closely to the ideological position of the Admonition than the bulk of the Laws. The Laws by themselves state diverse halakhic and communal prescriptions in a neutral fashion. One never gets the impression that the writers responsible for the Laws of the Damascus Document polemicised against opponents, be it opponents outside the movement or backsliders from within the movement. Only occasionally is the wickedness of the masses outside the movement referred to, and I would argue that these exceptional passages go back to a later redactor who tried to bring the Laws into line with the Admonition. The expression time of wickedness occurs in the Laws only in CD 15,7 and in 12,23. In the Admonition, the expression occurs in CD 6,10 and 6,14. Numerically, of course, the term occurs an equal number of times in the Admonition and the Laws. Once we look at the overriding concerns that dominate the Admonition as opposed to the bulk of the Laws it becomes clear that the concept of a time of wickedness is alien to the neutral position reflected in the legal part of the document, whereas it is simply one of several ways of expressing the dissatisfaction with the outside world in the Admonition, cf. for example CD 2,2-3a ('And now listen to me all who enter the covenant and I will open your ears concerning the ways of the wicked'). Elsewhere in the Admonition the 'princes of Judah' are criticised for 'not departing from the way of traitors' in CD 8,4-5 (par. 19,17) and in CD 8,9 (par. 19,21) for 'walking in the ways of the wicked'.

Unlike the Laws the Admonition is, moreover, preoccupied to a great degree with time schemes of both a historical and an eschatological nature. In fact, it would be true to say that reflections on God's dealings with Israel in the past and his dealings with the community—and those outside, i.e. the wicked—in the present and future are a key concern in the Admonition, and these reflections are frequently couched in temporal terms. Past, present and future conform to a divinely ordained scheme which is dominated by several important turning points in the course of time such as the exile, the emergence of a movement of pious survivors, the coming of the teacher, the death of the teacher, and lastly the final visitation of God and the coming of the Messiah of Aaron and Israel. Such temporal concerns are by and large alien to the Laws.[38] On the basis of these considerations I understand the reference to the time of wickedness in CD 15,7 as a secondary addition. The concerns and outlook behind this addition is close to that of the Damascus redactor. Even though CD 15,6b-7a does not form part of a transitional passage it nevertheless provides something of a link to the Admonition which is one of the chief characteristics of this redaction.

In the Cave 4 MSS of the Damascus Document, the expression occurs once in 4QD^f 2,12 par. 4QD^d 8 ii 5.[39] A composite text drawing on both MSS results in,

[ ] הנדה בקץ הרשע איש טה[ו]ר מ[כול טומאתו אשר יעריב א[ת]

] sprinkling in the time of wickedness by a man puri[fied from] all his uncleanness who waits for

It seems likely to me that the expression goes back to the work of the Damascus redactor. The surrounding material deals with the subject of ritual defilement and purification, and the reference to the age of wickedness at the end of this section seems to be intended to place the unpolemical halakhah that precedes it into the polemical context of the Damascus Document in its final form.[40] All the arguments adduced above about the alien place of the concept of a time of wickedness in the Laws apply equally in this instance. It seems probable, therefore, that we have here a further passage that can be assigned to the work of the Damascus redactor.

A further interpolation has entered our piece of legislation. We find in CD 15,8 a reference to 'the overseer over the many' (המבקר אשר לרבים). This reference to the many in the Laws of the Damascus Document is surprising. As is well known this designation is characteristic of the Community Rule, and it occurs very frequently indeed in 1QS 6-9. In 1QS 6,11-12 we even find a reference to 'the overseer over the many' (האיש המבקר על הרבים) and again in 1QS 6,19-20 we come across 'the overseer over the work of the many' (האיש המבקר על מלאכת הרבים).

---

[38] Cf. the following observation by Knibb, "The corpus of laws lacks any historical perspective, whereas such a perspective is characteristic of all parts of the Admonition.", 'Place of the Damascus Document', p. 153.
[39] Cf. Baumgarten, *Qumran Cave 4. XIII*, pp. 131 and 173.
[40] Cf. section 3.2.3 above.

It is further noteworthy that according to CD 13 it is one of the duties of the *overseer over the camp* to oversee the admission of new members, cf. the section heading in CD 13,7 וזה סרך המבקר למחנה ('And this is the rule for the overseer over the camp') and particularly the following prohibition in CD 13,12b-13,

אל ימשול איש מבני המחנה להביא איש אל העדה זולת פי המבקר אשר למחנה

No member of the camp shall have the right to bring anyone to the congregation without the consent of the overseer over the camp.

Thus the regulations on the duties of the *overseer over the camp* in CD 13 provide further evidence in favour of recognizing the incongruity of a reference to an *overseer over the many* in a context dealing with the admission process in CD 15,8.

The expression רבים occurs thirty four times in 1QS 6-9 and only four times in the mediaeval text of the Laws of the Damascus Document, i.e. in CD 13,7; 14,7.12; 15,8. The term is preserved five times in 4QD^a, of which one occurrence (4QD^a 10 i 5) preserves a text parallel to CD 14,12, one instance is from the penal code (4QD^a 10 ii 7), and three occurrences are found in the column that constitutes the end of the Damascus Document as preserved in 4QD, i.e. 4QD^a 11. 4QD^b contains one occurrence which preserves text parallel to CD 14,7 (4QD^b 9 v 11). 4QD^e preserves one occurrence of the term in the penal code (4QD^e 7 i 11). It emerges clearly from this overview that the expression the many is a favoured term to refer to the community in 1QS.[41] In the Damascus Document, by contrast, it is certainly not the most frequently used expression to refer to the community.

Furthermore, the overseer who is associated with the many in CD 15,8 is most commonly linked to the camp in the Laws, cf. 4QD^a 7 iii 3 [4QD^b 8,4]; CD 15,14; 13,7b.13.16; 14,8-9. Only in the present instance is he described as 'the overseer over the many'.[42] We even

---

[41] One of the most crucial variants in 4QS^d 1 over against 1QS 5 concerns the occurrence of 'the many' in 4QS^d in a passage where 1QS 5 has 'the sons of Zadok the priests'. For preliminary discussions of the differences between 1QS 5 and 4QS^d 1, cf. G. Vermes, 'Preliminary Remarks'; see also *idem*, 'Qumran Forum Miscellanea I', *JJS* 43 (1992) 299-305 and C. Hempel 'Comments on the Translation of 4QS^d I,1', *JJS* 44 (1993) 127-28. A third text that should be included in the discussion of this important variant is 1QSa 1,1-3, cf. C. Hempel, 'Earthly Essene Nucleus'.

[42] Baumgarten restores a further reference to the overseer over the many in 4QD^d 9,8 [par. 4QD^f 3,14-15] (*Qumran Cave 4. XIII*, pp. 132,175). I have argued above that the minute remains of what Baumgarten takes to be a *resh* in D^d 9,8 might be traces of a final *mem* which would result in a further attestation of the fre-

find a reference to the multitude of the *camp* in the present passage dealing with the admission process in CD 15,13-14. Although the traces of מחנה at the beginning of CD 15,14 are very faint this reading is now confirmed in the parallel text preserved in 4QD^a 8 i 4.

The presence of a number of references to the many in the corpus of the Laws of D posit a crucial interpretative problem in any analysis of the Laws as well as in determining the relationship of D and S. I have become convinced that these references are part of a further redactional process evident in the Laws, i.e. a redaction that is intended to bring the communal legislation of the Laws into line with S. I call this redaction Serekh redaction. I am aware that the term serekh occurs more widely in the scrolls outside of 1QS/4QS not least in D itself. I nevertheless adopted the shorthand Serekh redaction since Serekh has become the customary term for the S MSS.

A crucial piece of physical evidence that sheds new light on the question of the many in the Laws of D is found in the version of the penal code as preserved in 4QD^a. One of the offences mentioned both in 1QS and 4QD^a is very similar but not quite identical in both texts. 1QS 7,10b-11b reads,

כן לאיש הנפטר במושב הרבים אשר לוא בעצה וחנם עד שלוש פעמים
על מושב אחד

> Thus shall be the case for anyone who leaves the session of the many without consultation and without reason for up to three times in one session.

4QD^a 10 ii 6b-7 reads,[43]

[וכן לאיש הנ פ[ט]ר [אשר] לו בעצת הר[ב]י[ם] ו[ח]נם] עד שלוש
פע[מים על מושב] אחד

> [And likewise the one who lea]ves [with]out the consent of the ma[n]y [and with]out [cause] up to three tim[es during] a single [meeting].

Contrast particularly,

1QS 7,11   אשר לוא בעצה   4QD^a 10 ii 7   [אשר] לו בעצת הר[ב]י[ם].

---

quent phrase overseer over the camp, cf. the textual notes to l. 18 of the composite text pp. p. 67 above.

[43] The reading חנם is favoured here in analogy to the text of 1QS over against Baumgarten's reading הגם, *Qumran Cave 4. XIII*, p. 74. Baumgarten's reconstruction of [אשר] as the first word in 4QD^a 10 ii 7 is shorter than 1QS 7,10-11 (אשר במושב הרבים) presumably on the basis of the calculated length of the lines.

1QS 7,11 lacks 4QD^a's reference to the many and has בעצה in the absolute state. The parallel in 4QS^g 3,3 agrees with the reading of 1QS.[44] In 4QD^a עצה occurs unmistakably in the construct state and the *he* and the *resh* of הרבים are fairly clearly preserved. The difference in meaning is considerable as can be seen from the translations given for both versions in a number of recent translations.[45] This presence of a reference to the many in 4QD^a over against 1QS is significant indeed. On the one hand, we have a clear preponderance of references to the many in S, yet intriguingly in this passage from the penal code D includes a reference to the many absent from S in an otherwise identical offence.

It seems most unlikely to suppose that a reference to the many that was present in an earlier version of the penal code came to be left out in 1QS since, as we saw, this term occurs over thirty times in 1QS 6-9.[46] It seems more probable to me that the reference to the many in 4QD^a has been added to an earlier version of this offence. This instance from the penal code provides clear evidence that a reference to the many was secondarily inserted into a piece of legislation where it was originally lacking. This piece of physical evidence confirms that the kind of picture of redactional activity that I am painting is at least a realistic and conceivable one.

To return again to our present passage, it needs to be emphasized that the reference to the many in CD 15,8—quite apart from being confined to a limited stratum of the Laws as a whole—is also out of place in CD 15,5b-16,6a itself. In this whole rather lengthy passage prescribing for the admission of new members the many occur only once as part of the title the overseer over the many. If this designation were original in the context of the passage as a whole, it would be surprising not to find another reference to the body of the many in this piece of legislation. In other words, if the community into which members are admitted referred to itself as the many it would

---

[44] Cf. the recent edition of the text of the 4QS MSS by E. Qimron in J.H. Charlesworth ed., *The Dead Sea Scrolls. Hebrew, Aramaic, and Greek Texts with English Translations*, Tübingen: J.C.B. Mohr (Paul Siebeck)/Louisville: Westminster John Knox Press, 1994, p. 94.

[45] Cf. García Martínez, *Dead Sea Scrolls Translated*, pp. 11; 56; Vermes, *The Complete Dead Sea Scrolls*, pp. 107-108,151. The recent translations by Maier bring out the difference between both formulations clearly, cf. *Qumran-Essener*, 1995, I, p. 185, II, p. 229.

[46] Whereas in 1QS 5 we may have a case of an original reference to the many having been replaced by the inclusion of a reference to the sons of Zadok the priests who keep the covenant (for bibliographical details cf. p. 82 n. 41 above) the present penal code passage merely lacks the reference to the many altogether. The supposition of a process of deleting references to the many in S is not likely in the light of the frequent occurrence of the self-designation in 1QS 6-9.

be most unexpected not to find another reference to this self-designation in a piece of legislation that deals with the admission process into the community.

In sum, it seems probable to me that the reference to the many in CD 15,8 forms part of a reworking of the Laws of the Damascus Document in the light of S. Moreover, it seems possible that המבקר אשר לרבים replaced an original המבקר אשר למחנה, an expression that is frequently attested in the Laws of D.[47] On the other hand, it is equally possible that 15,8 originally only read המבקר.

Having isolated two secondary interpolations, which I have underlined in the Hebrew text and the translation, we are now left with the prescriptions on the admission of new members into the movement behind the communal legislation in the Laws of the Damascus Document. These prescriptions are found in CD 15,5b-6a and 15,7b-16,2a. New members are admitted by means of swearing the oath of the covenant.[48] The overseer plays an important role throughout this section. A major concern relating to the admission of new members is to establish their worthiness of membership. Prior to an examination by the overseer no halakhic knowledge must be passed on to the candidates. Although we are not directly informed what this examination involved—the Hebrew terms used are עמד לפני and דרש—it seems to have as its aim the identification of simple or foolish candidates, cf. especially CD15,11b.15a.

CD 15,15b-17a provides a summarizing statement of all the categories of people that should not be admitted into the congregation. Similar rules on the exclusion of certain categories of people can be found in the Rule of the Congregation (1QSa 2,4b-9a),[49] the War Scroll (1QM 7,4b-6a), 4QFlorilegium (4QFlor. 1,3b-5a) and *Miqsat Ma'aseh ha-Torah* (4QMMT B39-54).[50] Such lists of categories for exclusion are based on Lev. 21 which contains the purity regulations for the Aaronic priesthood. This summarizing statement appears in a new light in view of the now improved reading of CD 15,15b-17a with the help of 4QD^a 8 i 6-7. It emerges from the improved text that the connection of the general exclusion clause to what precedes is the catch phrase אל יבו 'shall not enter' which occurs in CD 15,15 and CD 15,16-17. From

---

[47] For references see p. 82 above.
[48] A similar procedure is described in 1QS 5,7c-9a. For a discussion of the relationship of that passage to the admission process in the Damascus Document cf. Hempel, 'Community Structures in the Dead Sea Scrolls'.
[49] On the significance of this correspondence between the Laws of the Damascus Document and the Rule of the Congregation cf. Hempel, 'Earthly Essene Nucleus'.
[50] For a detailed presentation of the evidence and discussion cf. Qimron and Strugnell, *Qumran Cave 4. V*, pp. 145-47.

the array of parallels in other texts listed above it clearly emerges that the exclusion rule was a tradition that circulated widely. It seems likely that the author(s) behind the material on the admission of new members in CD 15 incorporated this tradition here and applied it to the very specific circumstances dealt with in this passage.[51] Although almost all of CD 15,17b-20 has been lost,[52] it seems quite clear that 16,1b-2a forms a conclusion to the section dealing with the admission of new members. The legislation on the admission process concludes with CD 16,2b-6a. Rather abruptly, CD 16,2b-4a introduces the famous explicit reference to the Book of Jubilees. The book is referred to as 'the book of the divisions of the times into their jubilees and weeks' (ספר מחלקות העתים ליובליהם ובשבועותיהם) a title which is remarkably similar to a phrase used in the Prologue of Jubilees itself, as has often been pointed out.[53] Apart from the catchword מדוקדק it is difficult to see the connection of this reference to what precedes. It seems likely that the whole short section in CD 16,2b-6a has been added by a glossator seeking to promote the influence of the Book of Jubilees who is at work elsewhere in the Laws of the Damascus Document outside of this passage.[54]

The disruptive nature of this reference to Jubilees was already noted by Ginzberg who remarks on CD 16,2,

> This sentence interrupts the continuity, and its genuineness is very suspect. It probably comes from a reader for whom the Book of Jubilees possessed high authority...[55]

---

[51] On the exclusion passage in D cf. M.J. Davidson, *Angels at Qumran. A Comparative Study of 1Enoch 1-36, 72-108 and Sectarian Writings from Qumran*, Sheffield: Sheffield Academic Press, 1992, pp. 185-86 and L.H. Schiffman, *The Eschatological Community of the Dead Sea Scrolls. A Study of the Rule of the Congregation*, Atlanta: Scholars Press, 1989, pp. 47-48. Both Davidson and Schiffman understand the present passage to restrict access to the communal assembly rather than membership in general. It seems to me that now we can draw on 4QD*a*'s text in full that the exclusion passage as it now stands applies to membership of the covenant community. This was also the view favoured by Milik (*Ten Years of Discovery*, p. 114).

[52] Baumgarten's edition includes the following additional words מ[עטו שני האד]ם 'the years of the hum[an (lifespan)] were [sh]ortened' in 4QD*r* 6 ii 10 (*Qumran Cave 4. XIII*, p. 156 and Plate XXXI). It is difficult to see exactly how this phrase relates to its immediate context. As noted by Baumgarten (p. 157) the idea behind this statement is reflected also in CD 10,8b-10a. Moreover, 4QD*f* 4 ii 2-3a contains a number of words from the lost end of CD 15, cf. Baumgarten, *Qumran Cave 4. XIII*, pp. 178-79. There is not enough text for conclusive interpretations except to say that the end of page 15 dealt with the subject of the covenant. The first word of 4QD*f* 4 ii 3 (לאמור) marks out what follows as direct speech. Should we understand the overseer reciting these words as part of an entrance ceremony?

[53] This explicit reference to Jubilees was already noted by Schechter. cf. *Fragments of a Zadokite Work*, p. xv.

[54] Cf. CD 10,7b-10a (Jub. 23,9-11) and CD 12,2b-6a (Jub. 1,20; 10,12-14), cf. pp. 102-103 and section 8.3 below.

[55] L. Ginzberg, *An Unknown Jewish Sect*, p. 94.

Further on in his study Ginzberg returns to this passage and comments on CD 16,4,

> ...I have grave suspicions about the genuineness of this passage, for, apart from the reasons given above for excluding it as a later gloss, it is further to be noted that the constant designation of Satan in our document is 'Belial', and it would be very strange to find him in this passage as 'Mastema' or 'angel of Mastema'...[56]

The present occurrence constitutes indeed the only attestation of the name or even the noun Mastema, usually rendered 'hatred' or 'hostility', in both CD and 4QD.[57] In the Book of Jubilees, by contrast, the title 'prince of Mastema' occurs frequently, cf. 11,5; 17,16; 18,9. Finally and more importantly, quite apart from the unusual title prince of Mastema, the concept of the influence of angelic forces on one's decision to join the movement behind the Laws is alien to the preceding description of admission. In the preceding rather lengthy piece of legislation on the admission of new members angelic forces, be they benign or hostile ones, play no role whatsoever. To the author behind CD 16,4b-5, by contrast, the influence of angelic forces seems to lie at the heart of the admission process.[58] In other words, whereas the preceding legislation is thoroughly pragmatic and

---

[56] *Unknown Jewish Sect*, p. 177. Furthermore, P. von der Osten-Sacken argues, "Der Hinweis auf Jub. in CD XVI,2b-4a bildet jedoch einen sekundären Nachtrag." (*Gott und Belial. Traditionsgeschichtliche Untersuchungen zum Dualismus in den Texten aus Qumran*, Göttingen: Vandenhoeck & Ruprecht, 1969, p. 198). Von der Osten-Sacken regards the following reference to the angel Mastema as forming part of the original text on the admission process in CD however. Davies seems sympathetic to this view, cf. *Damascus Covenant*, p. 203. Most recently Baumgarten commented on this passage, "As suggested by Ginzberg, lines 3-4 appear to be a gloss inserted by someone who wished to point out that, while the law is specified (מדוקדק) in the Torah, the periods of blindness to the law are specified (מדוקדק) only in the Book of Jubilees.", Baumgarten in Charlesworth ed., *Dead Sea Scrolls*, II, p. 39 n. 132; see also *ibid*, p. 21.

[57] To my knowledge the name Mastema does not occur anywhere else in the non-biblical scrolls published to date. The noun, on the other hand, is applied to the angel of darkness in 1QS 3,23 and to Belial in 1QM 13,4.11. See also the plural term 'angels of mastemoth' in 4Q390 (Pseudo-Moses) 1,11 cf. Devorah Dimant, 'New Light from Qumran on the Jewish Pseudepigrapha—4Q390', in *The Madrid Qumran Congress* ed. Trebolle Barrera and Vegas Montaner, II, pp. 405-48. Dimant notes, "It would seem that the plural מלאכי משטמות denotes the evil angels under the authority of Mastema." (p. 426).

[58] In this respect the present interpolation is close to the covenant ceremony described in 1QS 1,16-2,25a. The latter material is thoroughly dualistic as is manifest in the frequent references to 'the reign of Belial' (ממשלת בליעל, cf. 1QS 1,18.23-24; 2,19) and 'the men of the lot of Belial' (אנשי גורל בליעל, cf. 1QS 2,4-5) who are contrasted to 'the men of the lot of God' (אנשי גורל אל, cf. 1QS 2,2). The ceremony described in 1QS 1,16-2,25a deals with the admission of new members as well as the reaffirmation of their pledges to the covenant on the part of already existing mem-

'down to earth', CD 16,4b-5a places a great deal of emphasis on the power of angelic influences.[59]
Apart from the strong influence of the Book of Jubilees on the scribe behind this passage a number of links to the Admonition of the Damascus Document are also evident. In general terms, the passage is closer to the Admonition than the bulk of the Laws in that it is overtly polemical towards Israel at large which is described as 'blind'. A close terminological link of this passage with the Admonition is constituted by the expression פרוש קציהם, cf. CD 2,9. Also, the idea that Israel at large is misled concerning the correct observance of the calendar is clearly stated in CD 3,12b-15a. These lines constitute one of the descriptions of the emergence of the community behind the Admonition and address the same issues raised in the present passage. CD 3,12b-15a reads,

12b   ובמחזיקים במצות אל
13   אשר נותרו מהם הקים אל את בריתו לישראל עד עולם לנלות
14   להם נסתרות אשר תעו בם כל ישראל vacat שבתות קדשו ומועדי
15a   כבודו

3,12b But with those who held fast to the commandments of God
   13 who were left over from them, God established his covenant with Israel for ever, revealing
   14 to them the hidden things in which all Israel had gone astray: his holy sabbaths, his glorious
   15a feasts...

The author behind CD 16,2b-6a was clearly as much preoccupied with the correct observance of the calendar as the author of CD 3,12b-15a. Furthermore, both passages emphatically criticize Israel for failing to observe the calendar correctly. The most important aspect of this correspondence between CD 16,2b-6a and CD 3,12b-15a for the present argument is the shared overt polemic against Israel at large. Such a stance clearly sets apart the present passage from the main part of CD 15,5b-16,2a. As I have shown above, the latter passage refers to Israel at large in a neutral, if not positive, manner.

---

bers, cf. 1QS 2,19; see also 1QS 5,20b-24a. In contrast to CD 15 the material contained in 1QS 1-2 explicitly refers to an annual event, has a pronounced dualistic orientation as well as a liturgical setting. The first two columns of 1QS belong to that part of the Community Rule that is absent from the version of the Community Rule as attested by 4QS^d. It's liturgical character distinguishes it clearly from the predominantly administrative procedures described in both CD 15-16 and 1QS 6.

[59] For a different view see J.C. VanderKam, *Textual and Historical Studies in the Book of Jubilees*, Missoula: Scholars Press, 1977, pp. 257-258 n. 91.

A further observation may be made. It seems questionable to me that one and the same person should lie behind the statement 'for in it [viz. the law of Moses] everything is laid down in detail' as well as the following qualification. (*'But the exact statement of their times with regard to the blindness of Israel concerning all these, behold they are laid down in detail in the book of the divisions of the times into their jubilees and weeks.'*). One would hesitate to build a case on this observation alone on the grounds that it may presuppose standards of consistency that are inappropriate in this literature. However, as a consideration over and above the more substantial arguments put forward already it may serve to provide further support for my case.

The interpolation ends, in my view, in CD 16,6a with the words *'Therefore, Abraham was circumcised on the day he received his knowledge'*. In his discussion of the reference to Jubilees in CD 16, VanderKam has made a convincing case for taking CD 16,6a as an integral part of the passage starting in 16,2b.[60] VanderKam draws our attention to Jubilees 15 which forms the background to CD 16,4b-6a,

> ...the circumcision of Abraham serves as an example of obedience to the law, for on the very day that he received the divine instructions regarding the rite he implemented them (Jub. 15: 23-24)... the preceding reference to the angel of animosity's turning aside is drawn from Jub. 15...[61]

VanderKam, thus, establishes the thematic unity of CD 16,2b-6a and is able to show that the whole of this passage is heavily influenced by the book of Jubilees.

Although it is probable that the movement behind the whole corpus of the Laws of the Damascus Document venerated the Book of Jubilees and adhered to the solar calendar, it emerges from this discussion that CD 16,2b-6a goes back to a different author from the bulk of the legislation on the admission process.

Finally, I would like to come back to the close links of this gloss to the Admonition, especially to CD 3,12b-15a. It would go far beyond the scope of this examination to examine the place of 3,12b-15a within the Admonition as a whole. For the moment it suffices to raise the possibility that the same glossator who interspersed the Laws with interpolations stressing the correct observance of the calendar may have been at work in a similar fashion in the Admonition.[62]

---

[60] *Textual and Historical Studies*, pp. 255-58.
[61] *Textual and Historical Studies*, pp. 256-57. Cf. also Baumgarten in Charlesworth ed. *Dead Sea Scrolls*, II, p. 41 n. 133.
[62] Interestingly Davies has argued that another reference to the festivals in the Admonition, i.e. CD 6,18-19, is a secondary gloss, cf. *Damascus Covenant*, pp. 130-31.

4.2 Summary

The main results of the analysis of CD 15,5b-16,6a may be summarized as follows:

a. CD 15,5b-6a.7b-16,2a contains communal legislation on the admission into the community by swearing the oath of the covenant. CD 15,15b-17a constitutes an originally independent, general statement on the exclusion of certain categories of people that is here applied to the admission process.
b. CD 15,6b-7a have been attributed to the work of the Damascus redactor.
c. The reference to the many (אשר לרבים) in CD 15,8 was assigned to the Serekh redaction.
d. Finally, it was argued that CD 16,2b-6a constitutes an interpolation promoting the ideology of the book of Jubilees.

CHAPTER FIVE

COMMUNITY ORGANIZATION PART TWO: ADMINISTRATION OF JUSTICE

This chapter deals with the communal legislation relating to lost or stolen property, witnesses, and the judges of the congregation.

5.1 The Procedure for Dealing with Lost or Stolen Property in the Camp

CD 9,10b-16a lays down the procedure for dealing with lost or stolen property in the camp.[1] 4QD^b 9 i and 4QD^e 6 iv contain material parallel to this section without providing any significant variants.[2]

A. *Text*
(CD 9,10b-16a; 4QD^b 9 i; 4QD^e 6 iv)

10b	וכל האובד
11	ולא נודע מי גנבו ממאד המחנה אשר גנב בו ישביע בעליו
12	בשבועת האלה והשומע אם יודע הוא ולא יניד ואשם
13	כל אשם מושב אשר אין בעלים והתורה המישב לכהן
14	והיה לו לבד מאיל האשם (הכל) וכן כל אבדה נמצאת ואין
15	לה בעלים והיתה לכהנים כי לא ידע מוצאיה את משפטה
16	אם לא נמצא לה בעלים הם ישמרו

B. *Translation*
9,10b Anything that is missing
   11 and it is not known who stole it from the property of the camp where it was stolen, let its owner pronounce
   12 a cursing oath. And anyone who hears it, if he has knowledge of it and withholds information, is guilty.
   13 Any guilt repayment which is made and there is no owner, let him who makes the payment confess to the priest,

---

[1] On this material see the discussion in Schiffman, *Sectarian Law*, pp. 111-32.
[2] Cf. Baumgarten, *Qumran Cave 4. XIII*, pp. 105 and 159.

14 and it shall be his apart from the ram of the guilt offering. And likewise any missing property that is found and there is no
15 owner shall be the priests', for the finder does not know the rules that apply to it.
16a If no owners are found for it, they shall keep charge of it.

C. *Textual Notes*
9,13 For והתורה המישב read והתודה המשיב.³

D. *Commentary*
This material has often been read alongside CD 9,8b-10a, a piece of halakhic exposition that is introduced in CD 9,8b with the heading 'Concerning the Oath' (על השבועה).⁴ Such an association is probably based on the reference to a cursing oath in the context of dealing with lost or stolen property in CD 9,10b-12. In this first part of our passage the cursing oath constitutes indeed a crucial part in the procedure for dealing with stolen property. However, no such link can be said to exist with the following two rules which lack reference to swearing an oath. I therefore agree with those scholars who have taken the present passage as a separate unit in the Laws.⁵

As has been noted by Baumgarten the specific topics dealt with in CD 9,10b-12 and CD 9,13-14a are linked by the catchword אשם.⁶ The section as a whole is held together also by its common occupation with property and the rights of those who properly own it. It is noteworthy that the term 'owner' (בעל) occurs four times in this short section (CD 9,11[par. 4QD^b 9 i 6].13.15.16) and nowhere else in the Laws of D.

The reference to the camp in CD 9,11 clearly establishes that we are dealing with a piece of communal legislation. This passage is important for our understanding of the community behind the communal legislation in the Laws of the Damascus Document. Firstly, these rules clearly presuppose a community the members of which owned private property. Secondly, the reference to the ram of the guilt offering in CD 9,14 constitutes an uncritical and unpolemical reference to the sacrificial cult. Finally, in this passage it is the priest who is invested with a key role in dealing with matters of lost or stolen property in the camp. The communal rules in the Laws of the

---

³ Cf. Qimron, 'Text of CDC', p. 27 nn. 11-12.
⁴ So, for example, Dupont-Sommer, *Essene Writings*, pp. 149-50; also Cothenet, 'Document de Damas', pp. 186-89.
⁵ So, for instance, Gaster, *Scriptures of the Dead Sea Sect*, p. 84 and Charles, *Apocrypha and Pseudepigrapha*, II, p. 824.
⁶ Baumgarten in Charlesworth ed., *Dead Sea Scrolls*, II, p. 43 n. 144.

Damascus Document mention several figures of authority for the camps. It may be that the particular task of dealing with cases of lost and stolen property fell into the realm of the priest's authority rather than the overseer's who is frequently assigned a key role in the communal rules, cf., for example, CD 9,16b-10,3. On the other hand, it seems equally possible that the authority structure of the camps underwent development and that the communal rules in D give evidence to several stages in this development. If that were the case then we would have here a piece of communal legislation that goes back to a time when it was the priest rather than the overseer who held the position of authority in the camp.[7] This tradition that attributes communal authority to the priest could, in theory, be an alternative tradition rather than an earlier tradition. Two reasons lead me to regard this piece of communal legislation as reflecting an earlier stage in the development of the communal legislation from those parts of the Laws that attribute ultimate authority in the community to the overseer. Firstly, the priest as an authority figure follows the traditional scriptural model of authority, whereas the office of the overseer is not known from the Hebrew Bible. The office of the overseer appears to have become the dominant one in the communal legislation of the Laws of D with only more sporadic references to the office of the priest. Secondly, a further argument in favour of considering the office of the overseer as a later development is the highly developed and complex character of pieces of communal legislation in which this office plays a central role, cf. especially the law of testimony in CD 9,16b-10,3.

5.2 Witnesses

CD 9,16b-10,3 regulates on cases where community members witness a fellow member transgressing the law.

A. *Text*
(CD 9,16b-10,3; 4QD^c 6 iv)

9:16b כול דבר אשר ימעל

9:17 איש בתורה וראה רעיהו והוא אחד אם דבר מות הוא וידיעהו

9:18 לעיניו *vacat* בהוכיח למבקר והמבקר יכתבהו בידו עד עשותו

9:19 עוד לפני אחד ושב והודיע למבקר אם ישוב וניחפש לפני

---

[7] Cf. my discussion of CD 13,2b-7a in section 6.2 below which may provide further support for the latter view.

9:20 אחר שלם משפטו vacat ואם שנים הם והם מעידים על
9:21 דבר אחר והובדל האיש מן הטהרה לבד vacat אם נאמנים
9:22 הם וביום ראות האיש יודיעה למבקר ועל ההון יקבלו שני
9:23 עידים נאמנים vacat ועל אחד להבדיל הטהרה ואל יקובל
10:1 עוד לשופטים להמית על פיהו אשר לא מלאו ימיו לעבור
10:2 על הפקודים ירא את אל vacat אל יאמן איש על רעהו
10:3 לעד עובר דבר מן המצוה ביד רמה עד זכו לשוב

B. *Translation*

9,16b Every case of a person transgressing
   17 the law and his neighbour witnesses it as a single witness, if it is a capital case, he shall report it
   18 in his presence and with reproving to the overseer. And the overseer shall record it in case he reoffends
   19 in front of a single witness and the latter again informs the overseer. If he offends a third time and is caught in front of
   20 another (witness) his case shall be complete. And if there are two (witnesses) and they testify concerning
   21 different cases the offender shall be excluded from the purity provided[8] that they are trustworthy.
   22 Each witness shall report to the overseer on the same day as they witness (the offence). In matters of property they shall accept two
   23 trustworthy witnesses, and one witness (suffices) to exclude from the purity. But the testimony
10,1 of anyone who has not reached the age to pass over to the mustered as one who fears God shall not be accepted by the judges
   2 to pronounce a death sentence on the basis of his testimony. A person shall not be trusted as a witness
   3 against his neighbour who has transgressed anything from the commandment high-handedly until he is pure to return again.

C. *Textual Notes*

9,23 4QD^e 6 iv 13 reads ועל פי עד אחד.[9] 4QD^e's fuller text is reflected in my translation. The text of CD may be due to haplographical error, or alternatively, CD may preserve a shorthand formulation that is equivalent in meaning to 4QD^e's text.

10,1 Read עֵד = עִיד for עוד.[10]

---

[8] On this translation cf. Qimron, 'Text of CDC', p. 26 n. 17.
[9] Cf. Qimron, 'Text of CDC', p. 26 n. 18-18 and Baumgarten, *Qumran Cave 4. XIII*, p. 159.
[10] Cf. Qimron, 'Text of CDC', p. 29 n. 1. See also Schiffman, *Sectarian Law*, pp. 55-56 for a full discussion in favour of this emendation.

D. Commentary

The present passage on the law of testimony has received a great deal of attention in scholarly literature.[11] The reading of the text itself is not straightforward. In particular, it is often difficult to be certain whether the text reads אחד or אחר, and whether in some cases one or the other of these two readings should be emended to the other. The choice of reading bears upon one's understanding of the meaning of the passage. The text and translation given above are based on Qimron's edition of the text of CD.[12]

A second area of debate concerns the question whether our passage requires two or three witnesses for a capital case to be complete (cf. CD 9,16b-20a). On the whole, the text itself as well as the arguments advanced by scholars lead me to believe that three witnesses are required to complete a capital case whereas the evidence of two witnesses suffices in matters of property. The scriptural basis for the legislation on the required number of witnesses is Dt. 17,6 and 19,15. The biblical law is formulated rather vaguely and lacks precision as regards the number of witnesses required. Dt. 17,6 reads,

על־פי שנים עדים או שלשה עדים יומת המת לא יומת על־פי עד אחד :

> On the evidence of two or three witnesses the death sentence shall be executed; a person must not be put to death on the evidence of only one witness.[13]

---

[11] Cf. F. García Martínez and J. Trebolle Barrera, *People of the Dead Sea Scrolls*, pp. 221-32; B.S. Jackson, '*Testes Singulares* in Early Jewish Law and the New Testament', in *idem, Essays in Jewish and Comparative Legal History*, Leiden: E.J. Brill, 1975, pp. 172-201; *idem*, 'Damascus Document IX,16-23 and Parallels', *RQ* 9 (1978) 445-50; J.L. Kugel, 'On Hidden Hatred and Open Reproach: Early Exegesis of Leviticus 19:17', *HTR* 80 (1987) 43-61; B.A. Levine, 'Damascus Document IX,17-22: A New Translation and Comments', *RQ* 8 (1972-75) 195-96; J. Neusner, '"By the Testimony of Two Witnesses" in the Damascus Document IX,17-22 and in Pharisaic-Rabbinic Law', *RQ* 8 (1972-75) 197-217; *idem*, 'Damascus Document IX,17-22 and Irrelevant Parallels', *RQ* 9 (1978) 441-44; N.L. Rabinovitch, 'Damascus Document IX,17-22 and Rabbinic Parallels', *RQ* 9 (1978) 113-16; L.H. Schiffman, *Sectarian Law*, esp. pp. 55-88; *idem, Reclaiming the Dead Sea Scrolls*, pp. 282-87; B.Z. Wacholder, 'Rules of Testimony'; Y. Yadin, *The Temple Scroll*, I, pp. 379-82. For a discussion of parallels in the codes of pagan associations of the Greco-Roman period see M. Weinfeld, *The Organizational Pattern and the Penal Code of the Qumran Sect. A Comparison with Guilds and Religious Associations of the Hellenistic-Roman Period*, Göttingen: Vandenhoeck and Ruprecht / Fribourg: Éditions Universitaires, 1986, pp. 38-39.

[12] 'Text of CDC', pp. 26-29. The recent edition of the text of the CD Laws by Baumgarten agrees widely with Qimron's readings apart from reading אחד as the first word in CD 9,20, cf. Baumgarten in Charlesworth ed., *Dead Sea Scrolls*, II, pp. 42-45.

[13] Both this translation and the following one are taken from the *NRSV*.

Similarly, Dt. 19,15 reads,

לא־יקום עד אחד באיש לכל־עון ולכל־חטאת בכל־חטא אשר יחטא על־פי שני עדים או על־פי שלשה־עדים יקום דבר:

> A single witness shall not suffice to convict a person of any crime or wrongdoing in connection with any offence that may be committed. Only on the evidence of two or three witnesses shall a charge be sustained.

The ambiguous phrase 'on the evidence of two witnesses *or* of three witnesses' poses an interpretative problem for exegetes of these passages. Schiffman has shown that the interpretation chosen by the author of our passage attaches a distinct significance to each number of witnesses, i.e. three witnesses are required to complete a capital case whereas matters of property can be solved on the basis of the testimony of two witnesses.[14] The view that the passage under discussion rules that three witnesses are required in capital cases seems preferable to me for two reasons. Firstly, the text of CD 9,19b-20 itself is most naturally taken to refer to a third witness (אם ישוב וניתפש לפני אחר שלם משפט). Secondly, Schiffman's reconstruction of the exegetical process which attaches a distinct meaning to each number mentioned in the Hebrew Bible is convincing and provides considerable support for taking CD 9,19b-20a as a reference to a third witness. Schiffman has shown that the same exegetical process lies behind the rules on the sabbath limits in CD 10,5-6 and 10,21 which are based on the mention to two figures (one thousand and two thousand cubits) in Num. 35,2-5, the description of the extent of the pasture land of the levitical cities.[15]

Finally, a great deal of scholarly discussion has focused on comparing the present passage with rabbinic evidence and the New Testament.

All of these areas of inquiry—interesting and important though they are—are only mentioned here for the sake of completeness since few of the questions that lie at the heart of the present study are touched upon there. In the context of my source critical analysis of the Laws the present passage has been assigned to the communal legislation stratum on the basis of the following considerations.

a. The Overseer
The important role assigned to the overseer (מבקר) throughout the passage firmly places this material alongside the legislation on the

---
[14] *Sectarian Law*, pp. 74-78.
[15] *Sectarian Law*, p. 74.

entry into the covenant community in CD 15,5b-16,6a discussed above as well as the material on the organization of the camps to be dealt with below. From the communal rules found in the Laws of the Damascus Document it emerges clearly that the overseer played an important role in the organizational structure of the community, cf. especially CD 13,7b-14,2 and 14,8b-12a and the discussion of each passage below.

In the context of his distinction between urban halakhah and camp rules in the CD Laws Rubinstein suggests that the present material probably belongs to the camp tradition because of the mention of the overseer. Thus, Rubinstein comments on this passage,

> Now although an urban Mebakker is a distinct possibility, it is equally possible that the Mebakker here is the *camp* Mebakker, having regard to the fact that this official is only mentioned elsewhere in the CDC in the rules specifically applicable *to the camps*.[16]

Esther Eshel has published a fascinating new text from Cave 4 in an article entitled '4Q477: The Rebukes by the Overseer' that appears to constitute an ancient document illustrating the procedure laid down in CD 9,16b-10,3.[17] This important new text consists of five fragments and seems to contain a written record of offences that have been brought before the overseer with reproof and recorded by him. Eshel's suggested title for the work—which is identical with the title of the article—is somewhat misleading. The title 'The Rebukes by the Overseer' would imply that the overseer does the reproving whereas it is clear both from 4Q477 itself as well as from CD 9,18b-19a that it is ordinary community members who bring rebukes to the attention of the overseer.[18]

b. The Judges

A second group in authority within the organizational structure of the community legislated for in the Laws of D are the judges. The fact that the present passage allots the role of executing the verdict on offenders to the judges indicates that this material originated with the same community as CD 10,4-10a, the rule for the judges of the congregation, to be discussed below. It is implied in CD 9,23b-10,2a that it was the judges who held ultimate juridical authority, whereas the role of the overseer was predominantly to be present when witnesses reproved a neighbour and to keep a record of all offences that

---

[16] 'Urban Halakhah and Camp Rules', p. 287.
[17] *JJS* 45 (1994) 111-22.
[18] Cf. C. Hempel, 'Who Rebukes in 4Q477?', *RQ* 16 (1995) 655-56; see also S.A. Reed, 'Genre, Setting and Title of 4Q477', *JJS* 47 (1996) 147-148.

were brought before him. This has been emphasized already by Jackson who comments on the role of the overseer as follows,

> Indeed, our passage [...] assigns to the mevaker no role greater than that of a clerk, taking the depositions of witnesses as the evidence becomes available.[19]

Schiffman describes the *mebaqqer* along the same lines as 'an administrative official'.[20] Wacholder, by contrast, argues that the overseer is assigned 'all the prerogatives of an absolute judge'.[21] Furthermore, the reference to the judges in CD 10,1 is explained by Wacholder as either belonging to a different source or as being of a more general application.[22] Wacholder's case seems unconvincing. His suggestion to take the reference to the judges as going back to a different source or referring to more general cases seems unnecessary. It is clear form several passages in the body of communal rules of the Laws that both the judges and the overseer occupied a role in the communal organization of the community. Thus, reference to one does not of necessity exclude the other, cf. especially the rules on the collection of charitable funds in CD 14,12-16 which mention the overseer and the judges side by side in CD 14,13 as the collectors of these funds. Finally, it is not clear to me on what evidence Wacholder arrived at the conclusion that the overseer is presented as an absolute judge in our passage. The only role attributed to the overseer is that of recording rebukes.

To sum up, both the role assigned to the overseer in the process of testifying on the one hand and the reference to the judicial authority of the judges on the other hand indicate that this section belongs to the communal legislation of the Laws of D which describe a movement in which both authorities have their respective roles.

c. Exclusion from the טהרה

Both L.H. Schiffman[23] and F. García Martínez[24] have argued that the reference to the exclusion from the purity (טהרה) in CD 9,21 refers to the relegation of full members to the status of applicants. This line of argument presupposes a two-stage admission process characteristic of parts of S but not D. While it seems correct that the

---

[19] 'Damascus Document IX,16-23 and Parallels', p. 449.
[20] *Sectarian Law*, p. 95.
[21] 'Rules of Testimony', p. 169.
[22] 'Rules of Testimony', p. 172.
[23] *Sectarian Law*, p. 76.
[24] F. García Martínez and J. Trebolle Barrera, *People of the Dead Sea Scrolls*, pp. 224 and 231.

term *tohorah* refers to some kind of pure food,[25] it is used in a variety of contexts in a number of documents, and each occurrence ought to be considered in their own context rather than read in the light of 1QS 6,13b-23 and associated with the complex admission process laid down there. It seems likely that in the present passage the term טהרה refers to table fellowship of some kind, and the use here may be compared to the use of the term in 11QT^a 63,14 where is occurs in the context of marriage with a woman who had been taken prisoner in war.

d. The Importance of Reproof

The importance of reproof which is stressed in the present passage as part of the communal rules in the Laws of the Damascus Document is also emphasized in CD 9, 2-8a. The latter forms part the stratum of halakhic exposition. Both passages attach great importance to the practice of reproof in the community. Apart from belonging to different literary strands in the Laws, i.e. communal legislation and halakhic exposition, a difference in procedure can also be noted between both sections. Whereas the present passage deals with the *witnesses' duty to reprove*, CD 9,2-8a rules that the covenanter who intends to accuse another member of the covenant of shortcomings is to reprove the offender *in front of witnesses*. Furthermore, whereas it is the figure of the overseer before whom the reproof is brought in the present passage, this office is not mentioned in the halakhic material in CD 9,2-8a which instead refers to the elders not mentioned in the passage under discussion. The elders are a traditional and scriptural body of authority which is in keeping with the scriptural basis of the halakhah stratum of the Laws. By contrast, the community as reflected in the communal legislation seems to have developed the office of the overseer over and above scriptural authority structures.

It seems likely that the halakhah in CD 9,2-8a was taken as a starting point in this instance for the formulation of a piece of communal legislation. Thus, the emphasis on reproof which the exegete based on Lev. 19,18 and Nah. 1,2 in CD 9,2-8a is taken up again by the legislator who was responsible for the piece of communal legislation in CD 9,16b-10,3. Such a situation should not come as a surprise. It is not unexpected that the sections containing halakhah in the Laws of the Damascus Document share some of the concerns echoed in

---

[25] For a discussion of the use of the term טהרה in the scrolls and in rabbinic sources on the Pharisaic *haburoth* see S. Lieberman, 'The Discipline in the So-Called Dead Sea Manual of Discipline', *JBL* 71 (1952) 199-206.

the communal rules.²⁶ One may assume that the halakhah was handed down side by side with the communal rules because the movement that lies behind the communal legislation venerated the halakhah and continued to preserve it. Thus, the present passage is illuminating with regard to the relationship between the halakhah and the communal rules strata of the Laws of D.

5.3 The Judges of the Congregation

CD 10,4-10a prescribe for the office of the judges of the congregation. 4QD^a 8 iii 4-9 and 4QD^e 6 iv 15-19 parallel this material with only minor variants.²⁷

A. *Text*
(CD 10,4-10a; 4QD^a 8 iii; 4QD^e 6 iv)

10:4 וזה סרך לשפטי העדה עד²⁸ עשרה אנשים ברורים
10:5 מן העדה לפי העת ארבעה למטה לוי ואהרן ומישראל
10:6 ששה מבוננים בספר ההגי וביסודי הברית מבני חמשה
10:7 ועשרים שנה עד בני ששים שנה ואל יתיצב עוד מבן
10:8 ששים שנה ומעלה לשפוט את העדה כי במעל האדם
10:9 מעטו ימו ובחרון אף אל ביושבי הארץ אמר לסור את
10:10a דעתם עד לא ישלימו את ימידם

B. *Translation*
10,4 And this is the rule for the judges of the congregation. Ten men shall be chosen
 5 from the congregation for a fixed term: four from the tribe of Levi and Aaron and from Israel
 6 six, learned in the Book of Hagi and the principles of the covenant, aged between twenty
 7 five and sixty years. *No one older than*
 8 *sixty years shall (be in a position to) judge the congregation, for because of the sin of human beings*
 9 *their days were shortened, and in his fierce anger against the inhabitants of the earth God commanded that*
 10a *their understanding depart before they complete their days.*

---

²⁶ This interplay is noted also by Schiffman who comments, "in this area of law [i.e. courts and testimony] we will encounter a greater nexus between the halakhic issues under discussion and the way the sect was organized." (*Reclaiming the Dead Sea Scrolls*, pp. 282-83).
²⁷ Cf. Baumgarten, *Qumran Cave 4. XIII*, pp. 66-67,159-60.
²⁸ On this use of עד, cf. Baumgarten in Charlesworth ed., *Dead Sea Scrolls*, II, p. 45 n. 151.

C. Commentary

This piece of communal legislation is introduced by a heading which describes what follows as a סרך. This term occurs frequently in the literature from Qumran, and in the present context has the meaning 'rule'.[29] Similar headings occur throughout the Laws of the Damascus Document to introduce, or at times conclude, pieces of communal legislation (cf. CD 12,22-3; 13,7 etc.). It is often difficult to know with certainty whether a heading belonged originally to the material it introduces or whether it goes back to a compiler. What can be determined more easily, however, is how smoothly the headings and concluding statements relate to the surrounding material. The present heading aptly introduces the material that follows and belongs to the first category of headings outlined in chapter two.

The remainder of this section can be divided into four parts.

a. CD 10,4b-6a Number and descent of the judges

Ten men are to be chosen from the congregation for a certain period, four from the tribe of Levi and Aaron and six from Israel. Whereas the camp community as a whole was made up of priests, levites, Israelites, and proselytes (CD 14,3-6a), judges must be either from the tribes of Aaron and Levi or Israelites. Thus, the requirements for holding the office of the judge were stricter than those for simple community membership as noted already by Schechter.[30]

b. CD 10,6b Knowledge and education

The judges must be learned in the Book of Hagi and the principles of the covenant. The enigmatic Book of Hagi occurs three times in the communal legislation of the Damascus Document (CD 10,6b [par. 4QD^a and c]; 13,2; 14,7-8 [par. 4QD^b]). Although a number of scholars have attempted to identify this book with one or other of the Jewish works known to us, the Damascus Document gives us no clues as to its contents. In view of this lack of information any attempt at identifying this work is speculative. Interestingly, this work is never mentioned in the Community Rule. Even the passage in 1QS 6,3b-4a which at times agrees with CD 13,2b-3a word for word lacks the reference to the Book of Hagi found in CD 13,2b. I, therefore, suggest that the Book of Hagi was a work that had authority in the parent movement of the *yaḥad*. Outside of the Laws of

---

[29] For a detailed discussion of the use of סרך in the DSS see L.H. Schiffman, *Halakhah at Qumran*, pp. 60-68. See also pp. 26-27 n. 8 above.
[30] *Fragments of a Zadokite Work*, p. xiv.

the Damascus Document it occurs only in the Rule of the Congregation (1QSa 1,7).[31] I have argued elsewhere that this part of the Rule of the Congregation also originated with the parent movement of the *yaḥad* and probably with the same community as the one reflected in the Laws of D.[32] The principles of the covenant are nowhere spelled out for us either. The covenant in question is probably the covenant we encountered in the rules on admission in CD 15,5b-6a.7b-16,2a above. This covenant is perceived in the Laws of the Damascus Document as a re-affirmation of Israel's covenant, cf. CD 15,5b and 16,1.

c. CD 10,6c-7a Age of the Judges

The judges are to be between twenty five and sixty years of age. A comprehensive discussion of the age limits of the judges in relation to other prescriptions on age limits in the corpus of the DSS, the Hebrew Bible, and rabbinic literature can be found in Schiffman.[33] The minimum age of twenty five years goes back to Num. 8,24-25 where the minimum age for the service of the levites is twenty five. The maximum age of sixty, on the other hand, is derived from Lev. 27,3.[34]

d. CD 10,7b-10a Theological explanation of the upper age limit

This theological explanation is based on Jubilees 23,9-11 which VanderKam renders as follows,

> 23:9 For the times of the ancients were 19 jubilees for their lifetimes. After the flood they started to decrease from 19 jubilees, to be fewer with respect to jubilees, to age quickly, and to have their times be completed in view of the numerous difficulties and through the wickedness of their ways—with the exception of Abraham. 23:10 For Abraham was perfect with the Lord in everything that he did—being properly pleasing throughout all his lifetime. And yet (even) he had not completed four jubilees during his lifetime when he became old—in view of wickedness—and reached the end of his time. 23:11 All the

---

[31] No further references to the 'Book of Hagi' are listed in *A Preliminary Concordance to the Hebrew and Aramaic Texts from Qumran Caves II-X*, Vols. I-V, prepared and arranged for printing by H.-P. Richter on behalf of J. Strugnell, privately printed in Göttingen 1988 (distributed by H. Stegemann). A reference to a 'vision of meditation' occurs in 4QSapiential Work A [4Q417 2 i/4Q418 43], cf. D.J. Harrington, *Wisdom Texts from Qumran*, London: Routledge, 1996, p. 53 and A. Lange, *Weisheit und Prädestination. Weisheitliche Urordnung und Prädestination in den Textfunden von Qumran*, Leiden: E.J. Brill, 1995, pp. 84-85.
[32] Cf. Hempel, 'Earthly Essene Nucleus'.
[33] *Sectarian Law*, pp. 30-37.
[34] Cf. Y. Yadin, *The Scroll of the War of the Sons of Light against the Sons of Darkness*, Oxford: OUP, 1962, esp. pp. 75-79.

generations that will come into being from now until the great day of judgment will grow old quickly—before they complete two jubilees. It will be their knowledge that will leave them because of their old age; all of their knowledge will depart.[35]

This derivation from Jub. 23 was already pointed out by Schechter[36] and has frequently been noted since.[37] J. Kugel has offered a thorough study of Jub. 23 and its use of Ps. 90.[38] Kugel goes as far as to say that CD 10,7-10 may be based entirely on Ps. 90 and not on Jub. 23 at all. Kugel's analysis of Ps. 90 as the background to Jub. 23 is entirely convincing. However, his suggestion that the Damascus Document draws here only on a particular interpretation of Ps. 90 is probably going too far. It seems more likely that the present passage is based on Jub. 23 since the theological point made here is a major concern in Jub. that is hardly developed in the Damascus Document at all. The present passage constitutes the only instance in the Laws where a theological explanation is given for the upper age limit of an office, contrast CD 14,6c-8a and 14,9. Moreoever, in general, the prescriptions on the organization of the community are simply stated without a justification or theological rationale being provided. It, therefore, seems very probable that CD 10,7b-10a is secondary and was added at the end of the section on the judges of the congregation by the same redactor who was at work in CD 16,2b-6a. As in the latter case, the present interpolation is similarly characterized by a strong interest in promoting the message of the Book of Jubilees.

Thus, the original text of the rule on the judges of the congregation ran from CD 10,4-7a. The passage belongs to the stratum of communal legislation. It is entirely unpolemical and conforms in tone and terminology to the remainder of the communal legislation in the Laws. I have already mentioned the likelihood of the Book of Hagi having been a work of authority in this movement. Furthermore, the term used to refer to the community behind this passage is 'congregation' (עדה). This term occurs throughout the communal legislation in the Laws, cf. for example CD 15,17 [reconstructed with the help of 4QD^a 8 i 9]; 10,4.5.8; 13,10-11.13; 14,10. As far as the Cave 4 MSS of the Damascus Document are concerned עדה occurs thirteen times altogether. Two occurrences

---

[35] J.C. VanderKam, *The Book of Jubilees*, Louvain: Peeters, 1989, II, pp. 138-40.
[36] *Fragments of a Zadokite Work*, p. xlviii n. XI,10.
[37] See Baumgarten in Charlesworth ed., *Dead Sea Scrolls*, II, p. 45 n. 154; also J.C. VanderKam, 'The Jubilees Fragments from Qumran Cave 4', in *The Madrid Qumran Congress* ed. Trebolle Barrera and Vegas Montaner, II, p. 648 where he remarks, "CD 10:8-10 echoes fairly closely the wording of *Jub.* 23:11."
[38] J. Kugel, 'The Jubilees Apocalypse', *DSD* 1 (1994) 322-37, esp. p. 336.

are from the Admonition and they need not concern us here. Eight occurrences of עדה in the Cave 4 MSS parallel the mediaeval text of the Laws in which, as we saw, the term is used frequently to designate the community behind the text. Apart from these ten occurrences of עדה that cover text that is paralleled in the mediaeval text of the Damascus Document, 4QD^a 10 i 4[39], 4QD^b 5 iii 6, and 4QD^c 7 i 4 contain one further mention of עדה respectively which have no parallel in the Genizah text. The self-designation congregation occurs frequently alongside camp in the communal rules. It is difficult to be sure whether both terms are synonymous or whether the latter is more comprehensive than the former. I am inclined to think that access to the congregation was more limited than access to the camp, since CD [15,17] and the parallel account in 4QD^a 8 i 6-9 exclude certain categories of people from the congregation.

5.4 Summary

In sum, the material contained in CD 9,10b-10,7a par. deals with the administration of justice in the commuity, and has been assigned to the communal legislation in the Laws. In particular, the procedure for dealing with lost or stolen property, the testimony of witnesses, and the office of the judges of the congregation are legislated upon in this section. What is more, the theological explanation of the upper age limit for judges in CD 10,7b-10a was attributed to the glossator intent on promoting concerns that are prominent in the Book of Jubilees.

---

[39] In the case of 4QD^a 10 i 4 the additional reference to the congregation occurs as a variant reading from CD 14,11, cf. the textual note *ad* CD 14,11 on p. 133 below.

CHAPTER SIX

COMMUNITY ORGANIZATION PART THREE: THE ORGANIZATION OF THE CAMPS

The organization of the camps is dealt with at some lengths in the Laws of D. I will discuss the announcement of statutes for the wise leader (משכיל) at the end of CD 12, the authority structure in the camps, the detailed regulations on the overseer over the camp, and finally the regulations applicable to all the camps. As will become apparent the material included here has undergone a considerable amount of redactional development.

6.1 Announcement of Statutes for the משכיל

CD 12,20b-22a announces rules for the wise leader. 4QD[a] 9 ii 7-8 contains remnants of two words that parallel this material but provides no variants.[1]

A. Text
(CD 12,20b-22a; 4QD[a] 9 ii 7-8)

12:20b ואלה החקים
12:21 למשכיל להתהלך בם עם כל חי למשפט עת ועת וכמשפט
12:22a הזה יתהלכו זרע ישראל ולא יוארו

B. Translation
12,20b And these are the statutes
    21 by which the wise leader shall deal with all the living according to the rule appropriate for every time. And according to this
    22a ordinance the seed of Israel shall walk and not be cursed.

C. Commentary
This heading displays close terminological similarities with a heading found in the Community Rule in 1QS 9,12 which reads,

---

[1] Cf. Baumgarten, *Qumran Cave 4. XIII*, p. 69.

אלה החוקים למשכיל להתהלך בם עם כול חי לתכון עת ועת למשקל איש ואיש...

These are the statutes by which the wise leader shall deal with all the living according to the rule appropriate for every time and according to the weight of each man...

In contrast to 1QS 9 which goes on to list some of the חוקים which the משכיל[2] is to follow, CD contains no such list. Instead, the Laws of the Damascus Document contain this announcement of חוקים without any rules following it. As I will argue more fully in my analysis of CD 13,7b-14,2 below the traditions on the duties of the משכיל have become merged with traditions on the overseer in CD 12-14 in its final form. Remnants of a section dealing with the duties of the משכיל have survived in the present heading (CD 12,20b-21a) as well as in CD 13,7b-8 and CD 13,22 to be discussed below.[3]

Commenting on CD 12,20-21 Cothenet notes,

> On attendrait l'énoncé des prescriptions à observer. Le texte serait-il lacuneux? ou plutôt, en citant l'incipit d'une section de la *Règle de la Communauté* (9,12-21), l'auteur n'y renverrait-il pas expressément, comme nous renvoyons au chapitre d'un livre en en donnant le titre?[4]

I cannot agree with Cothenet's overall evaluation of the relationship between 1QS and the Laws of the Damascus Document. It seems unlikely to me that 1QS in its present form predates the Laws of the Damascus Document. Rather, I am inclined to suppose that the text of the Laws of the Damascus Document is the result of a merging of traditions on the משכיל with traditions on the overseer. One possible explanation for this correspondence between D and S is that both documents independently drew upon pre-Qumranic material. In the case of the Laws of the Damascus Document parts of this material were merged with the material on the overseer and parts may have been lost.[5]

---

[2] For an overview on the use and meaning of the term see H. Kosmala, 'Maskîl', *Studies, Essays and Reviews*, Leiden: E.J. Brill, 1978, I, pp. 235-41.

[3] 4QD[a] 5 i 17b may preserve remnants of a further heading virtually identical to CD 12,20-21 and 13,22. Unfortunately what follows is very fragmentary and not much can be said about this passage, cf. Baumgarten, *Qumran Cave 4. XIII*, p. 48 and chapter ten, esp. p. 174, below.

[4] 'Document de Damas', p. 199.

[5] See pp. 123-125 below.

6.2 Questions of Authority

The legislation on the organization of the camp proper begins with a passage dealing with questions of authority.

A. *Text*
(CD 12,22b-13,7a; 4QD^a 9 ii)

12:22b	וזה סרך מושב
12:23	המח[נו]ת המתהלכים באלה בקץ הרשעה עד עמוד משוח אהרן
13:1	וישראל עד **עשרה** אנשים למועט לאלפים ומיאיות וחמשים
13:2	ועשרות ובמקום **עשרה** אל ימש איש כהן מבונן בספר ההגי על
13:3	פיהו ישקו כולם⁶ *vacat* ואם אין הוא בחון בכל אלה ואיש מהלוים בחון
13:4	באלה ויצא הגורל לצאת ולבוא על פיהו כל באי המחנה *vacat* ואם
13:5	משפט לתורת נגע יהיה באיש ובא הכהן ועמד במחנה והבינו
13:6	המבקר בפרוש התורה *vacat* ואם פתי הוא הוא יסגירנו כי להם
13:7a	המשפט

B. *Translation*
12,22b And this is the rule for the meeting of
   23 the cam[p]s. <u>Those who walk in these in the time of wickedness until the Messiah of Aaron and Israel</u>
13,1 <u>arises</u> (shall form groups) of at least **ten** men by thousands and hundreds and fifties
   2 and tens. And in a place of **ten** there shall not be lacking a priest learned in the Book of Hagi.
   3 All of them shall obey him. *Vacat.* But if he is not experienced in all these, and one of the levites is experienced
   4 in these, then the lot shall determine that all the members of the camp shall go out and come in at his word. *Vacat.* But if
   5 there is a case pertaining to the law of disease befalling a person, then the priest shall enter and stand in the camp, and the overseer
   6 shall instruct him concerning the exact meaning of the law. *Vacat.* And even if he is a simpleton, it is he who shall lock him up for theirs is
   7a the judgment.

C. *Commentary*
This section is the first in a series of passages on the communal organization of the camps. This first section on the organization of the

---

⁶ For the formulation על פיהו ישקו כולם cf. Gen. 41,40, cf. Rabin, *Zadokite Documents*, p. 64. and P. Wernberg-Møller, *The Manual of Discipline. Translated and Annotated with an Introduction*, Leiden: E.J. Brill, 1957, pp. 102-103 with reference to 1QS 6,4.

camps is introduced by a heading of the סרך-type, so typical of the communal rules in the Laws. This heading introduces a block of material on the organization of individual camps that runs to CD 13,20. The material in this first section prescribes for the organization of the members of the camps along the lines of the organization of the Israelite camp in the wilderness, cf. Ex. 18,21.25. A substantial part of the section deals, however, with the question of authority in the camps. What is more, the material on the authority structure in the camps is rather complex in this section which is indicative of developments in the literary history of this prescription.

As I have argued above in my discussion of CD 15,6b-7a there is a good case to be made for taking CD 12,23b-13,1a as a redactional phrase that goes back to the Damascus redactor. CD 12,23b-13,1a reads,

המתהלכים באלה בקץ הרשעה עד עמוד משוח אהרן וישראל

> Those who walk in these in the time of wickedness until the Messiah of Aaron and Israel arises...

As I have argued in the context of the earlier occurrence of a reference to the time of wickedness in CD 15,6b-7a[7] this expression corresponds closely to the ideological position of the Admonition and is alien to the bulk of the Laws which list diverse halakhic and communal prescriptions in a neutral fashion.

Furthermore, the expression עד עמוד משוח אהרן וישראל or a similar equivalent occur in CD 19,10-11 and 20,1 in the Admonition and in CD 14,19 (par. 4QD^a 10 i 12 and 4QD^d 11 i 2) in the Laws as part of the introduction to the penal code in D. In contrast to the two references to the coming of the Messiah of Aaron and Israel in the Laws the two occurrences of the expression in the Admonition form an integral part of their immediate context. I will discuss each of the two occurrences in the Admonition in turn.

The reference to the Messiah of Aaron and Israel in CD 19,10-11 forms part of a warning to heed the series of halakhic rules given in CD 6,11b-7,4a. CD 19,1-34 contains the text of MS B that is partially paralleled by CD 7,5b-8,21 in MS A. The more immediate context of our expression is the warning which is found in CD 19,5b-14. As is well known, the texts of MSS A and B vary considerably at this point. Whereas MS A is made up of a midrashic exegesis of citations from Isaiah, Amos and Numbers MS B contains a

---

[7] See pp. 79-81 above.

midrashic exegesis of citations from Zechariah and Ezekiel. The warning in MS B begins in CD 19,5b-7a by stating that all those who reject the commandments will suffer at the time of God's visitation. The text of MS B continues with a citation of Zech. 13,7 and its midrashic exegesis. The latter contains the reference to the coming of the Messiah of Aaron and Israel. Much has been written on the Admonition, and detailed comments on this material can be found elsewhere.[8] As far as our present purposes are concerned it suffices to stress that the reference to the coming of the Messiah of Aaron and Israel in CD 19,10-11 occurs in a *thoroughly eschatological context*. God's visitation of the earth is mentioned in CD 19,6, and again the time of the visitation is mentioned in CD 19,10. Thus, in CD 19 the Messiah of Aaron and Israel is referred to as part of a general warning about the fate of the wicked at the time of the visitation in which the Messiah will play his part.

The second reference to the Messiah of Aaron and Israel in the Admonition in CD 20,1 is again found in MS B. The context here is a description of the fate of backsliders, i.e. members of the community who have become apostates. This part of the Admonition presupposes the death of the teacher of the community and has been assigned by Davies to a Qumranic recension of the Admonition.[9] CD 19,33b-20,1a reads,

19:33b כן כל האנשים אשר באו בברית
19:34 החדשה בארץ דמשק ושבו ויבנדו ויסורו מבאר מים החיים
19:35 לא יחשבו בסוד עם ובכתבם לא יכתבו מיום האסף[10]
20:1a מורה היחיד[11] עד עמוד משיח מאהרן ומישראל

19,33b Thus shall it be for all those who have entered the new
   34 covenant in the land of Damascus who have turned and acted as traitors and turned away from the well of living waters,
   35 they shall not be counted among the council of the people and they shall not be entered into their records from the day of the gathering in

---

[8] Cf., for example, Davies, *Damascus Covenant*, esp. pp. 143-72 and further literature discussed there. See also Knibb, *Qumran Community*, pp. 56-63.

[9] *Damascus Covenant*, pp. 173-97.

[10] Here and at the beginning of the following line a few words were deleted by the copyist of the MS.

[11] The text as it stands reads 'the unique teacher'. I translate 'teacher of the community' following the reading מורה היחד which is the reading preferred by many scholars, cf., for example, Rabin, *Zadokite Documents*, p. 37 *ad loc.* who expresses cautious approval and Qimron, 'Text of CDC', p. 47 n. 1. None of the eight 4QD MSS preserves the relevant portion of D.

20,1a of the teacher of the community until there will arise the Messiah from Aaron and from Israel.

As was the case in CD 19,10-11 so here the reference to the coming of the Messiah is an integral part of its immediate context. With the death of the teacher as a starting point and the coming of the Messiah as a turning point, the reference to the Messiah is part of an eschatological time scheme in the Admonition. I have emphasized with reference to CD 15,6b-7a that the Admonition, in contrast to the Laws, is greatly preoccupied with time schemes of both a historical and an eschatological nature.[12]

J.C. VanderKam recently made an interesting observation regarding the function of references to the Messiah of Aaron and Israel in the Laws of D. Commenting on CD 14,18-19 he remarks, "The messianic function is once more to define a unit of time."[13] I would add to this observation that 'units of time' are not a genuine concern in the body of the Laws of D but occur only in transitional passages that are best assigned to the Damascus redaction.

In sum, I hope to have been able to show that the references to the coming of the Messiah in the Admonition are an integral part of a context of historical and eschatological reflection. In the Laws, by contrast, the references to the Messiah occur only in transitional passages that serve to link various pieces of legislation, and go back to the Damascus redactor.

Following the provision for the organization of the members of the camps into thousands, hundreds, fifties, and tens the section deals with the question of authority in the camps. CD 13,2b-3a is linked to the preceding material through the catchword 'ten' (עשרה) highlighted in bold script in the text and translation above. This passage displays close terminological overlap with 1QS 6,3 as has frequently been pointed out. Commenting on CD 13,2 É. Cothenet points out the correspondence between this passage and 1QS 6,

> Littéralement: et dans un lieu de dix. Ce passage très concis, ne s'explique que comme un résumé de la *Règle de la Communauté* 6,3-4 [...].

---

[12] See pp. 80-81 above.

[13] 'Messianism in the Scrolls', in *The Community of the Renewed Covenant. The Notre Dame Symposium on the Dead Sea Scrolls* ed. E. Ulrich and J.C. VanderKam, Notre Dame: University of Notre Dame Press, 1994, pp. 211-34, p. 229. More generally J.J. Collins observes, "In fact, the scrolls are tantalisingly reticent on the activities of the messiahs and in most cases merely assert that they will arise.", 'Patterns of Eschatology at Qumran', in *Traditions in Transformation. Turning Points in Biblical Faith* ed. B. Halpern and J.D. Levenson, Winona Lake: Eisenbrauns, 1981, pp. 351-75,

> Sans la *Règle de la Communauté*, le *Document de Damas* serait peu compréhensible; c'est une preuve de sa postériorité.[14]

While I would disagree with Cothenet's final remark he rightly stresses the link between the two passages under consideration. In my view the corresponding phrases in both documents are best explained as remnants of pre-Qumranic community legislation in 1QS. In the case of the Laws of the Damascus Document, on the other hand, the passage in question conforms to the overall pre-Qumranic provenance of the communal legislation in that collection. The most likely explanation for this overlap between 1QS 6,3 and CD 12,23-13,2 is the preservation of communal legislation drawn from the traditions of the parent movement of the Qumran community in both cases. It is impossible to be sure whether both documents drew upon earlier traditions independently or whether 1QS is dependent on CD. The former seems more likely because of the very concise formulation in CD. Cothenet's view that CD is dependent on and later than 1QS seems unlikely to me. I think it much more likely that 1QS in its present form post-dates most of the Laws of the Damascus Document and reflects a more institutionalized stage in the sociological development of the community. The text of CD, though briefer and more concise than 1QS, is comprehensible as it stands, and we may have here a shorthand expression the meaning of which was easily grasped in the original context of its occurrence.

The material on the authority in the camps may be divided into three parts:

a. CD 13,2b-3a

vacat ובמקום עשרה אל ימש איש כהן מבונן בספר ההגי על פיהו ישקו כולם

> And in a place of ten there shall not be lacking a priest learned in the Book of Hagi. All of them shall obey him. *Vacat.*

b. CD 13,3b-4a

ו**אם** אין הוא בחון בכל אלה ואיש מהלוים בחון באלה ויצא הגורל
לצאת ולבוא על פיהו כל באי המחנה *vacat*

> **But if** he is not experienced in all these, and a man from the levites is experienced in these, then the lot shall determine that all the members of the camp shall go out and come in at his word. *Vacat.*

---

p. 356. See also the remarks by Stegemann on this issue in *Die Essener, Qumran, Johannes der Täufer und Jesus*, Freiburg: Herder, 1994, p. 288.

[14] 'Document de Damas', p. 199.

c. CD 13,4b-7a

ואם משפט לתורת נגע יהיה באיש ובא הכהן ועמד במחנה והבינו המבקר
בפרוש התורה vacat ואם פתי הוא יסגירנו כי להם המשפט

> **But if** there is a case pertaining to the law of disease befalling a person, then the priest shall enter and stand in the camp, and the overseer shall instruct him in the exact meaning of the law. *Vacat.* And even if he is a simpleton, it is he who shall lock him up for theirs is the judgment.

This passage on the authority structure in the camps conveys the impression of having undergone a process of development. It seems likely that the first part of this section, here designated a., originally stood by itself and was elaborated upon by the addition of parts b. and c. CD 13,2b-3a attributes absolute authority to the priest ('All of them shall obey him'). Both additions that follow are introduced by ואם 'but if' and qualify the absolute authority attributed to the priest in CD 13,2b-3a.

As far as the first addition is concerned it seems probable that more than mere pragmatism lies behind this qualification. G.J. Brooke has examined the place of Levi and the levites in the Dead Sea Scrolls.[15] In this study, Brooke discusses a wide variety of texts from Qumran and finds evidence for a strand of traditions promoting Levi and the levites in both Qumranic and pre-Qumranic works. From his discussion on the place of the levites in the War Scroll(s) from Caves 1 and 4 (1QM and 4QM) Brooke concludes that,

> ...probably in the mid first century BCE certain Levites became prominent in the Qumran community in such a way that older materials needed to be adjusted to take account of their position.[16]

In the light of Brooke's observations it seems possible that CD 13,3b-4a was added here in order to enhance the importance of the levites among the leadership of the community after a number of levites had become influential in the community.

The second addition in CD 13,4b-7a deals primarily with the priestly prerogative of administering the law of disease. The most interesting feature of this passage for our present purposes is the tacit and abrupt introduction of the figure of the overseer (המבקר) in CD

---

[15] G.J. Brooke, 'Levi and the Levites in the Dead Sea Scrolls and the New Testament', *Mogilany 1989. Papers on the Dead Sea Scrolls* ed Z.J. Kapera, Kraków: Enigma, 1993, I, pp. 105-29.

[16] 'Levi and the Levites', p. 109; see also G. Brooke, 'The Temple Scroll: A Law Unto Itself?' in *Law and Religion. Essays on the Place of the Law in Israel and Early Christianity* ed. B. Lindars SSF, Cambridge: James Clarke, 1988, pp. 34-43, esp. pp. 38-40.

13,5b-6a : 'And the overseer shall instruct him [i.e. the priest] in the exact meaning of the law'. On this passage Brooke comments that,

> ...it is reasonable to suppose that the overseer [...] was a Levite, though the text does not actually say this.[17]

Although this view is possible it seems unlikely to me that the same motives of promoting the levites led to this second qualifying addition on the authority of the priest in the camps. If the overseer was to be a levite, and this passage did go back to the same tradition as CD 13,3b-4a, we would expect a more explicit statement as to the overseer's levitical descent. Furthermore, it is difficult to see why the new term overseer should have been used if what is meant here is איש מהלוים as in CD 13,3b-4a above.[18]

It seems more likely that the structure of communal organization in the community behind the Laws of D underwent development. Throughout the Laws of the Damascus Document that deal with matters of communal organization the overseer is most frequently referred to as playing a leading role (cf. 4QD^a 5 i 14; 7 iii 2; 7 iii 3 [4QD^b 8,4]; 4QD^f 3,14; CD 15,8.11.14; 9,18 (twice).19.22; 13,6.7. 13.16; 14,8-9.11.13; 4QD^a 11,16) mostly in connection with the camp structure (4QD^a 7 iii 3 [4QD^b 8,4]; CD 15,14; 13,7b.13.16; 14,8-9).

Thus, although the priests play an important role in some parts of the Laws of the Damascus Document, it was the office of the overseer which eventually became the focus of authority in the camps. Although it remained a priestly prerogative to deal with cases of disease CD 13,4b-7a presupposes the inauguration of the office of the overseer in the camps. CD 13,2b-3a, on the other hand, attributes absolute authority to the priest and probably predates CD 13,5b-6a and the installation of the office of the overseer.[19] The section dealing with cases of lost or stolen property in CD 9,10b-16a discussed above constitutes another piece of communal legislation that goes

---

[17] 'Levi and the Levites', p. 114.

[18] As Schechter pointed out already it seems unlikely in the light of the present passage that the overseer was a priest, cf. Fragments of a Zadokite Work, p. xiv n. 10 where he observes, "This is the impression one receives from p. 13, ll. 5,6, where the Censor is put in contradistinction to the Priest."

[19] J.J. Collins has argued that CD 13,6-7 reflects the dual leadership of the community, one priestly and one lay leader ('Patterns of Eschatology', p. 356). This interpretation, though not impossible, seems less likely to me. The material on the authority in the camp in CD 12,22b-13,7a reflects developments and rivalries, in my view, rather than depicting a contemporaneous and harmonicus collaboration between various figures as Collins envisages it.

back to the pre-overseer phase in the community's development where the figure in charge of the procedure is the priest.[20]

J.M. Baumgarten has recently drawn attention to a number of illuminating parallels in rabbinic literature (e.g. *m.Nega* 3,1) that mention the priestly prerogative to proclaim the diagnosis of diseases but allow for a competent Israelite to assist the priest in arriving at his judgment.[21] These parallels are illuminating and may well reflect some common traditions. The present passage appears somewhat distinctive because it places levites and the overseer rather than Israelites vis-à-vis the priest.

In sum, CD 12,22b-13,7a reflects a great deal of development. CD 12,22b-23a introduces the rule on the organization of individual camps that is concluded by CD 13,20. CD 12,23b-13,1a goes back to the Damascus redactor. The material on the authority in the camps in CD 13,2b-3a was developed by the addition of CD 13,3b-7a probably in the light of changes in the make up of the community.

6.3 THE OVERSEER OVER THE CAMP

CD 13,7b-14,2 contains a lengthy section on the duties of the overseer over the camp which again shows evidence of extensive reworking.

A. *Text*[22]
(CD 13,7b-14,2; 4QD^a 9 iii; 4QD^b 9 iv-v)

13:7b	וזה סרך המבקר למחנה ישכיל את הרבים במעשי
13:8	אל ויבינם בגבורות פלאו ויספר לפניהם נהיות עולם בפ֯ת֯ר֯י֯ה֯ם
13:9	וירחם עליהם כאב לבניו וישקוד לכל מדהובם כרועה עדרו
13:10	יתר כל חרצובות קשריהם לבלתי היות עשוק ורצוץ **בעדתו**
13:11	וכל הנוסף **לעדתו** יפקדהו למעשיו ושכלו וכוחו ונבורתו והונו
13:12	וכתבוהו במקומו כפי נחלתו בגורל האור *vacat* אל ימשול איש
13:13	מבני המחנה להביא איש אל העדה זולת פי המבקר אשר למחנה
13:14	*vacat* ואיש מכל באי ברית אל אל ישא ואל יתן לבני השחר כי
13:15	אם כף לכף *vacat* ואל יעש איש דבר למקח ולממכר כי אם הודיע
13:16	למבקר אשר במחנה ועשה בעצה ולא יש[ו]נו וכן] ל[כ]ל ל[וק]ח ל[וק]ח א[ש]ה
13:17	וה[וא] ∘∘∘ [ב]עצה וכן למנרש והוא יס[ר אח בניהם [
13:18	[וטפם ברוח]ענוה ובאהבת חסד אל יטור להם [באף ועברה [
13:19	[לפ]שעיהם ואת אשר איננו נקשר בש[

---

[20] See section 5.1 above.
[21] Baumgarten in Charlesworth ed., *Dead Sea Scrolls*, II, p. 55 n. 197.
[22] Unless otherwise indicated the reconstructions in CD 13,16-14,2 are taken from Qimron ('Text of CDC', pp. 35-37), and are based on 4QD^a 9 iii and 4QD^b 9 v. The latter MS provides parallel text from CD 13,22 onwards.

13:20	משפטיהם [	vacat [וזה מושב המחנות לכל ז]רע [
13:21	]	בא]לה לא יצליחו לשבת בארץ °[ ]
13:22	ממצוקות [	ו]אלה המש[פט]ים למש[כיל] להתהלך בם [
13:23	]	כאשר אמר יבוא עליך ועל עמך ימים]
14:1	אשר לא באו מיום סור אפרים מעל יהודה וכל המתהלכים באלה
14:2	ברית אל נאמנות להם להנצילם מכל מוקשי שחת כי פתאום$_{עב[רו]}$ ונענשו

B. Translation

13,7b And this is the rule for the overseer over the camp. He shall instruct the many in the works of

8 God and he shall make them understand his wonderful mighty deeds and recount before them the events of eternity with their inter$_{\text{pretations.}}$

9 And he shall be as kind to them as a father to his children and guard all those who have gone astray like a shepherd his flock.

10 And he shall undo all the fetters that tie them so that there shall not be anyone oppressed and broken in **his congregation**.

11 And he shall examine everyone who joins **his congregation** as to their[23] deeds, their insight, their strength, their might, and their property.

12 And they shall write them down according to their inheritance in the lot of light. *Vacat.* No member of the camp shall have the right

13 to bring anyone to the congregation without the consent of the overseer over the camp.

14 *Vacat.* And no member of the covenant of God shall buy or sell anything to the sons of dawn except

15 from hand to hand. *Vacat.* No one shall perform an act of trade unless he has informed

16 the overseer of the camp and acted on the advice, and they shall not si[n inadvertently. And thus shall be the case] for [every]one who ta[ke]s a wif[e]

17 and [ ]°°°[ ] counsel. And thus shall be the case for the one who divorces. And he shall discipli[ne their children]

18 [and their small children in a spirit of] humility and with kind love. He shall not bear a grudge [in anger and rage]

19 [for] their [s]ins so that there may not be anybody bound in [ ]

20 [their judgments] *Vacat.* And this is the meeting of the camps for all the s[eed of]

21 [in the]se they shall not be fit to dwell in the land in[ ]

22 [from afflictions And] these are the ordi[nan]ces for the wise leader [to walk in them]

---

[23] I have translated the third masculine singular suffixes with plural suffixes in English in an attempt at using inclusive language here. We know from 4QD^e 7 i 13-15 that women were present in the congregation.

23 [as he said, 'There will come upon you, and upon your people days]
14,1 such as have not come since the day that Ephraim departed from Judah'. But for all those who walk in these
2 the covenant of God shall be a permanent assurance for them to save them from all the snares of the pit whereas the weak-minded _{transgress[ed]} and they shall be punished.

C. *Textual Notes*

13,8 CD's text is corrupt at the end of this line. The letters of the last word in subscript are taken from 4QD^b 9 iv 5.[24]

13,9 The text is corrupt, and several emendations have been proposed. I follow the emendation endorsed by Rabin[25] and Lohse.[26] Thus, I translate 'those who have gone astray' and read נידחיהם for מרהובם. The parallel text in 4QD^b 9 iv 6 only preserves the last two letters of this word and is of limited value here.

13,15 Only faint traces of the last word in this line are preserved in CD.[27] Baumgarten does not include the last word in his Hebrew text, but it is clearly reflected in his English translation.[28]

13,22 The first word as well as the last two words in this line are not reconstructed by Qimron. The reconstructions are based on 4QD^a 9 iii 14 and 4QD^b 9 v 1. The reading and reconstruction המש[פט]ים follows the reading suggested by Rabin[29] and adopted by Baumgarten.[30]

13,23 Qimron reconstructs a fuller citation of Isa.7,17. However, neither 4QD^a 9 iii 17 nor 4QD^b 9 v 3 provide sufficient space for a full citation.[31] I have reconstructed this line along the lines of 4QD^a.

14,2 The word [ו]עבר is taken from 4QD^b 9 v 5.[32] 4QD^b 9 v 6 also reads ויענשו instead of CD's ונענש.

D. *Commentary*

This section on the organization of the camps is introduced by a heading of the סרך-type. The heading in CD 13,7b announces the rule for the overseer over the camp (המבקר למחנה). Yet, the first pre-

---

[24] Cf. Baumgarten, *Qumran Cave 4. XIII*, p. 109 and Qimron, 'Text of CDC', p. 35 n. 3.
[25] *Zadokite Documents*, p. 65.
[26] *Texte aus Qumran*, p. 94 n. b.
[27] Cf. Rabin, *Zadokite Documents*, p. 67 and Qimron, 'Text of CDC', pp. 34-35.
[28] Baumgarten in Charlesworth ed., *Dead Sea Scrolls*, II, pp. 54-55. Also, in CD 13,15 Baumgarten (following Rabin, *Zadokite Documents*, p. 67) reads חבר for דבר, a reading curiously not reflected in the translation (p. 55). In *Qumran Cave 4. XIII*, pp. 70-71 he follows Qimron's reading דבר however.
[29] *Zadokite Documents*, p. 67.
[30] Baumgarten in Charlesworth ed., *Dead Sea Scrolls*, II, p. 54. For a different reading cf. Qimron, 'Text of CDC', p. 35.
[31] See Baumgarten, *Qumran Cave 4. XIII*, pp. 70,109.
[32] Cf. Qimron, 'Text of CDC', p. 37 n. 3.

scription that mentions the camp, and indeed the overseer over the camp, does not occur until lines 12b-13. Directly following the heading, by contrast, we have an admonition for the overseer to instruct the many (הרבים). This abrupt reference to the many in a section of prescriptions that are announced as the rule for the overseer over the camp is surprising. I will argue below that the present passage seems to preserve an original core of rules on the duties of the overseer over the camp that has been elaborated upon and merged with other material. It does not seem possible to outline with confidence all the stages of the elaboration of this passage. It is possible, however, to make a good case for the delineation of the original core of this section, and to comment more tentatively on the additional material.

a. CD 13,7b.12b-13.15b-16a: The Original Core of the Rule for the Overseer over the Camp

וזה סרך המבקר למחנה
אל ימשול איש מבני המחנה להביא איש אל העדה זולת פי המבקר אשר למחנה
ואל יעש איש דבר למקח ולממכר כי אם הודיע למבקר אשר במחנה ועשה בעצה
ולא יש[ונו

> And this is the rule for the overseer over the camp.
> No member of the camp shall have the right to bring anyone to the congregation without the consent of the overseer over the camp.
> No one shall perform an act of trade unless he has informed the overseer of the camp and acted on the advice, and they shall not si[n inadvertently.]

Both in terms of form and terminology this block of material forms a unity and can be distinguished from the remainder of the passage. The heading as well as each prescriptive clause refer to the overseer over the camp. In addition, the first clause contains another mention of the camp by referring to the group guided by the overseer as 'the members of the camp' (בני המחנה). Thus, the terms of reference used in this unit on the communal organization are consistently the camp and the overseer over the camp. Furthermore, each clause has the same form and begins with אל plus jussive plus איש. Formally these clauses resemble the halakhic material in the Laws. The resemblance ends there, however, since in contrast to the halakhic exposition these clauses are clearly addressed to a particular organized community and lack a basis in scripture.

The first clause states in general terms the ultimate authority of the overseer in admitting new members to the congregation. The procedure of admission is described in more detail in CD 15,5b-

16,6a. In the course of the discussion of the former passage it was pointed out that the overseer plays a prominent role in the admission process.[33] The present passage, dealing expressly with the duties of the overseer over the camp, contains merely a simple statement affirming the overseer's authoritative role in this process.

The second clause rules that the members of the camp are to consult the overseer before embarking on any acts of trade. As may be concluded from several references to the private ownership of property in the communal legislation of the Damascus Document the movement described there did not practise communal ownership of goods. Nevertheless, the overseer over the camp had to be consulted and approve of trade deals. Although no reason for this state of affairs is given here it seems likely that concerns for the preservation of strictest standards of purity lie at the heart of this requirement. It emerges from a number of halakhic rules in the Laws of the Damascus Document that much care was needed to avoid defilement when trading with gentiles for example, cf. CD 12,8b-11a.

b. Elaboration of and Additions to the Original Core of the Rule on the Overseer over the Camp

i. CD 13,7c-8

ישכיל את הרבים במעשי אל ויבינם בנבורות פלאו

ויספר לפניהם נהיות עולם בפתריהם[34]

> He shall instruct the many in the works of God and he shall make them understand his wonderful mighty deeds and recount before them the events of eternity with their interpretations.

This passage follows immediately after the heading and, as I have pointed out above, the sudden introduction of the many is incongruous within the context of the rule for the overseer over the camp. This passage appears to be out of place within its present framework not only because of this important terminological feature, but also on account of its content. Whereas the original core of rules on the overseer over the camp is of a pragmatic orientation, the present passage has a pronounced theological orientation. Furthermore, the pragmatic stance of the original core of this passage is in line with the bulk of the communal rules in the Laws of the Damascus Document since the great majority of the communal rules focus on

---

[33] See chapter four above.
[34] On this reading see the textual notes *ad* CD 13,8 above.

the practical organization of everyday life in the community.

The present passage, by contrast, assigns a task to the overseer that is much more akin to the role assigned to the wise leader (משכיל) in 1QS 9,12-26a on the one hand, and to the overall preoccupation with God's dealings throughout the ages that characterizes the Admonition. As far as the affinities of this passage with the Admonition are concerned it will suffice to point out a few terminological links that serve to support the general case for an affinity in outlook between CD 13,7c-8 and the Admonition. The expression מעשי אל occurs in the present passage and in the Admonition in CD 1,1-2 [par. 4QD^c 1,9] and 2,14-15.[35] The expression נהיות עולם may be compared to CD 2,9-10.[36] These links between the present passage and the Admonition both in terms of general theological orientation as well as in terms of terminology are striking. Yet, a detailed discussion of their significance for the relationship of the Admonition to the Laws would lie beyond the scope of this study.

As far as affinities between the passage under consideration and the description of the duties of the wise leader (משכיל) in 1QS 9,12-26a are concerned it is instructive to compare the following two passages:

CD 13,7c-8a

ישכיל את הרבים במעשי אל ויבינם בנבורות פלאו

He shall instruct the many in the works of God and he shall make them understand his wonderful mighty deeds.

1QS 9,18

וכן להשכילם ברזי פלא ואמת

And thus to instruct them in wonderful and true mysteries.

At first sight the affinities of the present passage with 1QS 9,18 may seem obvious, yet not very far reaching or important. However, in conjunction with the vexed problem of the announcement of a list of duties for the משכיל in CD 12,20b-21a the presence of such affinities can gain much in importance. In view of the close correspondence between some of the duties of the wise leader in 1QS 9,18 and CD 13,7c-8 it seems probable to me that some of the traditions associated with the wise leader have become merged with the rules on the overseer over the camp. Instead of following the announcement of

---

[35] CD 1,1-2 reads, ועתה שמעו כל יודעי צדק ובינו במעשי אל and CD 2,14-15 reads, ועתה בנים שמעו לי ואגלה עיניכם לראות ולהבין במעשי אל.

[36] CD 2,9-10 is slightly corrupt and for improved readings cf. Qimron, 'Text of CDC', p. 13 nn. 6 and 7. The relevant words read, הוי עולמים ונהיית.

statutes for the wise leader in CD 12,20b-21a some of the duties of the wise leader follow the heading announcing the rule for the overseer over the camp in the Laws of the Damascus Document in their present form. It is conceivable that at some point before these traditions became merged the compiler of the Laws had a list of duties for the wise leader available to him that were not dissimilar to what we have in 1QS 9,12-26a.

My hypothesis on the merging of traditions on the duties of the wise leader with rules on the overseer over the camp receives further support from the presence of an otherwise awkwardly placed concluding statement on the duties of the wise leader in the fragmentary text of CD 13,22 in the midst of the סרך on the overseer over the camp. Not much is preserved of CD 13,22 but enough can be made out to see that it contained a concluding statement dealing with the wise leader: ו[אלה המש]פט[י]ם למשכיל. It would be possible to take CD 13,22 as another heading rather than a concluding statement but that seems less likely to me. Rather, I would suggest that CD 12,20b-21a; 13,7c-8.14-15a[37] and 13,22 constitute remnants of a block of material dealing with the wise leader—along lines similar to 1QS 9,12-26a—that have become merged with the rules on the overseer over the camp in the Laws in their final form.

One of the MSS of the Community Rule from Cave 4, 4QS^e, provides additional evidence indicating that the long section on the duties of the wise leader might have originated independently. As S. Metso has noted[38] the text of 4QS^e 1 iii 6 moves directly from the equivalent of 1QS 8,15 to the equivalent of 1QS 9,12 leaving out the famous reference to 'the coming of the prophet and the Messiahs of Aaron and Israel' in 1QS 9,11. What is of interest for our present purposes is the fact that 4QS^e's text picks up with the heading announcing the duties of the wise leader in 1QS 9,12 which suggests that the latter material circulated as an independent unit before being incorporated into the S tradition. I am arguing that traces of the same independent tradition have also been preserved in D where this block of material has become merged with and overshadowed by material dealing with the overseer.

A recently published text[39] contains further material associated

---

[37] On CD 13,14-15a see pp. 123-25 below.
[38] 'The Primary Results of the Reconstruction of 4QS^e', *JJS* 44 (1993) 303-308; see also the edition of 4QS^e by Qimron and Charlesworth in Charlesworth ed., *The Dead Sea Scrolls*, I, pp. 84-89, esp. pp. 88-89.
[39] Cf. S. Pfann, '4Q298: The Maskîl's Address to All Sons of Dawn', *JQR* 85 (1994) 203-35; see also M. Kister, 'Commentary to 4Q298', *JQR* 85 (1994) 237-249.

with the figure of the משכיל indicating the prominence of such traditions in the Qumran library.[40] The small, portable scroll 4Q298[41] contains a document in cryptic script recording an address by the משכיל to the 'sons of dawn'. Both Pfann[42] and Kister[43] suggest that this text addresses new members in the process of joining the community ('sons of dawn') and becoming full members ('sons of light'). Recently Harrington expressed agreement with this line of argument.[44] Although this interpretation is possible it seems somewhat speculative to build such a strong case on the occurrence of the expression 'sons of dawn'. It is equally possible that 'sons of dawn' was simply another self-designation used in the scrolls. It is noteworthy, moreover, that none of the texts at our disposal that legislate on the admission process in some detail (e.g. CD 15,5b-16,6a and 1QS 6,13b-23) contain any reference to the idea of a progression from dawn to light nor, indeed, any use of light and darkness imagery.

In his commentary on the reference to the משכיל in 4Q298 1-2 i 1 Kister quotes CD 13,7-8 and notes the relationship of that passage to this new text.[45] Kister rightly draws attention to the close relationship between 4Q298 and CD 13,7-8. However, he does not comment on the curious fact that in CD 13,7-8 the verbs elsewhere associated with the figure of the משכיל follow a heading announcing the rule for the overseer over the camp. This heading is cited by Kister but never commented on. In fact, the way in which Kister presents the evidence of CD 13,7-8 as part of his discussion of the משכיל plays down this difficulty. As I hope to have shown in the analysis put forward above this complex picture is best accounted for by a secondary combination of traditions associated with the משכיל with rules for the overseer.

---

[40] The figure of the משכיל further occurs in a number of liturgical texts from Qumran such as 4QShirShabb (see C. Newsom, *Songs of the Sabbath Sacrifice: A Critical Edition*, Atlanta: Scholars Press, 1985),1QSb (see D. Barthélemy and J.T. Milik, *Qumran Cave I* (DJD I), Oxford: Clarendon Press, 1955, pp. 432-433), and 4Q510-511 Songs of the Maskil (see M. Baillet, *Qumran Grotte 4. III*, pp. 215-262 + Plates LV-LXII). See also E. Glickler-Chazon's preliminary report on 4Q444 in 'New Liturgical Manuscripts from Qumran', in *Proceedings of the Eleventh World Congress of Jewish Studies. Division A: The Bible and Its World* ed. David Assaf, Jerusalem: World Union of Jewish Studies, 1994, pp. 207-14. According to Chazon this text contains "a magic rite for driving away evil spirits" (p. 207) and displays resemblance to 4Q510-511.
[41] Cf. Pfann, 'Maskil's Address', p. 213 and n. 14.
[42] 'Maskil's Address', p. 225.
[43] 'Commentary', p. 238.
[44] *Wisdom Texts from Qumran*, p. 65.
[45] 'Commentary', p. 237.

ii. CD 13,9-10

וירחם עליהם כאב לבניו וישקוד לכל מדהובם כרועה עדרו
יתר כל הרצובות קשריהם לבלתי היות עשוק ורצוץ בעדתו

> And he shall be as kind to them as a father to his children and guard all those who have gone astray like a shepherd his flock. And he shall undo all the fetters that tie them so that there shall not be anyone oppressed and broken in his congregation.

These lines attribute a pastoral function to the overseer. The passage is admonitory and as such unusual in the Laws. This was noted already by Rabin who comments on CD 13,9-10 as follows,

> The following passage [...] has the metrical structure and biblical diction of parts of the Admonition, of D [i.e. 1QS] x-xi , &c.[46]

This brief exhortatory passage consists of a pastiche of biblical material drawing on Ps. 103,13; Ez. 34,12; Isa. 58,6; and Hos. 5,11.[47]

Apart from stressing the biblical orientation and admonitory tone of this passage, and its close resemblance with the Admonition in these respects, it is not possible to be any more precise as to its provenance.

iii. CD 13,11-12a

וכל הנוסף לעדתו יפקדהו למעשיו ושוכלו וכוחו ונבורתו והונו
וכתבוהו במקומו כפי נחלתו בנורל האור

> And he shall examine everyone who joins his congregation as to their deeds, their insight, their strength, their might, and their property. And they shall write them down according to their inheritance in the lot of light.

This short sentence takes up—or rather preempts—the subject of the admission of new members dealt with in the original core of the rule for the overseer over the camp in CD 13,12b-13. In the discussion of the latter passage above I mentioned the regulations on the admission into the covenant community in CD 15,5b-16,6a. When comparing this rule with CD 15,5b-16,6a it becomes apparent that the present passage envisages a much more detailed examination than CD 15-16. Furthermore, the kind of detailed examination prescribed here has much in common with the process of examination and admission found in 1QS 6,13b-23. A written record of members, for example, is mentioned here and seven

---

[46] *Zadokite Documents*, p. 65.
[47] Cf. Rabin, *Zadokite Documents*, pp. 65-66.

times in 1QS, cf. 1QS 5,23; 6,10.22.26; 7,21; 8,19; and 9,2. To be sure, CD 14,4 constitutes a second reference to a written registration of the members of the camp in the Laws of the Damascus Document. However, in CD 14,4 it is a case of the organization of the members of the camp into priests, levites, Israelites, and proselytes. In 1QS and the present passage, on the other hand, each individual member is carefully examined as to merit, property, etc. Compare, for instance, 1QS 5,23a which is strikingly close to the present rule,

וכתבם בסרך איש לפני רעהו לפי שכלו ומעשיו

> And they shall write them down in the order, each one before another according to one's insight and one's deeds.

It seems very likely to me that what we have in CD 13,11-12a should be assigned to the Serekh redaction of the Laws. Possibly the redactional statement was triggered off in this particular instance by a reference to the admission into the congregation in the immediately following line which forms part of the original core of the rule on the overseer over the camp. This might explain the use of the term 'congregation' (עדה) in CD 13,11-12a. This term occurs frequently in the communal rules of the Damascus Document, whereas the typical self-designations for the community in 1QS are 'the many' (הרבים) and 'the community' (היחד). Apart from this exception the terminology of CD 13,11-12a is, as we saw, close to the terminology of 1QS. CD 13,11-12a appears to have been linked to the preceding statement in CD 13,9-10 by the catchword principle with the term **עדתו** providing the link. I have put the crucial words in bold script in the Hebrew text and translation above.

In sum, I suggest that the rule on the admission of new members in CD 13,11-12a is an interpolation that elaborates on the subject of admission already dealt with in the original core of rules on the overseer over the camp and forms part of the work of the Serekh redactor.

iv. CD 13,14-15a

ואיש מכל באי ברית אל אל ישא ואל יתן לבני השחר כי אם כף לכף

> And no member of the covenant of God shall buy or sell anything to the sons of dawn except from hand to hand.

The reading of this passage given here and the translation adopted above follow the suggestions of J.M. Baumgarten which radically transformed the understanding of this prohibition.⁴⁸ Although Schechter had read בני הׁשחר in the original edition of the Damascus Document,⁴⁹ the reading that was most widely followed subsequently was Rabin's reading בני הׁשחת 'the sons of the pit'.⁵⁰ Baumgarten argues that a careful examination of the photograph of the original MS clearly favours the reading הׁשחר. He, further, draws attention to the opening words of 4Q298 (The Maskîl's Address to All Sons of Dawn) discussed above⁵¹ which read,

[דברי?] מׂשכיל אׁשר דבר לכול בני ׁשחר האזינו

[Words?] of the wise leader which he spoke to all the sons of dawn, "Hear ..."⁵²

Rabin's reading בני הׁשחת resulted in taking the rule as a prohibition of certain kinds of trade with non-members of the movement. In particular trade with the sons of the pit was thought to be limited to cash deals, taking the expression כף לכף as synonymous with mishnaic מיד ליד meaning 'cash'.⁵³ Baumgarten's reading, on the other hand, leaves us with a radically different meaning. According to Baumgarten it emerges from the opening statement in 4Q298 that sons of dawn is a title for the members of the movement who are instructed in the present passage freely to exchange goods with one another rather than engage in trade. As Baumgarten himself puts it,

> This rule, it develops, concerns not avoidance of contacts with outsiders, but the internal economic relations among members of the community. These relations are to be predicated not on the commercial basis of buying and selling (יׂשא...יתן), but the fraternal concept of mutual help and exchange of services (כף לכף).⁵⁴

Baumgarten derives further support for his suggestions from a morning hymn found at Qumran praising God for the establishment of dawn (11QPsᵃ 26,1-5) as well as from two statements in Philo and Josephus confirming the Essene practice of free exchange of services with one another.⁵⁵ Baumgarten's case seems, on the whole, convincing.

---

⁴⁸ 'The "Sons of Dawn" in *CDC* 13: 14-15 and the Ban on Commerce among the Essenes', *IEJ* 33 (1983) 81-85.
⁴⁹ Fragments of a Zadokite Work, p. 13.
⁵⁰ *Zadokite Documents*, p. 67.
⁵¹ See pp. 120-21 above.
⁵² Cf. 'Sons of Dawn', p. 83; and J.T. Milik, 'Le travail d'édition des fragments manuscrits de Qûmran', *RB* 63 (1956) 49-67, esp. p. 61; and more recently Pfann, 'Maskîl's Address'.
⁵³ So Rabin, *Zadokite Documents*, p. 67.
⁵⁴ 'Sons of Dawn', p. 83.
⁵⁵ Philo, *Quod omnis probus liber sit*, 78; Josephus, *War*, II, 127.

What, in the light of these observations, can be said about the place of CD 13,14-15a in the context of CD 13,7b-14,2?

First of all, this prescription has a distinct terminology. It refers to the members of the community as 'all members of the covenant of God' (כל באי ברית אל) and uses the verbs נתן and נשא to refer to the exchange of goods. The original core of rules for the overseer over the camp contains a prohibition dealing with the subject of trade in the camp which follows immediately after the present passage in CD 13,15b-16a. In the latter prohibition we return to the camp terminology. Furthermore, the verbs used to refer to buying and selling in CD 13,15b-16a are מכר and לקח. These differences in terminology in two immediately adjoining rules which, moreover, cover the same subject indicate that the passage has undergone literary development. It seems likely that a similar process of elaboration took place in CD 13,14-16a as I suggested concerning CD 13,11-13. That is to say, a regulation belonging to the original core of rules for the overseer over the camp was elaborated upon by the addition of a prescription that deals with the same subject matter—admission of members in the case of CD 13,11-12a and trade in CD 13,14-15a. Neither addition mentions the overseer or the camp.

As far as the provenance of CD 13,14-15a is concerned it may be best to remain agnostic in as much as the prescription provides us with no clues on the matter. Yet, I would like to make a tentative suggestion which draws upon the connection of the title משכיל with the expression בני השחר in the opening words of 4Q298 quoted above. I argued earlier that one strand of material that has become merged with the original core of rules on the overseer over the camp is made up of traditions on the משכיל. It seems conceivable that the present passage belongs to that same strand of material since it employs the expression 'the sons of dawn' which occurs in conjunction with the משכיל in 4Q298. Before concluding this discussion I would like to spell out one further possible corollary from this. If the expression 'the sons of dawn' were part of the tradition complex associated with the משכיל, this would add a further nuance to the expression 'the men of the pit' which occurs twice in the section dealing with the משכיל in the Community Rule (1QS 9,16.22). It may be that in some of the material associated with the משכיל the members of the community are referred to as בני השחר ('the sons of dawn') and outsiders as אנשי השחת ('the men of the pit'). Thus, the distinction between insiders and outsiders would have been expressed by changing one crucial letter.

v. CD 13,16b-22

The material in this section is very fragmentary and has been bracketed together purely for that reason. It is included and translated above for the sake of completeness. Apart from a few observations it is not possible to examine these lines in detail because of their fragmentary state.

CD 13,16b-18a seems to envisage a role for the overseer in matters of marriage, divorce, and the disciplining of the children of community members. This may be compared to 4QD^d 9 par. where it falls to the overseer over the camp to select experienced women to examine prospective brides.[56]

I have already discussed CD 13,22 in connection with CD 13,7c-8 above. The only other part of this fragmentary section that I would like to comment on is CD 13,20. Although only fragmentarily preserved, it can easily be made out that we are dealing with a heading or concluding statement which reads,

[וזה מושב המחנות לכל ז]רע

And this is the meeting of the
camps for all the s[eed of

It seems likely to me that this line constitutes the concluding statement at the end of a long section dealing with the מושב המחנות. As I will argue below the remaining lines of the current section, i.e. CD 13,23-14,2, belong to the Damascus redaction of the Laws. Furthermore, the following long section (CD 14,3-18a) deals no longer with the running of individual camps but with *all the camps*, cf. the heading in CD 14,3a: וסרך מושב כל המחנות. Since the long section on the meeting of the camps was introduced in CD 12,22b-23a with the words וזה סרך מושב המח[נו]ת, the fragmentary remains of CD 13,20 would form a well placed and consistently phrased conclusion to this section. Finally, the heading in CD 13,7b (וזה סרך המבקר למחנה) may then be explained as introducing a sub-section within the long rule on the meeting of the camps.

vi. CD 13,23-14,2

[כאשר אמר יבוא עליך ועל עמך ימים]
אשר לא באו מיום סור אפרים מעל יהודה וכל המתהלכים באלה
ברית אל נאמנות להם להנצילם מכל מוקשי שחת כי פתאום $_{עברו]ן}$ ונענשו

---

[56] See p. 69 above.

[as he said, 'There will come upon you, and upon your people days] such as have not come since the day that Ephraim departed from Judah'. But for all those who walk in these the covenant of God shall be a permanent assurance for them to save them from all the snares of the pit whereas the weak-minded ₍transgress[ed]₎ and they shall be punished.

In CD 13,23-14,2 we are on firmer ground again at least as far as the text of the MS is concerned. Page 14 begins with the continuation of a citation from Isa. 7,17, and it is almost certain that this citation began at the end of page 13.

This passage forms a redactional conclusion to the long section on the meetings of the camps that began in CD 12,22b. It belongs to the material that I assign to the Damascus redactor. We have come across other manifestations of this redaction at major junctures in the Laws. It has the purpose of linking diverse components of the Laws together, and further of providing connections between the Laws and the Admonition of the Damascus Document. Rather than concluding the preceding long section on the meeting of the camps by referring back to points or terms that are characteristic of this section, this passage takes up the citation of Isa. 7,17 found in the Admonition in CD 7,10-12a as well as sharing much of the terminology and content of CD 7,4b-6a (19,1). The citation of Isa. 7,17 occurs in CD 7,10-12a and forms part of a warning to all those who fail to heed the instructions contained in the small halakhic section in CD 6,11b-7,4a. This list of rules is preserved in MS A. It is followed by a promise to all those who heed these rules which is preserved in MSS A and B, although the promise is substantiated only in MS B by a citation of Dt. 7,9. The warning that counterbalances the promise, on the other hand, is preserved in different forms in MSS A and B, and the quotation from Isa. 7,17 occurs in the text of MS A.

CD 7,9b-12a reads,

וכל המואסים בפקד אל את הארץ להשיב נמול רשעים עליהם בבוא
הדבר אשר כתוב בדברי ישעיה בן אמוץ הנביא אשר אמר יבוא עליך
ועל עמך ועל בית אביך ימים אשר באו[57] מיום סור אפרים מעל
יהודה

But all who reject (these) will receive the reward of the wicked when God visits the earth when the word comes into effect which is written in the words of Isaiah son of Amoz, the prophet, who said 'There will

---

[57] Read לא בא, cf. Qimron, 'Text of CDC', p. 23 n. 7.

come upon you and upon your people and upon your father's house days such as have (not) come since the day Ephraim departed from Judah'.

This warning counterbalances the promise in CD 7,4b-6a the language of which is also reflected in our redactional passage in CD 13,23-14,2. CD 7,4b-6a reads,

כל המתהלכים באלה בתמים קדש על פי כל יסורו[58] ברית אל נאמנות
להם לחיותם אלף דור

> All those who walk in these in perfect holiness according to all the instructions of the covenant, the covenant of God shall be a permanent assurance for them so that they may live for a thousand generations.

Both the promise and the warning in CD 7 are in line with the general eschatological standpoint of the Admonition. I have argued above in connection with the references to the Messiah(s) in the Laws, that the expected divine visitation is a key concern in the Admonition. In CD 7 both promise and warning are closely linked to the expectation of the divine visitation. In the Laws, on the other hand, such an eschatological orientation is generally absent with the exception of passages belonging to the Damascus redaction.

It is difficult to be sure whether or not the citation of Isa. 7,17 in CD 13,23-14,2 forms part of a warning because the introduction to and the beginning of the citation are lost. It seems clear, however, that CD 14,1b-2a constitutes a promise drawing on the language of CD 7,4b-6a.

Thus, there is little in this redactional conclusion that would allow one to associate it with the preceding material. If this concluding statement where not placed at the end of this section but had got detached from its context, I doubt very much that anyone would associate it, on the basis of its content, with the material it now serves to conclude .

What is more, this rather general conclusion is preceded by two more specific concluding statements in CD 13, 20 (וזה מושב המחנות) and CD 13,22 (ו[א]לה המש[פט]ים למשכיל) (לכל ז[ר]ע). Both of these concluding statements are discussed above. Suffice it to say at this point that CD 13,20 is a concluding statement that is much more appropriate to round off the section on the meetings of the camps.

---

[58] The text is slightly corrupt here. In my translation I follow Rabin, *Zadokite Documents*, p. 26 and Knibb, *Qumran Community*, p. 51 and read יסורי ברית ברית אל. The present text may thus be explained as having emerged from a haplography of ברית and a confusion of *yod* and *waw*.

The redactional conclusion in CD 13,23-14,2 is, therefore, not only characterized by a rather feeble connection to the material it serves to conclude but is also repetitive formally since CD 13,20 forms a much more appropriate conclusion to the section on the meetings of the camps. These considerations in conjunction with the strong links of CD 13,23-14,2 with the Admonition form the basis for assigning this material to the work of the Damascus redactor.

With CD 14,2b we leave that part of this passage behind that bears close terminological resemblance to the Admonition. The redactional passage concludes with the words,

להצילם מכל מוקשי שחת כי פתאום ונענשו
to save them from all the snares of the pit whereas the weak-minded transgress[ed] and they shall be punished.

The words להצילם מכל מוקשי שחת follow on naturally and continue the promise that began in CD 14,1b. Even though the terminology is no longer drawn from CD 7,4b-6a the polemical stance of these words is close to the Admonition. As is the case throughout the Admonition, the contemporary Jewish world is here perceived and portrayed as divided between those who belong to the movement and those who do not. Those who belong to the community behind the Admonition may look forward to salvation whereas the rest is ensnared, misled, and may expect to suffer the fate of the wicked. Compare, for example, the famous passage on the three nets of Belial that are ensnaring Israel according to CD 4,12b-5,15a. The actual words used in CD 4 are different. However, the same expression as occurs in the present passage (מוקשי שחת) is used in 1QH 2,20-22a where it is used in connection with the phrase 'the congregation of Belial'. Thus, 1QH 2 would seem to indicate that the expressions 'the snares of the pit' and the 'nets of Belial' may be part of the same complex of traditions. In the Laws, by contrast, such a polemical stance is largely absent. The preceding communal rules on the meetings of the camps may serve as an appropriate example since the present passage serves as a conclusion to these rules. With the exception of CD 12,23b-13,1a which was identified as also going back to the Damascus redactor, the section lacks all polemic against non-members. Of course, one is aware that boundaries do exist between community members and non-members, cf. for example the material on the admission of members in CD 13,12b-13, but these boundaries are dealt with in purely pragmatic terms. One does not gain the impression—so characteristic of the Admonition—that self-definition by polemicizing against outsiders and opponents is a driving force in the community behind the Laws.

What one makes of the final words of CD 14,2 (ונענשו פתאום עברה[ו] כי) is less straightforward. In the text as we now have it these words can be taken as a warning counterbalancing the promise of CD 14,1b-2a. Two considerations would indicate, however, that these last words go back to a different source. Firstly, whereas the points at issue in the preceding promise are of an existential nature, i.e. escape from the snares of the pit and the assurance of the covenant of God, these final words seem surprisingly pragmatic and constitute something of an anticlimax. The verb ענש is familiar to us from the penal code, versions of which are preserved in D,S, and 4Q265, where it refers to the infliction of punishments within the community the exact nature of which is not spelled out.

Secondly, I have stated already that it is difficult to know whether the citation of Isa. 7,17 formed part of a warning in CD 13,23. It certainly seems conceivable that it did. The same citation forms part of a warning in CD 7, a passage upon which the present material is heavily dependent as we saw. If this were the case—and my translation of וכל in CD 14,1 with '*but* for all those' reflects such an understanding—then the statement כי פתאום עברה[ו] ונענשו would also be formally incongruous. It reads like an afterthought. Thus, it seems likely in view of the awkward position of CD 14,2c in its present context, that these words originated separately from the remainder of CD 13,23-14,2b. However, on the basis of three words only it is impossible to comment on the provenance of CD 14,2c.

In conclusion, it emerges from this discussion that CD 13,7b-14,2 is a heavily reworked passage. It was argued that the heading in CD 13,7b and CD 13,12b-13.15b-16a. constitute the original nucleus of the rules on the overseer over the camp. A number of suggestions have been made concerning the material that has been added to this section. It was further proposed that CD 13,7c-8.14-15a.22 preserve remnants of traditions associated with the משכיל that have become merged with the rules on the overseer in the Laws of D. Moreover, CD 13,11-12a was assigned to the Serekh redaction. CD 13,20 contains the conclusion to the long section on the organization of individual camps that began in CD 12,22. It was suggested, also, that CD 13,23-14,2a form part of the Damascus redaction. It was, however, not always possible to arrive at certain conclusions on the delineation and provenance of some of the additional material.

6.4 The Meeting of All the Camps

CD 14,3-18a provides the legislation for all the camps.

A. *Text*
(CD 14,3-18a; 4QD^a 10 i; 4QD^b 9 v; 4QD^c 2)

14:3	וסרך מושב כל המחנות יפקדו כלם בשמותיהם הכהנים לראשונה
14:4	והלויים שנים ובני ישראל שלשתם והגר רביע ויכתבו בשמותיהם
14:5	איש אחר אחיהו הכהנים לראשונה והלויים שנים ובני ישראל
14:6	שלושתם והגר רביע וכן ישבו וכן ישאלו לכל והכהן אשר יפקד
14:7	ב[ר]אש הרבים מבן שלושים שנה ועד בן ששים מבונן בספר
14:8	ההגי ובכל משפטי התורה לדברם כמשפטם *vacat* והמבקר אשר
14:9	לכל המחנות מבן שלשים שנה [ו]עד בן חמשים שנה בעול בכל
14:10	סוד אנשים ולכל לשון רמ[ש]פחותם על פיהו יבאו באי העדה
14:11	איש בתרו ולכל דבר אשר יהיה לכל האדם לדבר למבקר ידבר
14:12	לכל ריב ומשפט *vacat* וזה סרך הרבים להכין כל חפציהם שכר
14:13	שני ימים לכל חדש למעיט ונתנו על יד המבקר והשופטים
14:14	ממנו יתנו בעד [פ]צעם וממנו יחזיקו ביד עני ואביון ולזקן אשר
14:15	יכר[ע ולאיש אשר ינו]ע ולאשר ישבה לנוי נכר ולבתולה אשר
14:16	[אי]ן לה ג[ואל] [ו]לנ[ע]ר אש[ר] אין לו דורש כל עבודת החבר ולא
14:17	[יכרת בית החבר מיד]ם *vacat* וזה פרוש מושב המ[חנות ואלה יסודות]
14:18a	[ ] אנשי הק[הל

B. *Translation*

14,3 And the rule for the meeting of all the camps: they shall muster all of them by their names, the priests first,

4 the levites second, the Israelites third, and the proselytes fourth. And they shall be registered by their names

5 each one after his brother: the priests first, the levites second, the Israelites

6 third, and the proselytes fourth. And thus they shall sit and be consulted about everything. And the priest who musters

7 _{at the he}ad of the many shall be aged between thirty [a]nd sixty years, learned in the Book of

8 Hagi and in all the ordinances of the law to pronounce them according to their rule. *Vacat.* And the overseer over

9 all the camps shall be aged between thirty and fifty years, master of all

10 the secrets of humanity and all the tongues according to their fam[i]lies. At his word the members of the congregation shall enter

11 everyone in their place. And everyone who has anything to say to the overseer shall speak (to him) about

12 any dispute or judgment. *Vacat.* And this is the rule for the many to cater for all their needs: the wages of

13 at least two days each month they shall give to the overseer and the judges.⁵⁹

14 From it they shall give to their [in]jured and with it they shall support the poor, the needy, those who [stoo]p

15 with old age, the one who is str[u]ck (with disease), the one who has been taken captive by a foreign people, the virgin who

16 [has] no re[la]tives, and the [boy w]ho has no one to take care of him. All the work of the association and no

17 [house of the association shall be cut off from] their [hand]. *Vacat.* And this is the exact statement on the meeting of the ca[mps and these are the foundations]

18a [the men of the ass]embly.

C. *Textual Notes*

14,4 4QDᵇ 9 v 7-8 reads שנים and שלשים where CD has שנים and שלשתם. 4QDᵇ 9 v 8 lacks the first reference to the proselytes.⁶⁰ However, the second reference to the proselytes in fourth place found in CD 14,6 is clearly paralleled in 4QDᵇ 9 v 10.

14,6 For לכל 4QDᶜ 2,2 reads על [כול]. More significantly, perhaps, 4QDᵇ 9 v 10 has a *vacat* following לכל.⁶¹

14,7 The first three letters in subscript are taken from 4QDᵇ 9 v 11 which reads ברואש. 4QDᵇ's reading confirms the reading proposed by Rabin with reference to CD alone.⁶²

14,8 4QDᵇ 9 v 12 reads לדברום with a *waw* apparently added later in the space above *resh* and *mem* where CD 14,8 has לדברם. Both forms of the third person plural pronominal suffix are attested in the DSS.⁶³ For CD's אשר (לכל) 4QDᵃ 10 i 1 reads ש(לכל).

14,9 4QDᵇ 9 v 13 lacks the article of המחנות.

14,10 A number of readings and reconstructions have been proposed for רמ[ש]פחותם. 4QDᵇ 9 v which provided parallel text earlier in this section unfortunately breaks off just before this word, and 4QDᵃ 10 i 3 which also covers this text has a lacuna at the crucial place. I have adopted the reading suggested recently by Baumgarten⁶⁴ and taken it to be a corruption of למשפחותם. Qimron reads רמ]פריה and asks whether this is a corrupt version of למשפחותם.⁶⁵ Recently G.W. Nebe suggested a new reading and transla-

---

⁵⁹ The translation "...a wage of two days every month at least shall be given to the Overseer. Then the judges will give some of it..." recently suggested by Cook assumes an unusual word order (Wise, Abegg, and Cook, *A New Translation*, p. 72).

⁶⁰ Cf. Baumgarten, *Qumran Cave 4. XIII*, p. 109 in contrast to Qimron, 'Text of CDC', p. 37 n. 7.

⁶¹ This vacat is not noted by Baumgarten, *Qumran Cave 4. XIII*, pp. 109-10 but is clearly visible on Plate XX of his edition.

⁶² See *Zadokite Documents*, p. 69.

⁶³ Cf. Qimron, *Hebrew of the Dead Sea Scrolls*, p. 39.

⁶⁴ Baumgarten in Charlesworth ed., *Dead Sea Scrolls*, II, p. 56.

⁶⁵ 'Text of CDC', p. 37 n. 13-13.

tion of this difficult passage based on the photograph of the MS reproduced in Qimron's edition.[66] Nebe reads ולכל לשון רמ[ה ו]פרוזון and translates this passage, 'und betreffs jeder hohen (רמה Ptz.f.) Sprache und der der Bauern'.
14,11 4QD[a] 10 i 4 reads [וכול הח]בר where CD reads ולכל דבר. 4QD[a] 10 i 4 further has לדבר לעדה for CD's לדבר למבקר. Although a genuine variant cannot be excluded here, scribal error seems equally likely. If the text of 4QD[a] preserves a genuine variant one might want to speak of an initially more democratic procedure (4QD[a]) having been superseded by a more authoritarian practice (CD) or *vice versa*. The following observations, however, would support the view that the reading of 4QD[a] is due to a scribal error. The overseer and the congregation are frequently mentioned together in the Laws. Thus, for example, in the immediately preceding material we read, 'At his [the overseer's] word the members of the congregation shall enter' (על פיהו יבאו באי העדה). It, therefore, seems probable that issues of dispute raised in the meeting of all the camps would be heard by and addressed to the congregation *and* the overseer. Thus, in practice, it would make little difference whether the text reads 'overseer' or 'congregation' at this point. Furthermore, in 4QD[a] 10 i the reading of לדבר לעדה occurs at the end of line 4, and the last word of the preceding line is also הע[ד]ה which forms part of the expression 'all the members of the congregation'. That is to say, the reading of 'congregation' instead of 'overseer' in 4QD[a] 10 i 4 may be explained as having arisen from a dittographical error which caused the scribe to copy the last word of line 3 at the end of line 4 also.
14,13 There is not sufficient space for the words לכל חדש in 4QD[a] 10 i 6. 4QD[a] 10 i 6 further reads וינתן where CD has ונתנו.
14,14 פ[צעם] has been reconstructed with the help of 4QD[a] 10 i 7. 4QD[a] 10 i 7 further reads והאביון with the article.
14,15 Both reconstructions in this line are taken from Qimron and are based on 4QD[a] 10 i 8.
14,16 The reconstruction [ו]לנער is based on the reading in 4QD[a] 10 i 9 (ולנער). Rabin reads ולע[למה א]שר אין לה דורש and translates 'and for the virgin who has no one to seek her *in marriage*'.[67] However, the photograph reproduced in Qimron's edition clearly supports the reading לו rather than לה. The reading ולנער in 4QD[a] 10 i 9 in conjunction with the masculine suffix make a good case for reconstructing ולנער in CD as well. 4QD[a] 10 i 9 further reads ולכול where CD has כל.
14,17 4QD[a] 10 i 10 reads זה where CD has חה. The reconstructions in CD 14,17-18 are taken from Qimron and are based on 4QD[a] 10 i 10-11. Note, however, that the partially restored reference to the camps מושב המ[חנות is not preserved in 4QD[a]. I differ from Qimron by restoring המ[חנות in the plural. García Martínez misses out line 11 in his translation of 4QD[a] 10 i (in his translation designated 4QD[b] 18 iii) and reconstructs 'the session of the Many' in the parallel fragment 4QD[d] 11 i (in his translation designated 4QD[f] 13).[68]

---

[66] 'Sprachvermögen', p. 290.
[67] *Zadokite Documents*, pp. 70-71.
[68] *Dead Sea Scrolls Translated*, pp. 56 and 69.

D. *Commentary*

This new section of communal rules deals with the meetings of all the camps in contrast to the preceding section (CD 12,22b-14,2) which had the meetings of individual camps as its subject.

The heading in CD 14,3a is again of the סרך-type, and its form corresponds exactly to the heading in CD 12,22b-23a. Furthermore, CD 14,3a is an appropriate rubric that aptly introduces the material that follows. It goes back either to the same author responsible for the following section or to an editor who skilfully superscribed this section. The discussion of the communal legislation in CD 14,3b-18a may suitably be divided into three parts.

a. CD 14,3b-6b Mustering of the members of all the camps

The section on the meeting of all the camps begins by ruling that the members of the camps are to be mustered by their names. This process of mustering is to proceed in the following order: priests, levites, Israelites, and proselytes. The passage further prescribes that the members of the camps shall sit and be consulted in this same order at the meetings of all the camps.[69] When one compares the make-up of the meetings of all the camps described here to the make-up of the meetings of individual camps described in CD 13,1b-7a, a difference in scale can be noted. Whereas CD 13,1b-3a mentions a minimum of ten members and a priest among them, the present passage clearly envisages a considerable number of priests, levites, Israelites, and proselytes to be present at the meetings of all the camps.

It was noted above that 4QD^b 9 v 8 lacks the first reference to the proselytes (CD 14,4) but clearly preserves the second reference (CD 14,6) in 4QD^b 9 v 10. Three possible explanations could account for the ambiguous evidence:

i. The first reference might have been lost accidentally.

ii It may indicate that at some point the meetings of all the camps lacked proselytes and 4QD^b preserves evidence of the older as well as the more recent state of affairs.

iii. A scribe/redactor was uncomfortable with the presence of proselytes in the text and/or movement and deleted the first reference.

Of these possible explanations the third seems least likely since we would have expected a removal of the second reference to proselytes

---

[69] It has been pointed out by a number of scholars that this material ought to be compared to 1QS 6,8b-10a, cf. Rabin, *Zadokite Documents*, p. 68; Dupont-Sommer, *Essene Writings*, p. 159 n. 1; and Cothenet, 'Document de Damas', p. 203 n. 5. I will discuss both texts in my forthcoming paper 'Community Structures in the Dead Sea Scrolls'.

as well. It seems clear in any event that 4QD^b in its final form did include proselytes in its account.

Philip Davies has argued that the term 'proselyte' (גר) here refers to someone who is not yet a full community member but who has begun the relatively long-winded process of initiation.[70] The admission process as described at some length in CD 15,5b-16,6a does not, however, mention a complex procedure of admission involving various stages. Such a procedure in known solely from 1QS 6,13b-23 and Josephus' description of the Essenes. Davies is aware of this but nevertheless decides "to infer such a process" for the community described in the present passage.[71] I can see no justification for such an inference which plays down some very illuminating differences in the communal legislation between D and S. Instead, it seems preferable to me to take this reference to proselytes quite literally here as indicating the presence of converts to the Jewish religion in the movement described in the Laws of D, cf. also CD 12,10-11.

We are not told in which order the individual members of each of the four groups were mustered and sat. One may assume, however, that the hierarchical structure of each group was clear to the contemporary audience addressed here. Possibly, the Israelites were divided into groups of thousands, hundreds, fifties, and tens as was the case at meetings of individual camps in CD 13,1-2. Whether these numbers reflect an idealised concept of the movement mirroring itself on the Israelite camp in the wilderness or whether they resemble reality is a moot point.

Nothing is said in the present passage about the frequency and date of the meetings of all the camps. However, two MSS of the Damascus Document from Cave 4 preserve the end of the document[72] and both contain a reference to a meeting of the members of the camps 'in the third month' cf. 4QD^a 11,17 par. 4QD^e 7 ii 11. We may assume, therefore, that the meeting of all the camps took place in the third month.

b. CD 14,6c-12a Leadership at meetings of all the camps

This passage deals with the question of authority at the meetings of all the camps. A new beginning is indicated in 4QD^b 9 v 10 by a

---

[70] P.R. Davies, 'The "Damascus" Sect and Judaism', in *Pursuing the Text. Studies in Honor of Ben Zion Wacholder on the Occasion of his Seventieth Birthday* ed. J.C. Reeves and J. Kampen, Sheffield: Sheffield Academic Press, 1994, pp. 70-84 reprinted in P.R. Davies, *Sects and Scrolls*, pp. 163-77.

[71] '"Damascus" Sect and Judaism', p. 168.

[72] See chapter eleven below.

vacat after לכול. As was the case in the preceding long section on the meeting of individual camps the material on the authority structure has undergone development. This is indicated by the description of the office of the priest who musters at the head of the many which precedes the legislation on the office of the overseer over all the camps. It seems likely that this sudden introduction of the term the many in CD 14,7 goes back to the Serekh redaction of the Laws. The office of 'the overseer over all the camps' that is referred to in CD 14,8-9, by contrast, is much more in line with the terminology of CD 14,3-6a, especially the heading in CD 14,3. Let us look at the description of each office in turn.

i. CD 14, 6c-8a The priest at the head of the many

והכהן אשר יפקד בֿ‍אשׁ[73] הרבים מבן שלושים שנה ועד בן ששים
מבונן בספר ההגי ובכל משפטי התורה לדברם כמשפטם

> And the priest who musters at the head of the many shall be aged between thirty and sixty years, learned in the Book of Hagi and in all the ordinances of the law to pronounce them according to their rule.

It seems likely that the office described here originally lacked the reference to the body of the many. Such an interpretation is suggested by the reference to the mustering of all the *camps* in CD 14,3 discussed above. The authority structure described in the rule on individual camps included a priest and an overseer, cf. CD 12,22b-14,2. The legislation on the meeting of all the camps, with the exception of the secondary reference to the many, is structured along the same lines as the legislation on the meetings of individual camps, i.e. as comprising a priest who is learned in the Book of Hagi and an overseer. The reference to the many forms part of the Serekh redaction endeavouring to bring the Laws into line with the Community Rule. Finally, a strikingly similar title to the one repeated in our text occurs in 1QS 6,14 (הואיש הפקיד ברואש הרבים) in conjunction with the admission of new members. Unlike in the Laws of the Damascus Document this title reads much more naturally in 1QS since the self-designation the many pervades the communal legislation of 1QS where, we may recall, it occurs more than thirty times.

---

[73] See the textual notes *ad loc.* above.

ii. CD 14,8b-12a The overseer over all the camps

והמבקר אשר לכל המחנות מבן שלשים שנה [ו]עד בן חמשים שנה
בעול בכל סוד אנשים ולכל לשון רמ[ש]פחותם[^74] על פיהו יבאו
באי העדה איש בתרו ולכל[^75] דבר אשר יהיה לכל האדם לדבר
למבקר ידבר לכל ריב ומשפט

> And the overseer over all the camps shall be aged between thirty [an]d fifty years, master of all the secrets of humanity and all the tongues according to their fam[i]lies. At his word the members of the congregation shall enter everyone in their place. And everyone who has anything to say to the overseer shall speak (to him) about any dispute or judgment.

With the prescriptions on the office of the overseer over all the camps we return again to the terminological framework established in the heading of this section in CD 14,3. Furthermore, this inclusion of a passage on the overseer over *all* the camps within the section on the meeting of *all* the camps corresponds to the layout of the preceding section on the meeting of individual camps. Both units contain the following corresponding formal elements. For the sake of clarity secondary additions as well as formal elements peculiar to one of the units have not been included.

A. *Heading*

CD 12,22b-23a	CD 14,3a
וזה סרך מושב המח[נו]ת	וסרך מושב כל המחנות
And this is the rule for the meeting of the camps.	And the rule for the meeting of all the camps.

B. *Organization of Members*

CD 13,1b-2a	CD 14,3b-6a
Groups of at least ten people by thousands, hundreds, fifties, and tens.	Groups of priests first, levites second, Israelites third, and proselytes fourth.

---

[^74]: See the textual notes *ad loc.* above.
[^75]: See the textual notes *ad loc.* above.

C. Sub-section on the Overseer

CD 13,7b.12b-13.15b-16a	CD 14,8b-12a
Sub-heading: CD 13,7b	Sub-heading: CD 14,8b-9a
וזה סרך המבקר למחנה	והמבקר אשר לכל המחנות
And this is the rule for the overseer over the camps...	And the overseer over all the camps...

The formal correspondences between these two units are considerable. It is conceivable that prior to the process of elaboration which this material underwent the formal correspondence would have been obvious at first sight.

The overseer over all the camps is to be aged between thirty and fifty years, master of all the secrets of humanity and all tongues. A discussion of these age limits as well as other age limits in the scrolls has been offered by Schiffman.[76] It is difficult to be certain about the exact nature of the other requirements mentioned here.

c. CD 14, 12b-18a Charity and social support

This final part of the legislation on the meeting of all the camps concerns the collection of two days' salary a month to provide for those in need of support in the community. We noted that 4QD^a 10 i 6 appears to have insufficient space for the words 'each month' (חדש לכל). 4QD^a's shorter text may preserve an earlier version of this regulation which originally referred to a one-off charitable collection and later became a regular monthly collection.

This material is introduced by a new heading in CD 14,12b which reads, 'And this is the rule for the many' (וזה סרך הרבים). There are strong grounds for allocating this heading to the Serekh redaction of the Laws of the Damascus Document. I have already discussed at several places the frequency of the expression the many in the Community Rule in contrast to the Damascus Document. More importantly, however, the individuals classed as in need of assistance in the material that follows this heading can be much more easily accommodated in the context of the camps as it emerges from the Laws of the Damascus Document than in 1QS and the body of the many as it appears from 1QS. In particular, the concern for 'the one taken captive by a foreign nation' (לאשר ישבה לגוי נכר) and 'the virgin who [has] no re[la]tives' (בתולה אשר א[ין] לה ג[וא]ל) paint a pic-

---

[76] *Sectarian Law*, esp. pp. 34-35.

ture of the community similar to that reflected elsewhere in the Laws of the Damascus Document. In the communal legislation of the Community Rule (1QS 5-9), on the other hand, neither 'the nations' nor women are mentioned at all. As regards the presence of women in the community, the position of the present study is to suppose that the members of the movement reflected in the Laws of the Damascus Document were married, whereas the community behind 1QS 5-9 either practised celibacy or attributed a peripheral role to women in the life of the community.[77] The very mention of two days' wages (שכר שני ימים) would be difficult to reconcile, moreover, with an association of these rules with the many. As is well known, there are several indications in the Community Rule that the community behind this document—which frequently refers to itself as the many—practised communal ownership, cf. 1QS 1,11b-13a; 3,2; 5,1-3; and 6,18-23a. In the Laws of the Damascus Document, by contrast, the private ownership of goods is presupposed in several rules, cf. for example CD 9,10b-16a and 13,15-16.

What is more, according to CD 14,13 the communal authorities responsible for the collection and distribution of the aid are 'the overseer and the judges' (המבקר והשופטים). Although the overseer is mentioned twice in the Community Rule, it is fair to say that he is intrinsically linked with the organization of the camps in the Laws of the Damascus Document, cf. 4QD^a 7 iii 3 [4QD^b 8,4]; CD 15,14; 13,7b.13.16; 14,8-9. The judges form part of the communal organization in the Laws of the Damascus Document (cf. CD 10,4-10a) whereas they are never mentioned with reference to 'the many' in the Community Rule. The reference to the judges as part of a rule associated by its present heading with the many in CD 14,12b-18a constitutes a further incongruity that is removed if we attribute the heading to the Serekh redaction.

In sum, there are good grounds for attributing the heading in CD 14,12b to the work of the Serekh redactor. As far as the original text is concerned, we cannot be sure whether there would have been a new heading at this point at all. It is possible that the material on the provision for the needy simply continued the section on the meeting of all the camps introduced in CD 14,3. On the other hand, it is equally possible that an earlier sub-heading that lacked the reference to the many was replaced by the present one.

---

[77] The Penal Code as preserved in 4QD preserves crucial new evidence on this issue, for a discussion cf. C. Hempel 'The Penal Code Reconsidered', in *Legal Texts and Legal Issues: Second Meeting of the IOQS, Cambridge 1995* ed. M.J. Bernstein and J. Kampen, Leiden: E.J. Brill, 1997, pp. 337-48.

Finally, CD 14,17b is only preserved in fragmentary form, but from what remains it seems likely that it incorporates a concluding statement on the meeting of the camps. CD 14,17b reads, 'And this is the exact statement on the meeting of the ca[mps' (וזה פרוש מושב המ]חנות). This conclusion comes right at the end of the section on the provision for the needy. Apart from indicating that the preceding rules are part of the material on the meeting of the camps, this conclusion further highlights the intrusive nature of the reference to the many in CD 14,12b.

6.5 Summary and Conclusions

The communal legislation dealing with the organization of the camps underwent a considerable amount of development. The following traditions and later developments were identified.

a. Communal legislation describing the organization of the camps proper is found in CD 12,22b-23a; 13,1b-7a (including some elaboration).7b.12b-13.15b-16a.20; 14,3-6b.8b-12a.12c-18a
b. Remnants of traditions dealing with the משכיל were identified in CD 12,20b-22a; 13,7c-8.14-15a.22.
c. CD 12,23b-13,1a; 13,23-14,2a were assigned to the Damascus redaction. To this CD 13,9-10 should perhaps be added because its admonitory tone resembles the Admonition.
d. CD 13,11-12a; 14,6c-8a.12b were attributed to the Serekh redaction.
e. It was not possible to associate a number of odd statements (i.e. CD 14,2b) and the fragmentary remains of CD 13,16b-19 with any of the larger blocks of material or redactional processes which have been identified in the Laws.

CHAPTER SEVEN

COMMUNITY ORGANIZATION PART FOUR: THE PENAL CODE

The beginning of the penal code is preserved in CD 14,18b-22 after which MS A of the Cairo text breaks off. The bulk of the code is found in 4QD[a,b,d and e]. I have produced a composite text of the penal code as preserved in the Damascus Document.

A. *Composite Text*[1]
(CD 14,18b-22; 4QD[a] 10 i-ii; 4QD[b] 9 vi; 4QD[d] 11 i-ii;[2] 4QD[e] 7 i)

1 וזה פרוש המשפטים אשר [יש]פטו בם עד ממוד משיח אהרון וישראל
2 ויכפר עונם מ[נ]חה וחטח [   ] vacat
3 וא[ש]ר ישקר בממון והוא יודע וה[בדילו]הו מן הטהרה
4 [שנה אחת ונ]ענש ששים יום ואשר ידב[ר   את רעהו במרום [

[lost material, perhaps compare to 1QS 6,26-7,8]

5 [   ] מאת[י]ם ימים ונענש מאה יום ואם בדבר מות ינטור ולו י[ש]וב
6 [עוד ואש]ר י[צ]חה את רעהו שלו בעצה [והו]בדל שנה אחת ונע[נ]ש
7 ש[ש]ה ח[וד]שים ואשר ידבר בפיה[ו] דבר נבל ונענש עשרים
8 יו[ם והובדל] שלושה חודשי[ם] ו[אשר י]דבר בתוך דב[ו]ר רעהו ו[פ]רע
9 [ונענש] ע[שרת] ימים [ואשר ישכ[ב] ו[ישן ב]מו[ש]ב הרבים [
10 [והובדל] שלושים יום [ו]נ[ענש עשרת ימים [וכן לאיש הנפ[טר
11 [אשר] לו בעצת הר[ב]י[ם ו[ה]נם [ ]ער שלוש פעמ[ים על מושב] אחד
12 ו[נענש] עשרה ימי[ם 'אם י]קפ[י] ונפטר [במושב ונענש שלושים [
13 יו[ם] ואשר יהלך לפני רע[ו]ם ערו[ם בבית או בשדה ה[לך] ע[רום לפני [
14 ה[ב]ריאות והובדל ששה [חודשים ונענש שלושים יום (?) ואשר [
15 יו[צא] {את} ידו מתחת בגדו והו[א]ה פוח ונראאתה ערותו והובדל שלו[שים

---

[1] The line numbers of this composite text do not correspond to the line numbers of any of its constituent texts. I have included those reconstructions which are not based on any remnants of text dealing with a particular offence in 4QD in smaller font. A number of these reconstructions appear possible in light of the penal code in 1QS but they should be used with caution.

[2] 4QD[d] 11 i-ii are only very fragmentarily preserved. As reconstructed by Baumgarten (*Qumran Cave 4. XIII*, p. 134) the sequence of offences in 4QD[d] 11 i differs considerably in this MS from the others. However, this difference in sequence is based purely on the way the text has been reconstructed. A great deal depends on the relative position one assigns to the individual fragments that make up 4QD[d] 11 i (cf. Baumgarten, *Qumran Cave 4. XIII*, Plate XXV).

16 [יו]ם ונענש עשרה והשוחק בסכלות להשמיע [קולו והובדל]
17 [ש]לושים ונענש חמשת [עשר] ימים והמוציא את י[דו השמאלית]
18 לשח בה ונענש [ ] עשרה ימים והאי[ש] אשר ילך [רכיל]
19 [בר]ע[הו והבדילוה]ו מן הטהרה שנ[ה אחת ונענש ששה ? חודשים ואיש ברבים]
20 ילך רכיל לשלח הוא ולא [ ] ישוב ע[וד ואם על רעהו ילון אשר לא במשפט]
21 ונענש ששה חודשים והאי[ש אשר תזוע] רוחו [
22 ו[הו]בדל שתי שנים ונ[ענש ששים [יום ובמלאות לו שנתים ימים]
23 [ישאלו הרבים] על דב[רו ואם יקרב] ויכתו[בוהו בתכונו ואחר ישאל אל המשפט]
24 ו[האיש אשר ימאס [א[ת משפט הרבים ויצא ו[לא ישו[ב עוד [ואשר יקח] va]cat
25 אוכלו חוצה מן המשפט והשיבו לאיש אשר לקחו מ[מנו va]cat ואשר יקרב
26 לזנות לאשתו אשר לא כמשפט ויצא ולא ישוב עוד vaca]t ואשר ילו[ן על האבות
27 [ישלח] מן העדה ולא ישוב [ואם] על האמות ונענש עשר[ת] ימים כי אין לאמו[ת]
    רוקמה בתוך
28 [העדה] vacat [אלה המ[שפטים א[שר ישפטו] בם כל המתיסרים

B. *Translation*

1. And this is the exact statement of the judgments by which they shall be [ju]dged until the Messiah of Aaron and Israel arises,
2. and he will forgive their sins. Gift] offering and guilt offering [ ] Vacat.
3. Who[ev]er lies knowingly in matters of money they shall ex[clu]de him from the purity
4. [for one year, and he shall be pu]nished for sixty days. And whoever spea[ks to his neighbour with insolence]

[lost material, perhaps compare to 1QS 6,26-7,8]

5. two [hund]red days, and he shall be punished for a hundred days. But if it is a capital case, and he bears a grudge he shall not [re]turn
6. [again. And anyone wh]o [ins]ults his neighbour without conferring [he shall be ex]cluded for one year and punish[ed]
7. for s[i]x m[on]ths. And anyone who speaks foolishly shall be punished for twenty
8. [da]ys [and excluded] for three month[s.] And [anyone who i]nterrupts [his neighbour's] speec[h and] lacks restraint
9. [shall be punished for] t[en] days. [And anyone who lies do]wn [and] falls asleep during [a mee]t[ing of the many]
10. [shall be excluded] for thirty days [and] punished for ten days. [And likewise the one who lea]ves
11. [with]out the consent of the ma[n]y and [with]out [cause] up to three tim[es during] a single [meeting]
12. sha[ll be punished] for ten days. And if [they are standing³], and he leaves [during the meeting he shall be punished for thirty]

---

³ For a different understanding of זקף cf. Weinfeld, *Organizational Pattern*, pp. 29-30.

13 da[ys.] And anyone who walks [nak]ed in front of [his] neigh[bour] in the house, or in the field walking na[ked] [in front of]
14 the[cr]eatures, shall be excluded for six [months and punished for thirty days (?). And anyone who]
15 [ta]kes out his hand from underneath his garment and, i[t becomes disarranged so his nakedness can be seen shall be excluded for thi]rty
16 day[s] and punished for ten. And the one who emits vulgar laughter to make [his voice] heard [shall be excluded]
17 [for th]irty (days) and punished for fif[teen] days. [And the one who takes out] his left hand
18 to gesticulate with it shall be punished [for ten days. And the one] who goes about [slandering]
19 [his neigh]bour, [they shall exclude] him from the purity for [one] yea[r and he shall be punished for six months. And he who goes about slandering]
20 [the many shall be sent away and not] return a[gain. And if he murmurs against his neighbour in a manner which is not according to the law]
21 [he shall be punished for six months. And h]e whose [spirit] deviates [ ]
22 he shall be ex[cluded for two years and pu]nished for sixty [days. And after the two years]
23 [the many shall be consulted] concerning [his] ca[se and if he is to rejoin] they shall wri[te him down in his place and afterwards he shall be asked about the law.]
24 *Va[cat.* And] the one who despises the judgment of the many shall leave and [not re]turn again. [And the one who takes]
25 his food in a manner that is against (lit.: outside) the law shall return it to the person from whom it was taken.[4] [*Va]cat.* And the one who approaches
26 his wife for fornication which is not according to the law[5] shall leave and not return again. *V[acat.* And he who murmu]rs against the fathers
27 [shall be sent away] from the congregation and not return. [And if] it is against the mothers he shall be punished for te[n] days for the m[o]thers have no *rwqmh*[6] in the midst of
28 [the congregation.] *Vacat.* [These are the or]dinances by wh[ich] all those who are disciplined shall [be judged.]

---

[4] Baumgarten plausibly suggests that the food in question belongs to an expelled member (*Qumran Cave 4. XIII*, p. 166).

[5] A number of suggestions have been offered regarding the exact nature of this offence, cf. Baumgarten, 'Laws of the *Damascus Document* in Current Research', p. 54; M. Kister, 'Notes on Some New Texts from Qumran', *JJS* 44 (1993) 280-81; Maier, *Qumran-Essener*, 1995, II, p. 229 n. 344; and S. Talmon, 'The Community of the Renewed Covenant: Between Judaism and Christianity', in *The Community of the Renewed Covenant* ed. Ulrich and VanderKam, pp. 3-24, p. 9.

[6] The meaning of this term is uncertain, cf. C. Hempel, 'Penal Code Reconsidered', p. 347 n. 54.

C. Textual Notes

2 Baumgarten reconstructs מ(מנ)חה and has argued that this passage advocates atonement through the agency of the messiah rather than through sacrifices.[7] This text is too fragmentary in my view to assess what is being said about the types of sacrifice mentioned in this line.

3 Only has the last two letters of ישקר are preserved in CD 14,20 but the reading is suggested by 1QS 6,24.[8] For יודע, the reading suggested by Qimron, Baumgarten reads נודע.[9]

11 For [הנ]ם Baumgarten reads [והנ]ם in 4QDᵃ 10 ii 7.[10]

19 The reference to 'six (months)' has been tentatively reconstructed in 4QDᵉ 7 i 6 by Baumgarten.[11]

22 4QDᵉ 7 i 9 includes the two superlinear letters *resh* and *s(h)in* after 'sixty' (ששים) the meaning of which is obscure.[12]

24 Baumgarten reconstructs ואשר לקח in 4QDᵇ 9 vi 3.[13] I have reconstructed an imperfect which is the dominant formulation in the penal code and occurs even in the immediately following line in 4QDᵇ 9 vi 4. Baumgarten himself reconstructs the imperfect in the equivalent passage in 4QDᵉ 7 i 11.[14]

D. Commentary

As is well known a penal code with a remarkably similar text has long been known from 1QS 6,24-7,25.[15] Subtle differences between both codes are of great interest for our understanding of the relationship between the Community Rule and the Damascus Document.[16] The material in ll. 24-28 of the composite text draws on MSS 4QDᵇ and ᵉ and includes a number of offences not found in the version of the penal code as preserved in 1QS. The text of the penal code as preserved in 4QDᵃ breaks off in 10 ii 15 (l. 19 of the com-

---

[7] Cf. J.M Baumgarten, 'Messianic Forgiveness of Sin in CD 14:19 (4Q266 10 i 12-13)', in *Proceedings of the International Conference on the Dead Sea Scrolls, Provo, Utah 1996* ed. D.W. Parry and E. Ulrich, Leiden: E.J. Brill, forthcoming.

[8] See Qimron, 'Text of CDC', p. 37 n. 24.

[9] Baumgarten in Charlesworth ed., *Dead Sea Scrolls*, II, p. 56. More recently Baumgarten adopted Qimron's reading in his reconstruction of 4QDᵃ 10 i 14 which is based on CD 14, cf. *Qumran Cave 4. XIII*, p. 72.

[10] *Qumran Cave 4. XIII*, p. 74.

[11] Cf. *Qumran Cave 4. XIII*, p. 162.

[12] Cf. Baumgarten, *Qumran Cave 4. XIII*, p. 163.

[13] *Qumran Cave 4. XIII*, p. 110.

[14] *Qumran Cave 4. XIII*, p. 163.

[15] Cf. Garcia Martinez, *People of the Dead Sea Scrolls*, pp. 152-57 and Schiffman, *Sectarian Law*, pp. 155-90. For a discussion of parallels in the codes of associations in the Greco-Roman period see Weinfeld, *Organizational Pattern*, pp. 23-43.

[16] For comparative studies see J. Baumgarten, 'The Cave 4 Versions of the Qumran Penal Code', *JJS* 43 (1992) 268-76 and C. Hempel, 'The Penal Code Reconsidered'.

posite text). Baumgarten has suggested that the penal code as preserved in 4QD^a might have lacked a number of offences dealt with in 4QD$^{b\ and\ e}$ but absent from 1QS.[17] It appears unlikely, however, that 4QD^a lacked all of 4QD$^{b\ and\ e}$'s material additional to 1QS. 4QD^a 10 ii breaks off in l. 15, and the average number of lines per column in this MS is twenty-four to twenty-five lines. According to Baumgarten, 4QD^a 10 ii would need to have accommodated 'either lines of close to fifty characters or a column with about twenty-seven lines'.[18] Baumgarten's calculation indicates that 4QD^a's text appears to be somewhat shorter than the text of 4QD$^{b\ and\ e}$ at this point. However, this difference covers around two lines, and the material preserved in 4QD$^{b\ and\ e}$ over and above the penal material in 1QS would cover approximately four to five lines in 4QD^a.

a. Ll. 1-2 Introduction to the penal code

The penal code is introduced in l. 1a with the heading 'And this is the exact statement of the judgments by which they shall be [ju]dged.' (וזה פרוש המשפטים אשר [יש]פטו בם). This concise heading was expanded by a reference to the coming of the Messiah of Aaron and Israel. As I have shown in the course of the earlier discussion of the messianic reference in CD 12,23b-13,1a the references to the coming of the Messiah are best assigned to the work of the Damascus redactor.[19] A phrase that is almost identical to the original heading in l. 1a forms part of the introduction to the penal code in 1QS 6,24 'And these are the judgments by which they shall be judged' (ואלה המשפטים אשר ישפטו בם). This phrase was expanded in 1QS by the subsequent phrase 'at an inquiry of the community' (במדרש יחד) which appears to be lacking in 4QS^g 2,2.[20] The presence of the same core phrase in the introductions to the penal code in both S and D lends further weight to our argument that this phrase constitutes the original heading of the penal code. What is more, the heading in l. 1a mirrors the concluding statement at the end of the penal code in l. 28b. The subsequent reference to the role of the Messiah in bringing about atonement is, as we saw, rather fragmentary and not much can be said with certainty on its place in the Laws, cf. my comments in the textual note to l. 2.

---

[17] *Qumran Cave 4. XIII*, p. 75.
[18] *Ibid.*
[19] See pp. 79-81 and 108-10 above.
[20] Cf. Qimron and Charlesworth in Charlesworth ed., *Dead Sea Scrolls*, I, pp. 94-95.

b. Ll. 3-28a Penal legislation

The penal legislation preserved here leaves little doubt that this code should be assigned to the communal legislation stratum in the Laws of D. Perhaps more than any other section of the Laws the penal code reflects the life of a particular community. However, since the bulk of this code is attested also in the Community Rule we need to ask ourselves which community is reflected in this legislation. Until the 4QD MSS became available to the scholarly public it was thought that the community reflected in the penal code was the sectarian Qumran community, the *yahad*, described in the Community Rule. Since 4QD preserves a penal code that resembles the code found in 1QS at times *verbatim* the situation is no longer so simple.[21] I have argued elsewhere that the most fruitful starting point for a comparative analysis of the penal code as preserved in S and D is a study of the offences, particularly since two MSS of 4QD preserve a number of offences not found in 1QS.[22] These offences not present in 1QS are found in ll. 24-28a of the composite text. Particularly revealing is the presence of two offences in 4QD that mention women, cf. ll. 25b-28a. As far as the communal legislation of the Damascus Document is concerned references to women in the penal code merely confirm the picture derived from other passages in the communal legislation. It is quite clear from passages like CD 15,5b-6a; 14,12c-16a that the community envisaged by the communal legislation of D included women. The Community Rule, by contrast, is silent on the subject of women. I have argued elsewhere that this silence is best explained by assuming that the community behind the Community Rule was either celibate or that women though present played a very peripheral part in the life of the community.[23] On either of these two interpretations it is clear that the visible role of women in the community distinguishes the Damascus Document from the Community Rule.

The most likely explanation for the different forms of the penal code in S and D is to argue that the penal code developed in the movement behind the communal legislation of D which allowed women to play an active and visible part in the life of the communi-

---

[21] A third text from Qumran that includes penal legislation is the still unpublished 4Q265 *Serekh Damascus*, cf. Garcia Martinez, *Dead Sea Scrolls Translated*, p. 72; Maier, *Qumran-Essener*, 1995, II, pp. 215-16; Vermes, *Complete Dead Sea Scrolls*, pp. 153-56; and Wise, Abegg, and Cook, *A New Translation*, pp. 278-81.

[22] Cf. Hempel, 'Penal Code Reconsidered'.

[23] Cf. Hempel, 'Earthly Essene Nucleus', pp. 262-66, for a fuller discussion of the evidence as well as bibliographical details.

ty. The penal code was then taken up by the author/redactor behind S who left out those offences that mention women because they were of little interest to his community.[24]

We noted already in the discussion of CD 15,8 that the penal code in D shows clear signs of having been revised by the Serekh redactor.[25] As is the case elsewhere in the communal legislation of D the work of the Serekh redactor is manifest in the frequent use of the self-designation the many (הרבים). The self-designations camp (מחנה) and congregation (עדה) used more frequently in the communal legislation are also present in D's penal code, cf. ll. 27-28 of the composite text. I have discussed at some length the reference to the many in l.11 of the composite text since this particular passage provides the clearest evidence for the work of the Serekh redactor.[26] Let me briefly summarize my earlier discussion. 4QD preserves here a reference to the many that is absent from an otherwise parallel offence in 1QS 7,11 par. 4QS^g 3,3. Since the self-designation the many occurs over thirty times in S it is doubtful that this particular reference has been omitted in S. The evidence is best accounted for by assuming that a reference to the many has been inserted into a passage that originally lacked it by the Serekh redactor. The work of the Serekh redactor is reflected in l. 11 of the composite text and possibly also in ll. 9, 20, and 23 were further references to the many have been reconstructed. A further reference to the many occurs in l. 24 in an offence that is absent from 1QS. It seems likely that this passage also goes back to the Serekh redaction because of its preference for the self-designation 'the many'. Furthermore, unlike all the other offences included in D's penal code which are addressing very specific practices l. 24 stands out because of its general character.

c. Ll. 28b Conclusion to the penal code
L. 28b of the composite text appears to conclude to the penal code proper, and as noted earlier this conclusion mirrors the heading in l. 1a. The transition between the end of the penal code and the beginning of the expulsion ceremony that makes up the final part of the Damascus Document is very smooth.

In sum, ll. 1a.3-28b of the composite text above provide us with D's version of the penal code and form part of the communal legis-

---

[24] Such a view of the development of the penal code in S is reflected in a reworking of the material represented by ll. 26b-28a of the composite text in 1QS 7,17b-18a, cf. C. Hempel, 'Penal Code Reconsidered' for a fuller discussion.

[25] See pp. 81-85 above.

[26] See note 25.

lation in D. Ll. 1b-2 have been assigned to the Damascus redaction. Finally, the reference to the many in l. 11 and the offence preserved in l. 24 were attributed to the Serekh redaction.

SUMMARY AND CONCLUSION TO CHAPTERS FOUR-SEVEN

The following picture emerges of the community behind the communal legislation in the Laws of D.[1]

a. Self-designations and Authority Structure of the Community

The communal legislation in Laws of D employs a distinctive set of terms to refer to itself and its officials. The community's self-designations are camp (מחנה), congregation (עדה), and covenant (ברית).[2] The authority structure in the community appears to have undergone development with the ordinary priest (כוהן) having been replaced by the office of the overseer (מבקר). Furthermore, a group of judges play a part in leading the community. Most of the terms used as self-designations are based on scripture, a point to which I will come back in the conclusion.[3] The authority structure seems to have moved away from the biblical paradigm by replacing the priest with the office of the overseer.

b. Admission Process

New members are admitted into the community by swearing the oath of the covenant, a process in which the overseer plays a crucial role.

c. Unpolemical Stance

The tone of the bulk of the communal legislation is non-polemical, and the community identifies itself positively with Israel at large.

d. Family Life, Property and Temple

Family life, the private ownership of property, and participation in the Temple cult are taken for granted.

---

[1] 4QD^a 7 ii-iii par. 4QD^b 8 contain further communal legislation although not enough text has survived to interpret these remains in any detail. For the text of these fragments see Baumgarten, *Qumran Cave 4. XIII*, pp. 62-63, 104-105. In his table outlining the contents of D Baumgarten includes 4QD^a 7 i-iii and 4QD^b 8 under the heading 'Overseer of Camp' and aligns this material immediately preceding CD 15, see pp. 32-33 n. 26 above.

[2] On the latter terminology see H. Stegemann, 'Gesetzeskorpus', p. 427.

[3] See chapter twelve below.

e. The Book of Hagi
The Book of Hagi was an authoritative work consulted in the community.

f. Administration of Justice
Justice was administered in the community as evidenced by the penal code as well as the material examined in chapter five.

g. Remnants of Traditions on the *Maskil*
Remnants of traditions on the *maskil* have been preserved in the communal legislation of D. Since only fragments of these traditions have survived it is not possible to reconstruct the role of the wise leader in the community. His role seems to have been supplanted by the dominant position of the overseer in the Laws in their final form.

It thus emerges that the communal legislation in D gives evidence of an organized community that differs in numerous respects from the community as described in the Community Rule. It seems likely to me that what we have here is the community structure of the parent group of the *yaḥad*.[4] These results call into question the contention that the Teacher of Righteousness provided leadership for an unorganized group as recently suggested by Talmon.[5] In the light of my analysis of the Laws of D there is plenty of evidence for the communal organization of the pre-Teacher group. Talmon's model only works if we—as has up to now been the norm—associate every piece of communal organization with the Teacher community, in origin if not application. It seems likely that this perception of the parent movement is based on the reference to the period of blindness prior to the Teacher's arrival in CD 1. I have argued elsewhere that this presentation of life before the Teacher as characterized by blindness and lack of orientation is best seen as the particular point of view of the followers of the Teacher.[6]

---

[4] These conclusions bear out the recent suggestion by H. Stegemann that the Damascus Document incorporates 'viele frühere Gemeinde- und Disziplinarordnungen' (*Die Essener, Qumran, Johannes der Täufer und Jesus*, p. 165. See also *idem*, 'Gesetzeskorpus' and P.R. Callaway, 'Qumran Origins: From the *Doresh* to the *Moreh*', *RQ* 14 (1990) 637-50, esp. pp. 645-46.

[5] Cf., for example, S. Talmon, 'Waiting for the Messiah—the Conceptual Universe of the Qumran Covenanters' in *idem*, *The World of Qumran From Within*, pp. 273-300, p. 284 where he speaks of the Teacher's role in "transforming the loose group-cohesion of the founding members into a structured sociorcligious system."

[6] Cf. C. Hempel, 'Community Origins in the Damascus Document in the Light of Recent Scholarship' in *Proceedings of the International Conference on the Dead Sea Scrolls, Provo, Utah 1996*, ed. D.W. Parry and E. Ulrich, Leiden: E.J. Brill, forthcoming.

SUMMERY AND CONCLUSION TO CHAPTERS FOUR-SEVEN

We further noted two major redactional processes that are evident in the communal legislation. A Damascus redactor inserted a number of statements that serve to present the Damascus Document as a whole as a unified composition and a Serekh redaction attempting to bring the Laws into line with the Community Rule. In this respect my own analysis of the Laws corresponds well with Philip Davies' identification of a redaction of the Admonition of the Damascus Document by the *yaḥad*.[7] Finally, a number of secondary additions seeking to promote the message of the Book of Jubilees have been identified.

---

[7] *Damascus Covenant*, pp. 173-201.

CHAPTER EIGHT

MISCELLANEOUS PIECES OF HALAKHAH

The passages included here constitute the most patchy part of the Laws of D. Different halakhic passages, sometimes mere statements, follow upon one another rather abruptly. The disparate nature of this material has already been noted indirectly by other scholars. Thus, A. Dupont-Sommer entitles CD 11,18c-12,22a as 'Various Regulations',[1] and J. Fitzmyer in his outline of the contents of the Damascus Document groups together CD 11,18b-12,11a under the heading 'Sundry Regulations'.[2] Although the exact delineations differ between both scholars—and I will suggest yet another way of delineating this section of miscellaneous rules—it seems quite clear that CD 11,21b-12,6a and 12,11b-20a contain the most disparate and haphazard collection of rulings in the Laws of D.

8.1 Rules on Entering the House of Worship

CD 11,21b-12,1a par. 4QD^f 5 i 15b-17a lays down rules on entering the house of worship.

A. *Text*
(CD 11,21b-12,1a; 4QD^f 5 i)

11:21b וכל הבא אל
22 בית השתחות אל יבא טמא כבוס ובהרע חצוצרות הקהל
23 יתקדם או יתאחר ולא ישביתו את העבודה כולה [כ]י בית
12:1a קודש הוא

B. *Translation*
11,21b And no one who enters
   22 the house of worship shall be unclean and in need of washing. And at the sound of the trumpets of assembly
   23 he shall arrive before or afterwards so as not to bring the whole service to a halt [f]or it is a holy
12,1a house.

---

[1] *Essene Writings*, p. 153.
[2] J.A. Fitzmyer, *Prolegomenon*, p. 18; see also *idem, The Dead Sea Scrolls. Major Publications and Tools for Study*, Atlanta: Scholars Press, 1990, p. 133.

C. *Textual Notes*
22 4QD^f 5 i 15 reads בית ההשתחוות.³
23 For the reading and reconstruction of the last two words in this line I follow the reading recently suggested by Annette Steudel.⁴

D. *Commentary*
This enigmatic rule has given rise to a variety of interpretations. My concern is the place of this passage in the Laws of the Damascus Document, and it will suffice to point out the difficulties that face the interpreter of this rule.

A key problem is to establish the meaning of the expression בית השתחות. It is unclear whether it refers to the Jerusalem temple, to a sectarian place of worship,⁵ or to a synagogue. Scholars are divided, and the emergence of a consensus seems unlikely in the foreseeable future. Furthermore, the meaning of the expression טמא כבוס is also disputed. L. Ginzberg who is followed by C. Rabin has argued that the text envisages uncleanness caused by a seminal emission.⁶ S. Talmon, by contrast, suggests that ritually unclean garments are at issue here.⁷ A further crucial question is posed by the second part of our passage and concerns the meaning of the term עבודה. It may have the meaning 'work' as in the Sabbath Code, cf. CD 10,19.20. On the other hand, it can be used in the sense 'religious service'. עבודה is used in the latter sense in the material on the disqualification of priests in 4QD^a 5 ii 4 and 6. I have chosen the latter meaning for my translation.⁸

What, in the light of these observations, can be said about the place of this passage in the Laws of D? Because of the brevity of the passage, the uncertainty over the meaning of key terms, as well as the lack of formal coherence the criteria of form and content yield few tangible results in the analysis of this passage. The vocabulary criteri-

---

³ Cf. Baumgarten, *Qumran Cave 4. XIII*, pp. 180-82.
⁴ 'The Houses of Prostration CD XI,21-XII,1—Duplicates of the Temple' *RQ* 16 (1993) 49-68, pp. 51-52.
⁵ Steudel suggests that locus 77 at Qumran might have functioned as both a dining room as well as בית השתחות or 'house of prostration'. ('Houses of Prostration', p. 60). I am not at all sure, however, that we should associate the community behind the Laws of D with the Qumran site.
⁶ L. Ginzberg, *Unknown Jewish Sect*, p. 72; cf. also C. Rabin, *Zadokite Documents*, p. 59.
⁷ 'A Further Link Between the Judean Covenanters and the Essenes?', in *idem*, *The World of Qumran from Within*, pp. 61-67.
⁸ A. Dupont-Sommer renders this passage differently: "And when the trumpets of Assembly sound, whether it is early or late all work shall not cease..." (*Essene Writings*, p. 15). Dupont-Sommer is followed by É. Cothenet, ' Document de Damas', esp. p. 194; cf. also Talmon, 'A Further Link', pp. 63-66.

on, on the other hand, can be applied to this passage regardless of these obstacles.

Two key expressions, one from each of the two parts of the passage, seem to indicate that this material falls outside the major literary strata found in the Laws of D.

a. The expression בית השתחות is a *hapax legomenon* not only in the Damascus Document but in the published non-biblical literature from Qumran. Leaving aside the question whether it is a designation for the Jerusalem temple or any other place of worship, this expression is clearly unique in the Laws.
b. Similarly, the reference to the sounding of the trumpets of assembly constitutes an isolated case in the Laws. The biblical regulations on the use of trumpets are found in Num. 10,1-10. What is more, trumpets play an important part in the description of the eschatological battle in the War Scroll, cf. 1QM 2,15-3,11; 7,12c-15 etc. Outside of the War Scroll the present instance constitutes to my knowledge the only reference to the blowing of trumpets in the published non-biblical scrolls. Thus, as in the preceding case this expression stands in isolation not only from the remainder of the Laws of the Damascus Document but also from a considerable body of halakhah and communal legislation in the corpus of the scrolls as a whole.

It is on the basis of these considerations that the present passage has been included with the miscellaneous halakhah in the Laws of D. It seems to have been linked to the preceding section dealing with preserving the purity of the altar in CD 11,18c-21a by the catchword טמא which occurs in CD 11,19 and 20 as well as in CD 11,22.

8.2 Prohibition of Sexual Relations in Jerusalem

CD 12,1b-2a par. 4QD^f 5 i 17b-18a contains a prohibition of sexual relations in Jerusalem.

A. *Text*
(CD 12,1b-2a; 4QD^f 5 i)

אל ישכב איש עם אשה בעיר המקדש לטמא את עיר המקדש בנדתם

B. *Translation*
No one shall lie with a woman in the city of the sanctuary so as to defile the city of the sanctuary with their uncleanness.

C. Commentary

This passage seems to prohibit sexual intercourse in the city of Jerusalem.[9] This reference to 'the city of the sanctuary' (עיר המקדש) is unique in the Laws of the Damascus Document. In the Temple Scroll, by contrast, a great deal of attention is devoted to the purity of the Holy City. Of particular interest for the discussion of CD 12,1b-2a is 11QT^a 45,11-12a[10] which reads as follows,

11 ואיש כיא ישכב עם אשתו שכבת זרע לוא יבוא אל כול עיר
12a המקדש אשר אשכין שמי בה שלושת ימים

> And if a man lies with his wife and has an emission of semen, he shall not come into any part of the city of the temple, where I will settle my name, for three days.[11]

As has been pointed out by Yadin a similarly stringent level of purity as is demanded by CD 12,1b-2a and 11QT^a 45,11-12a for everyday life in Jerusalem is required by Moses of the people in preparation for the revelation on Mount Sinai, cf. Ex. 19, 10-15.[12] The biblical law on the impurity after intercourse is found in Lev. 15,18. In the Laws of D this reference to the city of the sanctuary occurs rather abruptly and constitutes the only passage that deals with the purity of the city of Jerusalem. To be sure, the preservation of ritual purity can be found in other parts of the Laws. A particular emphasis on the special status of Jerusalem, however, is on the whole absent from the Laws of D. In the Temple Scroll, on the other hand, the passage we cited occurs within a wider context of material dealing with the unique standards of purity required for the temple and the temple city, i.e. 11QT^a 45-47. It seems probable, therefore, that CD 12,1b-2a constitutes an interpolation in the Laws of D which seems to have originated from the same milieu as 11QT^a 45-47.[13]

---

[9] For this view cf. Ginzberg, *Unknown Jewish Sect*, pp. 73-74. B.A. Levine has argued that the prohibition refers to the temple precincts rather than the whole city, cf. 'The Temple Scroll: Aspects of Its Historical Provenance and Literary Character', *BASOR* 232 (1979) 5-23. This is also the position taken by Schiffman, cf. *Reclaiming the Dead Sea Scrolls*, p. 131; idem, 'The Theology of the Temple Scroll', *JQR* 85 (1994) 109-23 and 'Exclusion from the Sanctuary and the City of the Sanctuary in the Temple Scroll', *HAR* 9 (1985) 301-20. For a critique see J. Milgrom, '"Sabbath" and "Temple City" in the Temple Scroll', *BASOR* 232 (1978) 25-27 and idem, 'The City of the Temple. A Response to Lawrence H. Schiffman', *JQR* 85 (1994) 125-28.

[10] For a discussion of the relationship of CD 12,1b-2a and 11QT 45,11-12 see M.O. Wise, *A Critical Study of the Temple Scroll from Qumran Cave 11*, Chicago: The Oriental Institute of the University of Chicago, 1990, pp. 139-47.

[11] Text and translation are taken from Y. Yadin, *Temple Scroll*, II, p. 193.

[12] Cf. Yadin, *Temple Scroll*, II, p. 192 n. 8.

[13] Interestingly, H. Hübner included a footnote on this passage in a study of celibacy at Qumran in which he already airs the suspicion that CD 12,1b-2a is a

8.3 The Spirits of Belial and Failure to Honour the Sabbath and the Festivals

CD 12,2b-6a par. 4Q D^r 5 i 18b-21a comprises two rules prescribing the appropriate treatment for those under the influence of evil angelic forces.

A. *Text*
(CD 12,2b-6a; 4QD^r 5 i)

2b כל איש אשר ימשלו בו רוחות בליעל
3   ודבר סרה כמשפט האוב והידעוני ישפט וכל אשר יתעה
4   לחלל את השבת ואת המועדות לא יומת כי על בני האדם
5   משמרו ואם ירפא ממנו ושמרוהו עד שבע שנים ואחר
6a יבוא אל הקהל

B. *Translation*
2b Everyone who is ruled by the spirits of Belial
3 and speaks rebellion shall be judged with the same judgement as the ghost or wizard. And everyone who goes astray
4 so as to desecrate the sabbath or the festivals shall not be put to death but people shall be appointed
5 to guard him. If he is healed from it then they shall guard him for seven years and afterwards
6a he may enter the assembly.

C. *Commentary*
CD 12,2b-3a stipulates that those who speak rebellion are to be judged as the ghost or wizard. The biblical law on the ghost or wizard is found in Lev. 20,27a,

ואיש או־אשה כי־יהיה בהם אוב או ידעני מות יומתו

A man or a woman who is a medium or a wizard shall be put to death.[14]

Thus, CD 12,2b-3a prescribes the death penalty for those who speak rebellion because they are ruled by the spirits of Belial. Dt. 13,6 (Hebrew) rules, moreover, that the prophet and the 'dreamer of

---

secondary addition. Regrettably Hübner refrains from giving reasons for this. He sets out by arguing that CD 12,1b-2a is part of the Sabbath Code in CD and qualifies this view with the following footnote, "Dies ist unter der Voraussetzung gesagt, daß diese Stelle in der Tat eine ursprüngliche Sabbathalacha war und nicht erst auf redaktionellem Wege später unter die anderen Sabbathalachot geraten ist.", 'Zölibat in Qumran?', *NTS* 17 (1970-71) 153-67, p. 167 n. 1.

[14] This translation is taken from the NRSV.

dreams' who speak rebellion against God are to be put to death. The same expression as in our passage, דבר סרה, is used in Dt. 13,6.

The Book of Jubilees contains numerous references to the belief in the presence and influence of evil spirits,[15] and this link between Jubilees and the present passage has often been noted by commentators, cf. Jub. 1,20; 11,4-6; 15,31-32 and 19,28. Jubilees 1,20 is particularly instructive. This line forms part of a prayer by Moses and mentions 'the spirit of Belial'. VanderKam's rendering of Jub. 1,20 reads as follows,

> May your mercy, Lord, be lifted over your people. Create for them a just spirit. May the spirit of Belial not rule them so as to bring charges against them before you and to trap them away from every proper path so that they may be destroyed from your presence.[16]

CD 12,3b-6a deals with the case of someone who desecrates the sabbath and the festivals. At first sight one may have thought that this passage served at one time as a concluding statement to the Sabbath Code. This possibility seems unlikely, however, in view of the reference to the sabbath *and the festivals* in this text. It seems more likely that the calendar dispute lies behind this material.[17] Since no festivals fell on a sabbath according to the solar calendar the Essenes were able to keep the sabbath rigorously. The strict observance of the sabbath was more problematic for the followers of the lunar calendar.

By rejecting the death penalty for violators of the sabbath this passage differs sharply from the Torah (cf. Ex. 35,2 and Num. 15,35) and the Book of Jubilees (cf. Jub. 50,8.12-13) both of which prescribe the death penalty for sabbath violation. This surprising apparent contradiction to the Torah has led both J. Maier[18] and L.H. Schiffman[19] to assume that our text deals with inadvertent sabbath violation.[20] C. Rabin, on the other hand, takes the passage at face value and argues,

> ...the sect had abolished the capital punishment for Sabbath-breaking.[21]

---

[15] Cf. B. Noack, 'Qumran and the Book of Jubilees', *SEA* 22-23 (1958) 191-207. p. 200.
[16] *Book of Jubilees*, II, p. 5.
[17] Cf. A. Dupont-Sommer, *Essene Writings*, p. 154 n. 6.
[18] *Texte vom Toten Meer*, 1960, II, p. 56 n. 314.
[19] *Halakhah at Qumran*, p. 78.
[20] For a similar view cf. also T.H. Gaster, *Scriptures of the Dead Sea Sect*, p. 88 and H. Bietenhardt, 'Sabbatvorschriften', pp. 56-57. Both Gaster and Bietenhardt assume mental illness to be envisaged here.
[21] *Zadokite Documents*, p. 60.

S.T. Kimbrough's solution to this problem is pragmatic.[22] Kimbrough argues that the passage at hand reflects a lenient treatment for sabbath violators in order to ensure the future existence of a community that was mostly celibate and had rigid requirements for admission. The rigid application of the biblical punishment for sabbath violators would have diminished the numbers of this movement and put its continued existence at risk. This view presupposes a legal pragmatism that seems quite out of keeping with the picture that emerges from the literature found at Qumran. It is difficult to arrive at a certain answer to the question why the biblical death penalty for sabbath violation is rejected here. It seems likely that this passage was composed in reaction to a contrary position and it may reflect a particular dispute. Without further evidence no more can be said.

I have treated CD 12,2b-6a together on the basis of the reference to 'healing' (רפא) of those who desecrated the sabbath and festivals in CD 12,5. According to Jub. 10,12-14 remedies revealed by the angels to Noah can cure evil spirits. In the light of this it seems likely that CD 12,2b-6a should be taken together, and that CD 12,3b-6a attributes the blame for the desecration of the sabbath and the festivals to the influence of evil spirits. Otherwise the reference to healing would make little sense. In Jubilees sinfulness is frequently attributed to the influence of evil spirits and demonic angelic beings.

It seems likely that we have here another interpolation in the Laws of D that seeks to promote the message of the Book of Jubilees.[23] Apart from the influence of Jub. 1,20 it was noted that a belief in the presence and power of spirits is largely absent in the Laws of D in contrast to Jubilees. The Laws tend to remain in the realm of the factual and practical.

---

[22] 'Sabbath at Qumran', pp. 499-500.
[23] Further interpolations that reflect concerns prominent in the Book of Jubilees have been identified in CD 16,2b-6a and CD 10,7b-10a.

8.4 Various Purity Regulations

CD 12,11b-20a par. 4QD^a 9 ii 1-7a comprises a small collection of purity regulations.[24]

A. *Text*
(CD 12,11b-20a; 4QD^a 9 ii)

11b	אל ישקץ איש את נפשו
12	בכל החיה והרמש לאכל מהם מעגלי הדבורים עד כל נפש
13	החיה אשר תרמוש במים והדנים אל יאכלו כי אם נקרעו
14	חיים ונשפך דמם וכל החנבים במיניהם יבאו באש או במים
15	עד הם חיים כי הוא משפט בריאתם *vacat* וכל העצים והאבנים
16	והעפר אשר יגאלו ב**טמאת** האדם לגאולי שמן בהם כפי
17	**טמאתם** יטמא הנ[ו]גע בם וכל כלי {מסמר} מסמר או יתד בכותל
18	אשר יהיו עם המת בבית וטמאו ב**טמאת** אחד כלי מעשה
19	*vacat* סרך מושב ערי ישראל על המשפטים האלה להבדיל בין
20a	הטמא לטהור ולהודיע בין הקודש לחול

B. *Translation*

11b No one shall defile himself
12 by eating any living creature or creeping thing from the larvae of the bees to all living
13 creatures which creep in water. And they shall not eat fish unless they have been split
14 alive and their blood has been poured out. And all the locusts in their different kinds shall be thrown into fire or water
15 while they are alive for this is how they are to be eaten. *Vacat*. And all wood, stones,
16 and dust that are defiled with the **uncleanness** of a corpse with stains[25] of oil on them
17 whoever t[ou]ches them shall be defiled according to **their uncleanness**. And every utensil, a nail or a peg in the wall,
18 which is in a house with a dead person shall be defiled in the same way (lit.: with one **uncleanness**) as a working tool.
19 *Vacat*. The rule for the meeting of the cities of Israel according to these laws to separate between
20a the unclean and the clean and to make known the distinction between the holy and the profane.

---

[24] For a discussion of this material cf. J.M. Baumgarten, 'The Essene Avoidance of Oil and the Laws of Purity', *RQ* 6 (1967-69) 183-92; S. B. Hoenig, 'Qumran Rules of Impurities', *RQ* 6 (1967-69) 559-67; and N. Golb, 'The Dietary Laws of the Damascus Document in Relation to Those of the Karaites', *JJS* 8 (1957) 51-69.

[25] On this meaning of גאל cf. Baumgarten, 'Essene Avoidance of Oil', pp. 184-85. For a different view see Hoenig, 'Qumran Rules of Impurities'.

C. Textual Notes

15 Qimron has suggested that בריאתם constitutes 'a phonetic spelling for בְּרִיָתָם "their eating".'[26] I have followed this suggestion in my translation.
16 The reading שמן בהם is based on a suggestion by J.M. Baumgarten.[27]

D. Commentary

This material has not been assigned to the halakhah stratum of the Laws since it largely lacks the formal coherence that characterizes the former group of texts. Nor are there any indications in CD 12,11b-18 par. that would warrant an association of these rules with the communal legislation in the Laws since nothing in these lines can be taken to refer to a particular organized community within Israel. CD 12,11b-20a begins with a prohibition of the form 'אל plus jussive plus 'איש that is reminiscent of Lev. 11,41-45, and CD 12,11b-15a is clearly based on Lev. 11. CD 12,15b-18 deals with the subject of corpse impurity. It seems likely that the second clause dealing with corpse impurity has been linked to the first clause through the catchword טמאה which occurs in CD 12,16-17 and CD 12,18. CD 12,19-20a constitutes a concluding statement that has in the past often been associated with that part of the Laws of CD that precedes this statement. I have discussed the problems involved with the distinction between urban rules and camp rules in the Laws as has been proposed by Rubinstein in the Introduction.[28] It seems more likely to me that CD 12,19-20a constitutes a concluding statement that goes back to a late stage in the literary development of D. The entire passage CD 12,19-23 seems to comprise a chain of concluding statements and headings that are difficult to attribute to the appropriate material. As far as CD 12,19-20a in particular is concerned it is not at all clear which passage or group of passages it serves to conclude. 'The cities of Israel' are not mentioned anywhere in the preceding material. What is more, I have pointed out in the Introduction above that the references to the city in the halakhah stratum of the Laws are often derived from scripture. The reference to the distinction between pure and impure, holy and profane, on the other hand, may refer back to the purity regulations in CD 12,11b-18 immediately preceding this concluding statement. The emphasis on the priestly duty to distinguish between pure and impure, holy and profane draws on Ez. 22,26 where the priests of Jerusalem are accused of having neglected these duties. The same

---

[26] 'Text of CDC', p. 33 n. 3.
[27] 'Essene Avoidance of Oil'.
[28] See pp. 11-12 above.

phrase as is used here in CD 12,19-20a also occurs in the Admonition in CD 6,17b-18a. Yet, it would go beyond the scope of this study to examine the complex issue of the relationship between CD 6,14c-7,4a and the Laws here. Suffice it to say that there seems to be some kind of literary dependence between CD 12,19-20a and CD 6,17b-18a.

It seems likely that the small collection of purity rules in CD 12,11b-18 originated independently and then became incorporated into the corpus of the Laws. The concluding statement in CD 12,19-20a is not easily associated with a particular section of the Laws and is best allocated to the Damascus redaction which aims to present the whole of D as a unified composition.

8.5 The Fragmentary Beginning of CD 15

For the sake of completeness reference must be made to CD 15,1-5a. Parallels in 4QD^e 6 i 20 and 4QD^f 4 i 6-7 are extremely fragmentary and are of limited value. These few lines have not been considered in my analysis of the Laws because of the lack of a context.[29]

8.6 Conclusion

The miscellaneous halakhah presented above comprises a number of isolated pieces of halakhah that have found their way into this collection and were handed down alongside the larger blocks of material that make up the Laws of D. CD 12,1b-2a was shown to be particularly close to the concerns and terminology of 11QT^a 45-47, and it was suggested that it constitutes an interpolation that reflects the same background as those columns of the Temple Scroll. CD 12,2b-6a was identified as an interpolation promoting the message of the Book of Jubilees.

---

[29] E. Qimron has devoted two studies to this difficult passage, cf. E. Qimron, 'שבועה הבנים in the Damascus Covenant 15.1-2' and 'Further Observations on the Laws of Oaths in the Damascus Document 15'.

CHAPTER NINE

CATALOGUE OF TRANSGRESSIONS

One of the portions of the Damascus Document that has not survived in CD but is preserved in 4QD is a section described as a 'Catalogue of Transgressors' in the official edition of 4QD. In an outline published previously the editor, J.M. Baumgarten, referred to this material as a 'catalogue of transgressions'.[1] I have adopted here the earlier terminology. This catalogue is preserved in 4QD^r 2 i 9—ii 21 and has already been discussed in a number of studies before its official publication.[2] In his synoptic description of the contents of D Baumgarten, following an earlier suggestion by Milik, assigns this material to the Admonition rather than the Laws.[3] This placement as part of the Admonition is based on the presence of a call to hearken at the end of this catalogue that strongly resembles similar calls in the Admonition of the document,[4] cf. CD 1,1; 2,2.14 and probably again in 4QD^a 1 a-b 5 if we follow Baumgarten's partial reconstruction of that passage. One might add to this criterion a further characteristic that aligns the conclusion of the catalogue to the Admonition, and that is the soteriological concerns that come to the fore in the last lines of this catalogue. Nevertheless, the placement of the catalogue as part of the Admonition is not entirely clear-cut. Side by side with the features, particularly prominent in the concluding part, that point to an association with the Admonition, the body of the catalogue reflects a number of concerns that are developed more fully in the Laws. This ambiguity is reflected in the developments that can be observed in Baumgarten's successive outlines of the contents of D. In an earlier outline Baumgarten took the catalogue to form part of the Laws whereas he chose to include it as part of the Admonition in his official edition of 4QD.[5]

---

[1] 'Laws of the *Damascus Document* in Current Research', p. 53.
[2] See, for example, J.M. Baumgarten, 'A Fragment on Fetal Life and Pregnancy in 4Q270', in *Pomegranates and Bells. Studies in Biblical, Jewish, and Near Eastern Ritual, Law, and Literature in Honor of Jacob Milgrom* ed. D.P. Wright, D.N. Freedman and A. Hurvitz, Winona Lake: Eisenbrauns, 1995, pp. 445-448 and O. Betz, 'The Qumran Halakhah Text Miqsat Ma'ase Ha-Torah (4QMMT) and Sadducean, Essene, and Early Pharisaic Tradition', in *The Aramaic Bible. Targums in Their Historical Context* ed. D.R.G. Beattie and M.J. McNamara, Sheffield: JSOT Press, 1994, pp. 176-202.
[3] Cf. *Qumran Cave 4. XIII*, pp. 3,12-13.
[4] Cf. *Qumran Cave 4. XIII*, p. 13.
[5] Cf. Baumgarten in Charlesworth ed., *Dead Sea Scrolls*, II, p. 5 and Baumgarten, *Qumran Cave 4. XIII*, p. 3.

CHAPTER NINE

This ambiguity does not characterize the catalogue in its entirety, and it is necessary to distinguish between the concluding lines of the catalogue, which are closely related to the Admonition, and the body of the catalogue which has more in common with the Laws of D. In its present form, and in particular in the light of its conclusion, I would agree with Baumgarten's placement of the catalogue as part of the Admonition. However, the body of the catalogue, that is to say the actual list of transgressions, shares a great deal with the Laws. It seems likely to me that the list of transgressions originated independently, and that the concluding statement was attached at a later stage, probably by the Damascus redactor. I, therefore, divide the catalogue into two parts in the discussion that follows.

9.1 The List of Transgressions

The list of trangressions is found in 4QD^e 2 i 9-ii 17a and reads as follows,

A. *Text*[6]
(4QD^e 2 i 9—ii 17a)

[יעבור או ישל]ח ש[מש]	2 i 9
שע[ירים או ידרוש באוב ובידעונים]	2 i 10
[והר]וחו[ת או אשר יחלל את השם]	2 i 11
[ ]ל[ ]ooooo	2 i 12
	2 i 13
	2 i 14
[oooo ניו]	2 i 15
או אשר עליה שם רע ב[בתוליה בבית]	2 i 16
אביה] או אלמנה אשר [ישכב אחר עמה]	2 i 17
או יק[רב אל אשתו ביום]	2 i 18
[ ]ה או אשר י[ ] [	2 i 19
	2 i 20
[כל]	2 i 21
על קדו[ ] [oo] [	2 ii 1
°את חק[[	2 ii 2
אל מקור [ ] oo[[	2 ii 3
[ו]אל [ ] °°ק[[	2 ii 4
[מחא להרים] את הקודשים ? [	2 ii 5
לחת [לבני אהרון המטעת [הרביעית [	2 ii 6

---

[6] Text and reconstructions are taken from Baumgarten, *Qumran Cave 4. XIII*,pp. 142-45

CATALOGUE OF TRANSGRESSIONS

[   ] ראש[ית כל אשר להם ומעשר בה[מתם מן הבקר   ]   2 ii 7
[וראשית נז אדם והצון ופדו]י בכור הבה[מה הטמאה ופדוי בכ]ור   ]   2 ii 8
[אשר מושב אשם וכל] vacat [הצון וכסף הערכים לפדוי נפשם   ]   2 ii 9
[אין להשיבה וחומשה עליה או י[   ]   2 ii 10
[בשמותם לטמא את רוח קודשו[°   ]   2 ii 11
[או   או ינוגע בנגע צרעת או זוב טמ[אה   ]   2 ii 12
[עמו או ידבר   אשר ינלה את רז עמו לנואים או יקלל א[ת   ]   2 ii 13
[אמתו בהמרותו   סרה על משיחי רוח הקדש ותועה ב[חוזי   ]   2 ii 14
[עם אשר ישכב עם   את פי אל או ישחט בהמה וחיה עבר]ה בה או   ]   2 ii 15
[אחיו או ישכב עם זכר אשה הרה מקיץ דם [או יקרב א[ל בת   ]   2 ii 16
משכבי אשה vacat   2 ii 17a

B. *Translation*

2 i 9 [   ] passes over or sends [out   s]un
2 i 10 [hairy de]mons or enquires from a necromancer or soothsayers
2 i 11 [   ] and the sp[iri]ts or one who profanes the name
2 i 12 [   ]
2 i 13 [   ]
2 i 14 [   ]
2 i 15 [   ]
2 i 16 [or she who has a bad name in] her youth in the house of
2 i 17 [her father   or a widow] with [whom] another lies
2 i 18 [or he ap]proaches his wife on the day
2 i 19 [   ] or the one who [   ]
2 i 20 [   ]
2 i 21 [   ]
2 ii 1 [   ]
2 ii 2 [   ]
2 ii 3 to a source [   ]
2 ii 4 [and] not (or: God; or: towards) [   ]
2 ii 5 [ob]jects to setting aside [the holy things   ]
2 ii 6 [to give] to the sons of Aaron [the fourth (year)] planting
2 ii 7 [the fir]st of all that which is theirs and a tenth of [their] ani[mals from the herd]
2 ii 8 and the flock and a ransom [for the firstborn of the] unclean [ani]mals and a ransom for the [human] fi[rstborn and the first of the wool]
2 ii 9 of the flock and the silver of the priestly estimates for the ransom of their life. *Vacat*. [And any restoration for guilt]
2 ii 10 is not to be returned and a fifth in addition to it or [   ]
2 ii 11 with their names to defile his holy spirit [   ]
2 ii 12 or the one afflicted with the disease *saraʿat* or an im[pure] discharge or]
2 ii 13 he who reveals a secret of his people to the gentiles or profanes [his people or speaks]
2 ii 14 rebellion against those anointed with the holy spirit and apostasy against [his seers of truth when he rebels]
2 ii 15 against the mouth of God; or slaughters an animal carrying a youn[g or he who lies with]

2 ii 16   a pregnant woman, a woman who no longer menstruates [or he who approaches] the daughter of [his brother or lies with a man]
2 ii 17a   as one lies with a woman. *Vacat.*

C. *Commentary*

The following transgressions are clearly preserved in the fragmentary catalogue:[7]

a. 4QD^e 2 i 10

Seeking advice from unorthodox sources such as necromancers and soothsayers, cf. CD 12,3.

b. 4QD^e 2 i 11

Profaning the divine name (which may be a consequence of the transgressions mentioned under a. rather than a separate act), cf. CD 15,3.

c. 4QD^e 2 i 16-18

Various sexual transgressions the exact nature of which is unclear from the remaining material. The Laws of D contain a number of passages that deal with the relation between the sexes, cf. the penal code esp. 4QD^e 7 i 12b-13a and the halakhah dealing with marriage and sexual relations in 4QD^a 12-13 and 4QD^e 4-5 par.

d. 4QD^e 2 ii 5-10

The priests' due. Noteworthy here is the terminology 'sons of Aaron' which links this section with the halakhah dealing with the priesthood in 4QD^a 5 ii par. Compare also the laws on tithing in 4QD^f 2 par. Baumgarten further notes that the same topic is dealt with in 11QT^a 60,3; 4QMMT B 63-64; and 4Q159 1 ii 6.[8]

e. 4QD^e 2 ii 12

Affliction with skin disease or flux, cf. the material on skin disease and flux in 4QD^a 6 i-iii par.[9]

---

[7] For a comparable list cf. Baumgarten, *Qumran Cave 4. XIII*, pp. 12-13.

[8] *Qumran Cave 4. XIII*, p. 146.

[9] Baumgarten has argued that, "those afflicted with skin disease and fluxes [...] were presumably viewed as symptomatic of sin." (Baumgarten in Charlesworth ed., *Dead Sea Scrolls*, II, p. 61), an interpretation preferable to the suggestion by O. Betz of viewing the catalogue as, "a strange mixture of physical defects and moral sins." ('Qumran Halakhah Text', p. 189).

f. 4QD^e 2 ii 13
Revealing a secret of his people to the gentiles, cf. 11QT^a 64,6-9 and the inscription of the En Gedi synagogue [10]

g. 4QD^e 2 ii 13-14
Agitating against the prophets followed by further examples of apostasy, cf. CD 12,3 par. 4QD^f 5 i 18. There is also some terminological overlap with CD 5,21-6,1 par. 4QD^b 2,5-6. However, the context of the occurrence of the same phrase is markedly different in CD 5,21-6,1. There rebellious talk is attributed to the 'builders of the wall' and the context is a historical one. The wider context in CD 5,20-6,1a deals with the activities of the builders of the wall in the period immediately preceding the description of the emergence of a reform movement, the period of wrath (CD 5,20). In the present passage the historical perspective which is characteristic of the Admonition is absent as is the case for the overwhelming majority of stipulations that make up the legal part of the document. Rather than forming part of an historical review rebellious behaviour is mentioned here as a concern of the present.

h. 4QD^e 2 ii 15
Slaughtering pregnant animals, cf. 4QMMT B 38 and 11QT^a 52,5.[11]

i. 4QD^e 2 ii 16-17
Various sexual transgressions are listed here the first of which is intercourse with a pregnant woman. Although in Hebrew two different terms are used it seems likely that this transgression follows the transgression regarding the slaughter of pregnant animals because of the common topic of pregnancy. I take מקיץ דם in l. 16 to refer to a woman who no longer menstruates as a result of being pregnant which appears to be Qimron's understanding of the phrase.[12] On this view מקיץ is taken to be the noun 'end' (קץ) with the preposition מן meaning 'at the end of'. It is possible in Qumran Hebrew to have a *yod* accompanying a *sere*.[13] From what remains of the other sexual

---

[10] See M. Weinfeld, *Organizational Pattern*, p. 25 and Baumgarten, *Qumran Cave 4. XIII*, p. 146.
[11] The scriptural basis for this passage is Dt. 22,6. For comments see Yadin, *Temple Scroll*, I, pp. 312-13 and Baumgarten, 'Fetal Life', p. 445.
[12] Cf. Baumgarten, *Qumran Cave 4. XIII*, p. 146. For a different view compare Baumgarten's translation ("a pregnant woman, causing blood to stir (?)") and explanatory comments *ibidem*, pp. 145-46 as well as his earlier comments in 'Fetal Life', p. 447 and n. 8.
[13] Cf. Qimron, *Hebrew of the Dead Sea Scrolls*, p. 19.

transgressions niece marriage and homosexual relations appear to be at issue following the reconstructions proposed by Baumgarten based on Milik's earlier work. The last transgression, i.e. homosexuality, has been reconstructed on the basis of a fragment of the Damascus Document from Cave 6 (6QD 5).[14] As noted by Baumgarten, this position conforms to one of the elements in Josephus' description of the Essenes.[15] For criticism of the practice of niece marriage cf. CD 5,7b-11, 11QT^a 66,15-17 and 4QHalakhah A (4Q251).[16]

It emerges from this outline that the list of transgressions deals with issues raised elsewhere in the Laws of D, particularly in the halakhah stratum of the Laws, as well as in 11QT and MMT. Two possibilities suggest themselves. On the one hand, the list may constitute an originally independent document that has been incorporated here into the Damascus Document but which was available also to the compilers of the Temple Scroll[17] and 4QMMT. Baumgarten has pointed out parallels to both 11QT and 4QMMT. Moreover, O. Betz has commented on the issues treated in 4QD^e, 4QMMT, and 11QT.[18] On the other hand, it seems equally possible that this catalogue was created as a kind of summary of the topics dealt with in the Laws (skin disease, flux, marriages, etc.) somewhat along similar lines to the list found in CD 6,11b-7,4a. It seems impossible to come to a definite answer on the two possibilities raised above.

If the catalogue existed independently and pre-dated the rest of the Laws it could be crucial for our understanding of the growth of the Laws or at least parts of the collection. The catalogue may have provided a kind of 'skeleton' and a number of more detailed portions of the Laws may have originated by providing flesh for the bones. This is no more than a possibility the probability of which it would be worth testing in the light of further study.

The relationship of our catalogue to Dt. 27 is noteworthy. Baumgarten has observed,

> The genre of the catalogue is broadly comparable to the list of curses (ארור) of particular sinners found in Deuteronomy 27, although the

---

[14] See M. Baillet, *Les 'Petites Grottes' de Qumrân*, pp. 128-31.
[15] 'Fetal Life', p. 447.
[16] See also M. Broshi, 'Anti-Qumranic Polemics in the Talmud' in *Madrid Qumran Congress* ed. Trebolle Barrera and Vegas Montaner, II, pp. 589-600, p. 596.
[17] A number of studies have been devoted to the composite character of the Temple Scroll, cf. A. Wilson and L. Wills, 'Literary Sources of the Temple Scroll', *HTR* 75 (1982) 275-88 and M. Wise, *A Critical Study of the Temple Scroll*.
[18] Betz, 'Qumran Halakhah Text', pp. 188-89.

sins listed here reflect the special concerns of Qumran legists.[19]

The term 'Qumran legists' is not a term I would want to use. It implies sectarian authorship which seems questionable for at least some of the transgressions, especially those also found in 4QMMT and 11QT, both of which I would not class as sectarian compositions, nor do I regard all of the Laws of D as of sectarian origin. Baumgarten is surely right, however, to point to the list of curses in Dt. 27 as a comparable composition.

The relationship of the petite code in CD 6 and the list of transgressors here to the collection of Laws in D appears to be rather comparable to the relationship between the Ten Commandments in Dt. 5 and the list of curses in Dt. 27 to the Law Code in Deuteronomy. In both cases the lists take up concerns expressed at greater length elsewhere.[20] Apart from the formal similarity with Dt. 27 a closeness in terms of content is also notable. Both Dt. 27 and the catalogue of transgressions in 4QD° include a large proportion of sexual offences.

9.2 The Conclusion to the Catalogue

The text of the conclusion to the catalogue reads as follows.

A. *Text*[21]
(4QDᵉ 2 ii 17b-21)

17b vacat עוברי א[ת   [
18 בם חקק אל להעביר בח[רון אפו בק[ץ   ]   [
19 ועתה שמעו לי כל יודעי צדק ו[שימו] תור[ת אל בלבכם ואגלה] [
20 לכם דרכי חיים ונתיבות שחת אפתחה ל[עיניכם ובמוקשי שחת]
21 אל תתפשו ובהבינכם במעשי דור ודור]   [

B. *Translation*
17b *Vacat.* Those who transgress [ ]
18 in them God has laid down to provoke [his furious anger in the tim]e of [ ]
19 And now listen to me all who know righteousness and [place] the law [of God in your heart and I will reveal]

---

[19] *Qumran Cave 4. XIII*, p. 143.
[20] Cf. A.D.H. Mayes, *Deuteronomy*, London: Marshall, Morgan & Scott, 1979, pp. 345-46.
[21] Text and reconstructions are taken from Baumgarten, *Qumran Cave 4. XIII*, p. 145, except the last letter of במעש in l. 21 where my reading differs.

20   to you the ways of life and the paths of destruction, I will open [your eyes, and in the snares of the pit]
21   you shall not be caught, and when you understand his works from generation to generation [   ]

C. *Commentary*
Although it is difficult to arrive at a detailed analysis because of the fragmentary character of the material 4QD^e 2 ii 17b-21 is probably best divided into two parts. Ll. 17b-18 provide a conclusion to the preceding catalogue. Ll. 19-21, on the other hand, bear little relation to the preceding catalogue and are best taken as an introduction to what follows. Ll. 19-21 are made up of a call to hearken that resembles four comparable calls to attention in the Admonition, cf. 4QD^a 1 a-b 5; CD 1,1; 2,2.14.[22] These lines provide a close link to the Admonition on the basis of which Baumgarten placed the catalogue at the end of the Admonition. They are best regarded as marking a new beginning rather than concluding the preceding catalogue. In support of this interpretation it is noteworthy that in all the other passages in D where a comparable call to hearken occurs the call always introduces a new section.

In sum, the catalogue of transgressions is best regarded as forming a part of the Laws of D. The concluding call to hearken which is reminiscent of a number of similar calls to attention in the Admonition is best taken as an introduction to what follows and should not be taken to be a determinative factor in evaluating the preceding catalogue.

---

[22] Such calls to attention are also attested in 4Q298, cf. S. Pfann, 'Maskîl's Address' and M. Kister, 'Commentary'. See also 4Q185, cf. Lange, *Weisheit und Prädestination*, p. 253 n. 83.

CHAPTER TEN

TRANSITIONAL PASSAGE INTRODUCING THE LAWS

In his synoptic outline of the contents of D Baumgarten lists this material under the heading 'The overseer, the priests, introduction to laws', and locates it after the catalogue of transgressions and preceding the rules on the disqualification of priests.[1]

The text provided below is that of 4QD^a based on Baumgarten's edition which includes restorations based on the shorter parallel in 4QD^b.[2] Any of Baumgarten's substantial restorations, disregarding odd letters, that are not based on a parallel in 4QD^b are printed in smaller font in the Hebrew text and the English translation.

A. *Composite Text*[3]
(4QD^a 5 i par. 4QD^b 5 ii)[4]

	[א[ה]קנת ○ ○]	1
	[○ אל אנוס]ם	2
	[ור את המשפטי]ם	3
	[בי לא vacat נם]	4
	[○ [ ] לאחרון [ ]	5
	[ס ע"ם ○ [ ]	6
	[ש[○]	7
[ ]	[ה]לננב כוח ואמיצי [ ]	8
[ ]	[ ] המחזי[קים בשם קודשו הם]	9
[ ]	קשר [נמ]צא[ ] ביהודה כי [יה"]	10
[ד]	[ ] בעומד לישראל [על ענה אביהם] לשוב	11

---

[1] *Qumran Cave 4. XIII*, pp. 3-5.
[2] Cf. *Qumran Cave 4. XIII*, pp. 47-49.
[3] The small group of fragments 4QD^a 5 i c-d the placement of which is tentative deserves mention. Baumgarten points out that the placement of this group of fragments at the end of this column goes back to a suggestion by Milik and is uncertain (*Qumran Cave 4. XIII*, p. 49). He notes some terminological similarities to CD 20,33, cf. *Qumran Cave 4. XIII*, p. 49. One might add that the fragmentary remains of line 3 resemble the Admonition in their historical perspective, cf. the use of the perfect tense "his statutes they declared righteous" (את חוקי הצדיקו ב] [).
[4] The line numbers of the composite text correspond to the line numbers of 4QD^a 5 i.

CHAPTER TEN

```
[           ] vacat ביושבי ירו[שלים] וכול הנשארים [           ]   12
[           ] איש {ל}  לפי רוחו [יקר]בו  ° °[           ]         13
[           ]וח י᾿חק{ו}ו לפי המבקר ו[כו]ל[           ]            14
[           ]° כול שבי ישראל יחהל[כו בם vacat [           ]       15
[           ] ב[נ]י צדוק הכהנים הנה המ[ה [           ]            16
[מדרש ה] תורה האחרון vacat ואלה הח[ו]ק[י]ם למש[כיל]              17
א  [           ]° ° [ח כל] בם לכול ישראל כ' לו יוש[י]ע אל [       ]  18
[           ] בדרכו להתהלך ת[מ]ים [           ]                    19
```

B. *Translation*

1 [   ] she (or: you) shall be innoce[nt   ]
2 [   ] forced not (or: God?) [   ]
3 [   ] the law[s   ]
4 [   ] *Vacat*. He shall not [   ]
5 [   ] the latter [   ]
6 [   ] with (or: a people) [   ]
7 [   ]
8 [   ] and mighty strength through that which is reveal[ed   ]
9 [those who hold] fast to his holy name they [   ]
10 [   ] for in Judah has been found conspiracy [   ]
11 to return [to the sins of their fathers   ] for Israel when it arises [   ]
12 [among (or: against) the inhabitants of Jeru]salem. *Vacat*. And all those who are left over [   ]
13 [every]one according to their spirit [shall draw] near
14 [ ] they shall leave according to (the decision) of the overseer and [   ]
15 [they shall wa]lk in them. *Vacat*. All the converts of Israel [   ]
16 [the so]ns of Zadok the priests behold the[y]
17 [the] latter [interpretation of the] law. *Vacat*. And these are the statu[te]s for the wise lea[der]
18 [   ] in them for all Israel for [God] will not sa[ve   ] all [   ]
19 [   ] in his way to walk perfec[tly   ]

C. *Commentary*

This material has no parallel in CD and combines features typical of the Admonition and the Laws in a unique manner. Because of the fragmentary state of this material it is not possible to offer anything but a tentative assessment of its contents. What is preserved of 4QD[a] 5 i 1-7 is very fragmentary indeed, and I will therefore limit my comments to ll. 8-19.

In common with the Admonition and a number of redactional passages in the Laws this material displays the following features:
a. A polemical tone, note the reference to 'conspiracy' (קשׁר) in l. 10.
b. A concern with the end time and salvation, cf. the occurrence of

the root ישע in l. 18. Such concerns are absent from the bulk of the Laws but prominent in the Admonition. Note further the references to 'all those left over' (כול הנשארים) in l. 12, to the arrival of one or several future figures in l. 11, and the partially preserved reference to salvation in l. 19.

c. The expression 'the converts of Israel' (שבי ישראל) in l. 15 is a term highly characteristic of the Admonition where it occurs in CD 4,2; 6,5; and 8,16. A related expression 'those who turn back from transgression' (שבי פשע) is found in CD 2,5. By contrast, this expression never occurs in the Laws of D.

d. The expression 'the sons of Zadok' (בני צדוק) is again reminiscent of the Admonition where it is found in CD 3,24 and 4,4. It never occurs in the Laws. The terminology preferred for the priests in the Laws is either simply '(the)priest(s)' (כוהן), e.g. CD 16,14; 9,13.15; 13,2.5; 14,3.5.6; 4QD^a 6 i 2.4.9.10; 11,8; 4QD^c 4,5; 7 i 16; 4QD^g 1 i 8 or 'the sons of Aaron' (בני אהרון), e.g. 4QD^a 5 ii 5.8.12; 6 i 13; 4QD^e 2 ii 6; and 4QD^g 1 ii 2. Particularly noteworthy is the multiple use of the terminology 'the sons of Aaron' in the legislation on the disqualification of priests in 4QD^a 5 ii, the very next column of 4QD^a.

e. The language used in l. 9, for example, suggests an admonitory purpose. For an implicit exhortation to be faithful to His holy name that is reminiscent of the language employed in l. 9 cf. CD 20,20.34.

f. Finally, the reference to נגלה in l. 8 reflects the claim to have received special divine revelation that is characteristic of the Admonition, cf. CD 3,13-14.

Taken collectively this evidence points strongly towards regarding this material as forming part of the exhortatory discourse introducing the Laws. 4QD^a 5 i 13-14.17b are at odds with this overall picture, however, and mitigate against associating this passage exclusively with the Admonition.

Firstly, although only a number of words survive, it is fairly clear that these lines contain legislation dealing with the day to day life of the community, in particular the procedure of entry into the community.[5] The Hebrew verbs used in ll. 13-14 (קר[ב]; רחק) are used with reference to admission into the community in 1QS 6,16.[6] What

---

[5] This topic has led Vermes to entitle his translation of 4QD^a 5 i 'Initiation Rules' (*Complete Dead Sea Scrolls*, p. 146). On the interpretation offered here this title aptly describes certain elements within this text rather than the text as a whole.

[6] This terminological correspondence has been noted already by Baumgarten, cf. *Qumran Cave 4. XIII*, p. 49.

is more, the overseer who is mentioned in 4QDᵃ 5 i 14 is attributed a key role in the legislation dealing with entry into the community in the Laws of D, cf. CD 15,5b-16,2a; 13,12b-13. Further, part of the lengthy sections on the admission process in CD 15,5b-16,6a is attested in 4QDᵃ 8 i. This MS contains an improved text of CD 15,15 in 4QDᵃ 8 i 6 where it reads "and according to his knowledge he shall draw near" (ולפי דעתה יקרב). This formulation is particularly close to 4QDᵃ 5 i 13-14 and leaves little doubt that the latter refers to entry into the community.

Secondly, 4QDᵃ 5 i 13-14.17b includes references to the offices of the wise leader ([מש]כיל) and the overseer (מבקר), both familiar from the legal part of the Damascus Document, cf. CD 12,21; 13,22 for the former and CD 15,8.11.14; 9,18.19.22; 13,6.7.13.16; 14,8.11.13; 4QDᵃ 7 iii 3; 11,16; 4QDᶠ 3,14 for the latter. Neither office is referred to in the Admonition. A note of caution is required here, however, since the reading of the letter *sin* in [מש]כיל is no more than a possible reading.

Finally, the formulation used in 4QDᵃ 5 i 17b closely resembles the rubrics found at various points in the legal part of the Damascus Document, cf. especially CD 12,20-21 and 13,22 where a phrase virtually identical to the one partially preserved in l. 17b recurs. Baumgarten's reading and partial restoration of the possible reference to the wise leader in this line is almost certainly based on the recurring phrase in the passages cited here. Nevertheless, even if we disregard the reference to the wise leader at the end of this line, the words preceding it suffice to show the resemblance of this phrase with CD 12,20-21 and 13,22.

In sum, this fragmentary passage combines vocabulary, style, and concerns from the Admonition and the Laws, and it is difficult to see how 4QDᵃ 5 i 13-14.17b relates to the remainder of this passage. I would, therefore, attribute it to the work of the Damascus redactor. Baumgarten's placement of this material as well as the section containing the catalogue of transgressions in 4QDᵉ 2 i-ii at the end of the Admonition and the very beginning of the legal part respectively ties in with our results to some degree since these portions of 4QD have been shown to contain material that may have formed something of a bridge between both parts of the work. This judgment must of necessity be a tentative one because the fragmentary nature of the passage does not allow any firm conclusions.

CHAPTER ELEVEN

EXPULSION CEREMONY AND THE END OF THE DOCUMENT

Following the penal code as preserved in 4QD is a section that can be described as the end of the Damascus Document since the end of this section constitutes the end of the Damascus Document as attested in the Cave 4 MSS. This material is preserved in MSS D^a and D^e. The end of the document is marked by six empty ruled lines and a bottom margin clearly visible in 4QD^e 7 ii. I have produced a composite text drawing on both MSS.

A. *Composite Text*[1]
(4QD^a 11; 4QD^e 7 i-ii)

כל אי[ש] אשר [ ] יבוא וידיעהו לכהן [המ]ופקד	0
על הרבים וקבל את משפטו מרצונו כאשר אמר ביד	1
מושה על הנפש אשר תחטה בשגגה אשר יביאו את	2
חטתו ואת אשמו ועל ישראל כתוב אלכה לי	3
אל קצי השמים ולו אריח בריח ניחוחכם ובמקום אחר	4
ובמקום [אח]ר כתוב קרעו לבבכם ואל בנדיכם	5*
כתוב לשוב אל אל בבכי ובצום וכול המואס במשפטים	5
האלה על פי כול החוקים הנמצאים בתורת מושה לו יחשב	6
בכול בני אמתו כי נעלה נפשו ביסורי הצדק vacat ובמרד מלפני	7
הרבים ישתלח וידבר בו הכוהן המופקד [ע]ל הרבים וענה	8
[וא]מר ברוך את הכול און הו ובידיך הכול ועושה הכול אשר יסדחה	9
[ע]מים למשפחותיהם ולשנונת לאומותם ותתעם בתהו ולו	10
(ולו) דרך ובאבותינו בחרתה לזרעם נתתה חוקי אמתכה	11
ומשפטי קודשכה אשר יעשה האדם וחיה ונבולות הנבלתה	12
לנו אשר את עובריהם ארותה ואנו עם פדוחכה וצון מרעיתדה	13
אתה ארותה את עובריהם ואנו הקימונו ויצא המשתלח והאיש	14
אשר יוכל מהונם ואשר ידרוש שלומו ו{המשתלח} ואשר יאות עמו	15
ונכחב דברו על פני המבקר בחרת ושלים משפטו וכול {יו}	16
[יושבי] המחנות יקהלו בחודש השלישי ואררו את הנוטה ימין	17
[ושמאול מן ה]תורה והזה פרוש המשפטים אשר יעשו בכול קץ	18
[הפקודה] את אשר [יפ]קידו [בכו]ל קצי החרון ומסעיהם לכול	19
יושב [מ]חניהם וכול י[ושב ערי]הם הנה הכול כ[תוב] על מדרש התורה	20

---

[1] The line numbers of the composite text correspond to the line numbers of 4QD^a 11 with a number of words preceding 4QD^a 11 added from 4QD^e and referred to as line number zero.

האחרון 21

B. *Translation*
0 Any[one] who [ ] shall enter and make it known to the priest [in cha]rge
1 over the many, and he shall receive his judgment with goodwill as he has said through
2 Moses concerning the one who sins unintentionally that they shall bring
3 his sin-offering and his guilt-offering. And concerning Israel it is written, I will depart
4 to the ends of heaven and I will not smell the sweet scent of your soothing odours. And in another place
5* And in [anoth]er place it is written, Rend your hearts and not your garments.
5 it is written to return to God with weeping and with fasting. And anyone who despises these
6 judgments according to all the statutes found in the law of Moses shall not be counted
7 among all the sons of his truth for his soul loathes all the instructions of righteousness. When he rebels before
8 the many he shall be sent away. And the priest in charge [ov]er the many shall speak concerning him, answer, and
9 say, Blessed are you, almighty God, everything is in your hands, (you are) the maker of everything, (it is) you who has established
10 [n]ations according to their families, and tongues for their tribes. And you led them astray in a wilderness with no
11 path. And you chose our fathers and to their descendants you gave your true statutes
12 and your holy laws which humankind must act upon and thereby live. You set up boundaries
13 for us, those who transgress them you have cursed. But we are the people of your deliverance and the flock of your pasture.
14 You have cursed those who transgress them, but we have upheld (the correct observance of the law.) And the person being sent away shall depart. Anyone
15 who eats from their food, or the one who seeks his well-being, or the one who agrees with him
16 his case shall be written down with ink in front of the overseer, and his case shall be complete. And all
17 [the inhabitants of] the camps shall assemble in the third month and curse the one who turns aside to the right
18 [or to the left from the] law. And this is the exact statement of the ordinances which they shall act upon in all the time of

---

* Supralinear in 4QD^a 11.

19 [the visitation with which they shall be visi]ted [during al]l the periods of wrath and their travels for all
20 the inhabitants of the [c]amps and all the in[habitants of] their [cities]. Behold everything is wri[tten] according to the latter interpretation of the
21 law.

C. *Textual Notes*

0 Baumgarten tentatively suggests reading and reconstructing [יחיס]ר for the *lacuna* in the centre of this line which is based on the first word of 4QD^c 7 i 16.[2]

5* This superlinear line seems to preserve clear traces of the *resh* in [אח]ר which is the reading adopted here. Baumgarten does not include this word in his transcription of the superlinear writing in 4QD^a and appears to take the remains of the letter to belong to the final *mem* of מקום.[3]

5 4QD^c 7 i 19 reads וכתוב 'and it is written' for the first word in this line and seems to lack the third occurrence of the formula 'and in another place it is written'.

7 4QD^a 11,7 reads במרד whereas 4QD^c 7 i 21 has a large *vacat* followed by וב[מ]רד. I have followed 4QD^c's text here because in 4QD^a 11,7 במרד follows on rather abruptly from what precedes.

11 The scribe of MS A repeated the first word of the last line (ולו), presumably a simple dittographical error.

16 Baumgarten reads כחרת but a *beth* seems more likely. Baumgarten notes the possibility of reading a *beth* in his comments[4] and suggests the translation 'with a graving tool'. He draws attention to a comparable expression that occurs in 1QH 1,24.

20 According to Baumgarten's text and reconstruction there does not appear to be sufficient space in 4QD^a 11,20 for the word [כ]תוב.[5] The photograph of 4QD^a 11 reproduced on Plate XIV reveals that l. 20 is only fragmentarily preserved and it is difficult to be certain of its reading. Traces of the *kaph* seem to be preserved in 4QD^c 7 ii 14 although the reading is not certain.[6]

D. *Commentary*

It is not easy to determine where the epilogue to the penal code ends and where the expulsion ceremony begins or indeed the precise relationship of both sections to each other. Although it is difficult to be sure about the beginning of a new section following the penal code it

---

[2] *Qumran Cave 4. XIII*, p. 163. In the recent translation by Vermes (*Complete Dead Sea Scrolls*, p. 152) the *lacuna* is not noted which considerably affects the meaning of the passage.
[3] Cf. *Qumran Cave 4. XIII*, p. 76 and Plate XIV.
[4] *Qumran Cave 4. XIII*, p. 78.
[5] *Qumran Cave 4. XIII*, p. 76.
[6] See the comments in Baumgarten, *Qumran Cave 4. XIII*, p. 167.

seems fairly clear that with 4QD^c 7 i 16 we have left behind the penal code proper.[7]

This text may be divided into five sections.

a. ll. 0-5a Admonition to accept one's judgment willingly

Ll. 0-5a are here included in the discussion of what follows although they may also function as an epilogue to what precedes. Ll. 5b-14b follow on rather naturally from ll. 0-5a, and the title 'the priest in charge over the many' (הכוהן המופקד על הרבים) occurs in l. 0 and l. 8, thus constituting something of a link between ll. 0-5a and ll. 5b-14b. The latter considerations led me to include ll. 0-5a with what follows.

The text begins with the instruction for the priest in charge over the many to be informed about something or someone specified in *lacuna* in line 0 of the composite text. We encountered a similar title in CD 14,6-7 (הכהן אשר יפקד ברואש[8] הרבים) where it was identified as part of the Serekh redaction.[9] It seems likely that both occurrences of this title in the present text (l. 0 and l. 8) also reflect the communal organization as described in the Community Rule rather than the movement as it emerges from the communal rules in D. We have noted earlier that the designation the many (הרבים) occurs with great frequency as a designation for the community in 1QS 5-9 whereas the most common designation for the community in the communal rules of the Damascus Document is the camp (מחנה), and the official in authority in the camps is the overseer (המבקר). It is noteworthy that the title overseer occurs also in l. 16 of this text, and a reference to the camps is found in the following line (l. 17). It seems likely to me, therefore, that both phrases in ll. 0 and 8 that refer to the priest in charge over the many go back to the work of the Serekh redactor. We have encountered traces of such redactional activity at several instances including in the preceding penal code.

The instruction to inform the priest in charge over the many is

---

[7] For a slightly different delineation cf. Vermes, *Dead Sea Scrolls in English*, 1995, pp. 115-18. In the most recent edition of his translation (*Complete Dead Sea Scrolls*, pp. 150-53) Vermes treats the penal code and the end of D together. Furthermore, Baumgarten has remarked with regard to ll. 0-5a of the Composite Text, "The following text occurs at the end of the penal code ...", 'A "Scriptural" Citation', p. 95. This statement seems to imply that Baumgarten understands these lines as going with the preceding penal code.

[8] This reading is based on 4QD^b 9 v 11.

[9] See p. 136 above.

followed by an admonition to accept one's punishment and a string of four references to scripture. The admonition to accept one's allotted punishment would, on the one hand, follow naturally after the penal code which prescribes the penalties to be inflicted for diverse transgressions. On the other hand, it is equally possible to take this admonition as a prologue to the following expulsion ceremony, i.e. the one who is inflicted with the punishment of expulsion is here being encouraged to accept his fate.

The four references to scripture are each introduced with an introductory formula. This string of citations is distinct from the references to scripture in the halakhah stratum of the Laws since here one citation follows upon the next without any halakhic exposition. In the halakhic material, by contrast, the halakhic exposition that is based on the references to scripture lies at the heart of each exegetical passage.

The first reference to scripture likens the willing acceptance of punishment to the offering of a sin-offering or a guilt-offering as legislated in Lev. 4-5.[10] The second reference to scripture is introduced as if it were a citation but the exact wording is nowhere to be found in scripture. Baumgarten has shown that this second 'citation' should be seen as the result of scriptural exegesis drawing on Dt. 30,4 and Lev. 26,31.[11] Thirdly, we have a supralinear citation of Joel 2,13, and finally a reference to Joel 2,12.

Of these four references to scripture only the first can, it seems to me, fruitfully be connected with what precedes, i.e. the admonition to accept one's punishment. The last three references seem to have been appended to the first citation with little regard for its overall context. Although the first two scriptural references share the subject matter of 'sacrifice' it is only the latter that display a critical attitude towards sacrifice. The first conveys the impression of a neutral if not positive attitude to sacrifice.[12] It seems likely that the last three references to scripture gradually came to be added to the first. They may each go back to different authors or, equally, they may go back to a single author who worked in a 'stream of consciousness' fashion adding more references as they occurred to him or her. Whether the last three references to scripture go back to one or several writers the introductory formulae that are used are rather appropriate for a process of gradual additions, cf. esp. ll. 4-5 and 5* (ובמקום אחר כתוב).

---

[10] Cf. Baumgarten, 'A "Scriptural" Citation', p. 96.
[11] 'A "Scriptural" Citation', p. 96.
[12] Baumgarten seems to see a connection between the second reference to scripture and the overall context, cf. 'A "Scriptural" Citation', p. 96.

b. ll. 5b-14b Expulsion ceremony

In delineating this second section to run from l. 5b (וכול המואס) to l. 14b (המשתלח ויצא) I follow Milik.¹³ This lengthy section seems to describe a ceremony for expelling anyone who despises the law of Moses and presumably the interpretation of the law as favoured by the community behind this text.

It is difficult to determine exactly how this expulsion ceremony relates to the preceding penal code. At first sight one could argue that since permanent expulsion is the most severe punishment that is mentioned in the penal code this ceremony was intended to be used when such a punishment was applied. As the text stands at the moment, however, l. 5b of the composite text above specifies that the candidate to be expelled in this ceremony is one who 'despises these judgments'. It seems, therefore, that the rather more fundamental issue of challenging the authority of the community's scripturally derived laws is at stake here. This impression is confirmed by the contents of the prayer that lies at the heart of the ceremony and emphasizes God's punishment of transgressors of the law. Finally, the formula used to refer to expulsion in the penal code 'he shall leave and not return' (יצא ולוא ישוב עוד) as well as the lesser penalties for less severe infringements ring of prompt action. It seems unlikely that offenders were punished only once a year in a ceremony in the third month, cf. l. 17 below. Whereas it is conceivable, on the other hand, that an annual expulsion ceremony took place to deal with the severe cases of betrayal by despising the laws of the community which is tantamount to challenging the law of Moses, cf. ll. 6.11-12. Such a public ceremony would serve at the same time to punish the traitor as well as to admonish everybody else to be faithful. Finally, as far as its literary function at the end of the document is concerned this ceremony and the warnings expressed in the course of it serve as a fitting conclusion to the document as a whole.

The bulk of this section is taken up by a prayer¹⁴ to be pronounced by the priest in charge over the many.¹⁵ The prayer begins

---

¹³ 'Milkî-sedeq and Milkî-resaʿ', p. 136.

¹⁴ For an excellent methodological survey of liturgical material from Qumran see Eileen Schuller, 'Prayer, Hymnic, and Liturgical Texts from Qumran' in *The Community of the Renewed Covenant* ed. Ulrich and VanderKam, pp. 153-71. See also E. Glickler Chazon, 'Prayers from Qumran and Their Historical Implications', *DSD* 1 (1994) 264-85. Of the seven form critical categories distinguished by Chazon the present prayer seems to fall into the second category 'ceremonial liturgies', at least in its present context.

¹⁵ For a discussion of this title cf. my comments on l. 0 above. The formula introducing the prayer in 4QDᵃ occurs frequently in the scrolls, cf. J.M. Baumgarten, 'A New Qumran Substitute for the Divine Name and Mishnah Sukkah 4.5', *JQR* 83

with a hymnic section[16] (ll. 9b-10a) and continues with a short historical review of God's dealings with Israel in the past (ll. 10b-13a). This review culminates in God's gift of the law. The prayer ends (ll.13b-14a) with a recollection of how God cursed transgressors of the law in the past and an affirmation that the community represented by the 'we' in the prayer upheld the correct observance of the law. Our section ends with the words ויצא המשתלח which seem to constitute an instruction to be adhered to in the expulsion ceremony, i.e. the expelled person is to leave after the foregoing prayer has been spoken.

The hymnic section in ll. 9b-10a probably comprises traditional liturgical material in praise of God that has been incorporated here. It shares much with other liturgical passages in the scrolls, cf., for example, 1QM 10,8-12.

Another reference to the many which should also be assigned to the Serekh redaction occurs in ll. 7b-8a. The brief statement of ll. 7b-8a occurs after a large *vacat* in 4QD^c 7 i 21. 4QD^a 11,7, by contrast, lacks both the *vacat* and the conjunction and reads instead simply במרד. 4QD^a's text is rather abrupt at this point which may speak in favour of identifying redactional activity here.

A number of concepts and expressions used in the historical review part of the prayer are familiar from the Admonition of the Damascus Document.

i. Cf. Ll. 10-11   ותתעם בתהו ולו דרך
   and CD 1,15   ויתעם בתוהו לא דרך.

Both passages are based on Job 12,24 and Ps. 107,40. The present passage follows the original meaning of scripture more closely in that it has God as the subject of the verb תעה. In CD 1,15, on the other hand, it is the scoffer (איש הלצון) who leads Israel into a pathless waste.

Even though both passages are ultimately derived from scripture it seems likely to me that the writer responsible for this phrase in the present passage would have been aware of its use in CD 1,15 or *vice versa*. The probability of a conscious link between this prayer and the Admonition increases in the light of two further correspondences.

(1992) 1-5, p. 3 and Schuller, 'Prayer', p. 163 n. 40. See also M. Abegg, 'Messianic Hope and 4Q285: A Reassessment', *JBL* 113/1 (1994) 81-91, esp. p. 83. Abegg lists numerous examples to which the present text should now be added.

[16] See Baumgarten, 'A New Qumran Substitute for the Divine Name'.

ii. Cf. L. 12 ...אשר יעשה האדם וחיה
   and CD 3,15-16 ...אשר יעשה האדם וחיה

Again the phrase shared by both texts is derived from scripture, in this case Lev. 18,5 and Ez. 20, 11.13.21.

iii. Ll. 12-13 of the prayer in the composite text refer to God's act of setting up boundaries. Boundaries and removers of the boundary are a frequent theme in the Admonition. In CD 1,16, for example, one of the actions of the scoffer is described as removing the boundaries which the ancestors had set up in their inheritance (ולסיע גבול אשר גבלו ראשנים בנחלתם). Furthermore, both CD 5,20 and CD 19,15-16 apply the phrase removers of the boundary (מסיגי גבול) to past apostates and traitors. This phrase is taken from Hos. 5,10 and in CD 19,15-16 it is part of a citation of this verse from the book of Hosea. Finally, CD 20,25 contains a warning against those who have broken through the boundary of the law (פרצו את גבול התורה). Thus, the symbolism of the law as the boundary and of transgressors as removers of the boundary which is rather prevalent in the Admonition is taken up again in this text at the end of our document.

These examples provide ample evidence to show the close relationship of the historical review in ll. 10b-13a to the Admonition.

c. ll. 14c-16a Treatment of those who fail to ostracise the expelled member

The material that immediately follows after the description of the expulsion ceremony deals with the treatment of those who fail to keep apart from expelled former community members. These lines are characterized by a change in terminology. Whereas the person in charge of the procedures thus far was called the priest in charge over the many l. 16 introduces the title the overseer (חמבקר).

The procedure described here is in some respects reminiscent of the procedure prescribed in the law of testimony in CD 9,16b-10,3. In both cases the overseer keeps a written record of misdeeds, and both passages use the expression שלם/שלים משפטו. In the present case the use of the latter expression makes little practical sense, however. Are we to understand that someone who associates with an expelled former member is merely recorded in writing by the overseer and thus his case is complete? It seems probable that parts of this passage have been lost and that at some stage some further specifications preceded the expression שלים משפטו. What is more, the juncture from l. 14b to 14c is rather harsh. One would have expected a concluding statement bringing the description of the expulsion ceremony to an end or a prohibition for anyone to mix with those expelled. Instead the text goes on, rather abruptly, with the case of someone who has infringed a prohibition that has not been spelled out. It seems likely that a prohibition along the lines of 1QS 5,14b-20a and 7,24b-25, passages that share a number of terminological links with the present passage, has been lost here. 1QS 7,24b-25 comes at the end of the penal code in 1QS and rules that anyone who mixes with a traitor is to be expelled. A relationship with 1QS 5,14b-20a is further indicated by the plural suffix in מהונם in l. 15 (cf. 1QS 5,16) as has been observed by Baumgarten.[17]

On the basis of these observations it seems to me that ll. 14c-16a draw on a number of passages both from the Laws of the Damascus Document and the Community Rule, and that parts of this material have been lost.

d. ll. 16b-18a The annual assembly of the members of the camps in the third month

These lines refer to an annual festival and probably provide the overall context for the expulsion ceremony described in ll. 5b-14b. However, in its immediate context this note on an annual gathering follows on abruptly after משפטו in l. 16. This harsh transition lends further support to the possibility raised above that some material has dropped out, and that ll. 14c-16a constitute the incomplete remains of an originally clearer passage.

Attention needs to be drawn, moreover, to the reference to the camps (המחנות) in l. 17. Unlike the designation the many which was used twice to refer to the group behind this text, the choice of the camps brings us again much closer to the terminology found predominantly in the communal rules in the Damascus Document. We saw a similar shift from using the title the priest in charge over the many in l. 0 and l. 8 to the use of the title the overseer in the preceding passage in l. 16. Again the latter title is familiar from the communal rules where it is associated with a position of authority in the camp.

e. ll. 18b-20 The end of the document

These lines present a concluding statement not only to the immediately preceding passage but to the Damascus Document as a whole.

---

[17] *Qumran Cave 4. XIII*, p. 78. For a perceptive commentary on 1QS 5, 10b-20a see Knibb, *Qumran Community*, pp. 109-12. For a comparison with 1Cor. 5,11 see K. Berger, *Jesus and the Dead Sea Scrolls. The Truth under Lock and Key?*, Louisville: Westminster John Knox Press, 1995, p. 64. Berger seems to misunderstand the reference to the third month in l. 17 as referring to an expulsion ceremony every three month.

As has been pointed out by Baumgarten 4QD^a 11 is followed by an empty column.[18] The last words of this passage as preserved in 4QD^e 7 ii are, moreover, followed by six empty ruled lines.[19] These features attested in two different MSS indicate that we are dealing with the end of the document.[20] These lines resemble the concerns of the Admonition by emphasizing the division of time into a sequence of periods.

J.T. Milik has drawn attention to a number of striking correspondences between the language used at the end of the Damascus Document and 1QS 2,25-3,6.[21] There is no need to repeat here all the examples given by Milik. However, I would like to draw attention to one further correspondence between these two texts that is not specifically spelled out by Milik, and this one example may suffice to illustrate Milik's case here.

Cf. l. 7	כי נעלה נפשו ביסורי הצדק
and 1QS 2,26b-3,1a	כיא נעלה נפשו ביסורי דעת.

Milik concludes from his comparison that both texts should be associated with the annual Essene festival of covenant renewal as described more fully in 1QS 1,16-3,12. This suggestion does seem very plausible especially in the light of the reference to an annual gathering in l. 17 of the composite text. Whereas I would fully agree with Milik about the influence of traditions and traditional language from the covenant renewal festival on our text, I would further like to emphasize that this complex of traditions is not the only influence that shaped the end of the Damascus Document.

It seems to me that the text discussed here goes back *in its present form* to a late stage in the composition of the Laws of the Damascus Document. Such a late date is indicated by the numerous links of this material with other parts of the Damascus Document, including the Admonition, and with the Community Rule. The links with the Admonition outlined above could conceivably be explained as resulting from both texts using the same scriptural passages or from parts of the Admonition drawing on the present passage. However,

---

[18] Cf. Baumgarten, *Qumran Cave 4. XIII*, Plate XIV.

[19] Cf. Baumgarten, *Qumran Cave 4. XIII*, Plate XXXV.

[20] H. Stegemann has suggested that ll. 20b-21 preserve the title of the Damascus Document, cf. *Die Essener, Qumran, Johannes der Täufer und Jesus*, p. 78. It is not clear to me why we should read ll. 20b-21, Stegemann's suggested title, in isolation from ll. 18b-20a.

[21] 'Milkî-ṣedeq and Milkî-reša'', p. 136. See also B. Nitzan, '4QBerakhot^{a-r} (4Q286-290): A Covenantal Ceremony in the Light of Related Texts', *RQ* 16 (1995) 487-506. Note that Nitzan uses the earlier nomenclature when referring to the MSS of 4QD. For a conversion table see Baumgarten, *Qumran Cave 4. XIII*, p. 1.

the presence in our text of a number of expressions characteristic of the Community Rule—notably the use of the designation the many (הרבים) in ll. 0 and 8—makes it seem likely that this material goes back to a late stage in the literary growth of the Damascus Document. These links with the Admonition may therefore be assigned to the work of the Damascus redactor. Although the text as we now have it looks like a rather late compilation, a number of earlier traditions seem to have been incorporated. Thus, apart from including material that is reminiscent of and probably reflects the same background as parts of the Admonition of the Damascus Document and 1QS three further blocks of tradition have been incorporated into our text. Firstly, we already mentioned the influence of traditions associated with the covenant renewal festival on our passage. Such traditions also lie behind 1QS 1,16-3,12. It seems likely that both 1QS and D are drawing on and incorporating older material associated with the covenant renewal tradition. Secondly, traditional liturgical material influenced parts of the prayer by the priest in charge over the many. Finally, the use of terminology familiar from the communal rules in D such as the overseer (המבקר) and the camp (המחנה) indicates the presence of a certain amount of communal legislation in this text.

In conclusion, the end of the Damascus Document as preserved in 4QD[a and e] appears to be a late compilation that is made up of a number of disparate passages. A number of abrupt transitions were noted as well as evidence of redactional activity both by the Serekh redactor as well as the Damascus redactor whose work is evident in the close relationship of this text to the Admonition. It was argued, finally, that the expulsion ceremony included here deals with the severe case of anyone challenging the authority of the law, both the law of Moses as well as the laws of the community expounded previously.

CHAPTER TWELVE

CONCLUSION

My analysis of the Laws of the Damascus Document has identified two main literary strata, a number of miscellaneous laws and traditions as well as a considerable amount of redactional activity. The main results of this study may now be summarized as follows.

12.1 Halakhah[1]

The presentation of the material that has been assigned to the halakhah stratum in the Laws was divided into three sub-sections: halakhic exposition of scripture in CD par. 4QD, halakhic exposition lacking an explicit reference to scripture in CD, and halakhah in the additional legal material from 4QD. The following passages have been attributed to this stratum:

a. Halakhic Exposition of Scripture in the Laws of CD par. 4QD
CD 16,6b-9   The Binding Oath
CD 16,10-12   Women's Oaths
CD 16,13-17a; 9,1 par.   Freewill Offerings
(tentatively also CD 16,17b-20)
CD 9,2-6a   The Requirement of Reproof
CD 9,8b-10a   Oaths
CD 10,14-11,18b   The Sabbath Code
CD 11,18c-21a   Preserving the Purity of the Altar

b. Halakhic Exposition Lacking an Explicit Reference to Scripture
CD 10,10b-13   Purification with Water
CD 12,6b-11a   Restrictions on Relations with Gentiles

c. Halakhah in the Additional Legal Material in 4QD
4QD^a 5 ii par.   Torot: The Disqualification of Priests
4QD^a 6 i-iii par.   Torot: Skin Disease, Fluxes, and Childbirth
4QD^a 6 iii a. iii-iv par.   Agricultural Halakhah
4QD^e 3 i
4QD^f 2 par.
4QD^d 8 i-ii par.   Ritual Defilement and Purification
4QD^e 4 par.   The Suspected Adulteress and the Betrothed Slave Woman

---

[1] For clarifications on my use of the term halakhah cf. p. 25 above.

4QD^f 3 par. The Jubilee Year, Transvestism, Ethical Standards in Business, and Marriage Arrangements

This stratum of halakhah contains halakhic material of a general orientation that does not presuppose a particular organized community within Israel. Instead, it has a national frame of reference. The halakhah stratum is further characterized by a strong basis in scripture, and caution needs to be exercised in attempts at using this material as evidence for the life of a particular community. Moreover, the halakhah stratum displays a considerable amount of formal cohesion with a preference for headings of the type 'על plus x', the formulation 'אל plus jussive plus איש', as well as explicit references to scripture introduced by introductory formulae.

The majority of the halakhot reflect priestly concerns. A priestly background is particularly evident in the material on priestly disqualifications and skin disease from 4QD for which I have adopted the term *torot*. These sections deal very obviously with issues concerning the priesthood. However, other parts of the halakhah stratum also reflect priestly concerns such as the agricultural halakhah, for example. The great majority of regulations dealing with agricultural matters relate to the time of the harvest and the religious obligations required at that time. It seems likely that priestly groups lie behind such halakhot.

In terms of form, frame of reference, and terminology the material that forms part of the halakhah stratum of the Laws shares a great deal with other halakhic works from the corpus of the scrolls such as 4QMMT, 4Q159 Ord^a,[2] and 11QT.

It was further noted that the material that forms part of the halakhah stratum shows few signs of redactional activity and updating in contrast to the communal legislation. Rather, the halakhic material appears to have been preserved and handed on rather more faithfully. A number of reasons suggest themselves for this difference in the transmission of halakhah and communal legislation. Firstly, the need to update communal rules is tied up closely with the issue of power. It is easy to see how passages dealing with matters of authority would be regularly up-dated. Secondly, in terms of terminology communal legislation is out of date quickly whereas it is conceivable that material preserving halakhic traditions may be preserved as it stands over a longer period of time.

---

[2] See my paper '4Q Ord^a (4Q159) and the Laws of the Damascus Document' in the Proceedings of the International Congress *The Dead Sea Scrolls. Fifty Years After Their Discovery*, Jerusalem: Israel Exploration Society, forthcoming.

It seems likely that the material in this stratum comprises traditional halakhic exegesis that was cherished and handed on in priestly circles, and that these traditions were shared by, though not confined to, the community reflected in the communal legislation.

12.2 Community Organization

The second major literary stratum in the Laws comprises communal legislation. The following material has been attributed to this stratum:

CD 15,5b-6a.7b-16,2a par.	Admission into the Community by Swearing the Oath of the Covenant
CD 9,10b-16a par.	Property Lost or Stolen from the Camp'
CD 9,16b-10,3 par.	Witnesses
CD 10,4-7a par.	The Judges of the Congregation
CD 12,22b-23a; 13,1b-7a.b.12b-13. 15b-16a.20 par.	The Organization of Individual Camps
CD 14,3-6b.8b-12a.12c-18a par.	The Organization of All the Camps
CD 14,18b.20-22; 4QD^a 10 i-ii and 4QD^r 7 i par.	The Penal Code

The material that has been attributed to the community organization stratum in the Laws regulates the organization of a particular community within Israel. Unlike the halakhah stratum the communal organization shows signs of extensive redactional activity and reworking which are dealt with below.

12.3 Miscellaneous Halakhah

Apart from these two main literary strata a number of miscellaneous pieces of halakhah were identified:

CD 11,21b-12,1a par.	Rules on Entering the House of Worship
CD 12,1b-2a	A Prohibition of Sexual Relations in Jerusalem
CD 12,11b-18	Various Purity Regulations

12.4 Miscellaneous Traditions and Redactional Passages

The following miscellaneous traditions and redactional passages have been identified:

a. Remnants of traditions dealing with the duties of the משכיל that have been merged with the material on the overseer are found in CD 12,20b-22a; 13,7c-8.14-15a.22 par.

190 CHAPTER TWELVE

b. Passages promoting the concerns reminiscent of the Book of Jubilees have been identified in CD 16,2b-6a; CD 10,7b-10a par.; 12,2b-6a.
c. Passages that have been assigned to the Serekh redaction of the Laws are the references to 'the many' in CD 15,8 and 4QD^a 10 ii 7; 11,1. Further, CD 13,11-12a; 14,6c-8a.12b par.; 4QD^e 7 i 11a; 4QD^a 11,7b-8a.
d. Passages that have been attributed to the Damascus redaction are preserved in 4QD^a 5 i par.; the reference to the time of wickedness in 4QD^f 2,12 par.; CD 15,6b-7a; 12,19-20a.23b-13,1a; 13,23-14,2a; 14,19 par.
e. A catalogue of transgressions the main body of which is reminiscent of the laws, particularly the halakhah stratum, in 4QD^e 2 i 9—ii 21. The conclusion, by contrast, is close to the Admonition, and it was suggested that the call to hearken at the end of the catalogue is best understood as an introduction to the now lost material that followed. It was proposed that the main body of the catalogue may have originated independently in which case it would be of fundamental importance for the growth of collections of laws. Since the catalogue briefly lists a number of issues that are dealt with at greater length elsewhere in the Laws the possibility was raised that it inspired the addition of more elaborate halakhic sections. These additions may, in turn, have originated independently but the reference in the catalogue to particular issues may have inspired their inclusion in the collection.
f. The expulsion ceremony and the end of the Damascus Document in 4QD^a 11 par. This text draws on a number of traditions such as the covenant renewal ceremony as well as displaying a number of striking links to the Admonition. It was argued, moreover, that the text appears to be carelessly edited and probably goes back to a late stage in the growth of the document.
g. A number of odd statements, mostly very fragmentary, which it was not possible to assign to any of the literary strata, traditions or redactional processes identified in the Laws are CD 15,1-5a; 13,9-10.16b-19; 14,2b.

The results of my source and redaction critical analysis of the Laws of the Damascus Document may provide an answer to a problem raised by Philip Davies in a recent paper.[3] Having outlined the different traditions preserved in 1QS 5,1-4 and 4QS^d 1,1-3 Davies ponders on the significance of alternative traditions in the communal legislation from Qumran and asks,

---

[3] 'Redaction and Sectarianism in the Qumran Scrolls', in *The Scriptures and the Scrolls. Studies in Honour of A. S. van der Woude on the Occasion of his 65th Birthday* ed. F. García Martínez, A. Hilhorst and C.J. Labuschagne, Leiden: E.J. Brill, 1992, pp. 152-63.

The fact of apparently 'obsolete' texts being present in the Qumran corpus creates severe difficulties when such texts are being used to reconstruct the structure, practice and belief of a community. If such texts are to be understood as rules for a living community, we have to ask why older versions of such a rule should be *copied* [Davies' emphasis] (not merely preserved) when newer versions are apparently in existence and presumably in effect?[4]

In the light of the foregoing analysis of the Laws of the Damascus Document it seems possible to attempt an answer to Davies' question. It emerged from my analysis of the Laws that the communal legislation underwent a process of redaction in order to bring it into line with the community behind the Community Rule. In other words, the community behind S revised and updated the communal legislation of D. Thus, the Laws of the Damascus Document continued to be *revised and brought up to date* rather than merely copied by the S community. In Davies' terminology, 'apparently obsolete texts' continued to be edited and revised by 'living communities'. This type of literary scenario receives some support from the analogy of Christian communities continuing to copy and revise, or copy for the sake of revising, Jewish texts.

One may further ask why the up-dating process of the communal terminology is not more complete and some of the older terminology was preserved. It seems to me that something of an answer may be found in the development of the terminology used by the communities to refer to itself as well as its officials. The communal terminology employed in the communal legislation of the Laws is rather 'biblical', e.g. camp (מחנה), congregation (עדה), covenant (ברית). In the secondary material which is close to the language of 1QS 5-9, by contrast, the terminology is more removed from biblical usage, e.g. the many in a technical sense (הרבים) and *yaḥad* (יחד). All the groups that lie behind the DSS, and most contemporary Jews, shared a pronounced reverence for scripture. It seems likely, therefore, that they would have cherished the older terminology even after a new set of terms had come into use. Finally, standards of consistency might not have been rated as highly then as is the case today.

12.5 Outlook

A number of areas for further study seem required in the light of the present study. I will mention only two here.

---

[4] 'Redaction and Sectarianism', p. 157.

a. I noted on numerous occasions that passages were linked to each other by means of a catchword, a process identified independently also by Prof. Baumgarten.[5] This method of linking material is used widely in all parts of the Laws, cf. CD 15,15-17 as improved with 4QD^a 8 i 6-7 (אל יבוא); CD 16,2-3 (מדוקדק); CD 9,12-13 (אשם); CD 10,9-11 (מעט); CD 10,11-13 (מרעיל); CD 11,17a-17b (יעל); CD 11,17-18 (מזבח; עולה); CD 11,19.22; 12,1 (טמא); CD 12,17-18 (טמאה); CD 13,1-2 (עשרה); CD 13,10-11 (עדתו). I am sure I have overlooked further examples. What is more, Philip Davies has tentatively suggested a similar process for 1QS 9,7-11 based on the term הון.[6] I suspect, moreover, that the catchword principle is much more widely attested in the DSS and beyond. It is of great importance for our understanding of the growth of documents, and its attestation deserves to be investigated more comprehensively.

b. A study of the literary development of the Damascus Document as a whole is now to be desired. Of particular interest will be the relationship of the Laws to the legal material in the Admonition. I have only touched upon the Admonition in as far as it was essential for my argument, and I am well aware that I was not able to do justice to all the important issues concerning the growth of the Damascus Document as a whole. However, my neglect of the Admonition should be seen in the context of decades of neglect of the Laws, notable exceptions excluded.

---

[5] Cf. Baumgarten in Charlesworth ed., *Dead Sea Scrolls*, II, pp. 43,49 nn. 144, 176.

[6] 'Communities at Qumran and the Case of the Missing "Teacher"', *RQ* 15 (1991) 275-86, p. 280.

BIBLIOGRAPHY

Abegg M. G. Jr., 'Messianic Hope and 4Q*285*: A Reassessment', *JBL* 113 (1994) 81-91
Allegro J.M. with the collaboration of A.A. Anderson, *Qumran Cave 4. I (4Q158-4Q186)* (DJD V), Oxford: Clarendon, 1968
A Preliminary Concordance To The Hebrew And Aramaic Texts From Qumran Caves II-X, 5 Vols., prepared and arranged for printing by H.-P. Richter on behalf of J. Strugnell, Göttingen: Privately printed in 1988 (distributed by H. Stegemann)

Baillet M., *Qumrân Grotte 4. III (4Q482—520)* (DJD VII), Oxford: Clarendon, 1982
Baillet M., J.T. Milik, and R. De Vaux, *Les "Petites Grottes" de Qumrân: Exploration de la falaise, Les grottes 2Q, 3Q, 5Q, 6Q, 7Q à 10Q, Le rouleau de cuivre* (DJD III), Oxford: Clarendon, 1962
Barthélemy D. and J.T. Milik, *Qumran Cave I* (DJD I), Oxford: Clarendon, 1955
Baumgarten J.M., 'The Essene Avoidance of Oil and the Laws of Purity', *RQ* 6 (1967-69) 183-92
Idem, Studies in Qumran Law, Leiden: E.J. Brill, 1977
Idem, 'The "Sons of Dawn" in *CDC* 13: 14-15 and the Ban on Commerce among the Essenes', *IEJ* 33 (1983) 81-85
Idem, 'Halakhic Polemics in New Fragments from Qumran Cave 4', in *Biblical Archaeology Today. Proceedings of the International Congress on Biblical Archaeology, Jerusalem, April 1984* ed. Janet Amitai, Jerusalem: Israel Exploration Society, 1985, pp. 390-99
Idem, 'The Laws of ʿOrlah and First Fruits in the Light of Jubilees, the Qumran Writings, and Targum Ps. Jonathan', *JJS* 38 (1987) 195-202
Idem, 'The Essene-Qumran Restraints on Marriage', in *Archaeology and History in the Dead Sea Scrolls* ed. L.H. Schiffman, Sheffield: JSOT Press, 1990, pp. 13-24
Idem, 'The 4Q Zadokite Fragments on Skin Disease', *JJS* 41 (1990) 152—65
Idem, 'A New Qumran Substitute for the Divine Name and Mishnah Sukkah 4.5', *JQR* 83 (1992) 1-5
Idem, 'A "Scriptural" Citation in 4Q Fragments of the Damascus Document', *JJS* 43 (1992) 95-98
Idem, 'The Cave 4 Versions of the Qumran Penal Code', *JJS* 43 (1992) 268-76
Idem, 'The Disqualifications of Priests in 4Q Fragments of the "Damascus Document", a Specimen of the Recovery of pre-Rabbinic Halakha', in *The Madrid Qumran Congress. Proceedings of the International Congress on the*

Dead Sea Scrolls, Madrid 18 -21 March 1991 ed. J. Trebolle Barrera and L. Vegas Montaner, 2 Vols., Leiden: E.J. Brill, 1992, II, pp. 503-13

Idem, 'The Laws of the *Damascus Document* in Current Research', in *The Damascus Document Reconsidered* ed. M. Broshi, Jerusalem: Israel Exploration Society, 1992, pp. 51—62

Idem, 'Liquids and the Susceptibility to Defilement in New 4Q Texts', *JQR* 85 (1994) 91-101

Idem, 'Purification after Childbirth and the Sacred Garden in 4Q265 and Jubilees', in *New Qumran Texts and Studies. Proceedings of the First Meeting of the International Organization for Qumran Studies, Paris 1992* ed. G.J. Brooke with F. García Martínez, Leiden: E. J. Brill, 1994, pp. 3-10

Idem, 'Zab Impurity in Qumran and Rabbinic Law', *JJS* 45 (1994) 273-77

Idem, 'A Fragment on Fetal Life and Pregnancy in 4Q270', in *Pomegranates and Bells. Studies in Biblical, Jewish, and Near Eastern Ritual, Law, and Literature in Honor of Jacob Milgrom* ed. D.P. Wright, D.N. Freedman and A. Hurvitz, Winona Lake: Eisenbrauns, 1995, pp. 445-48

Idem, 'A Qumran Text with Agrarian Halakhah', *JQR* 86 (1995) 1-8

Idem, 'The Laws About Fluxes in 4Q Tohora^a (4Q274)', in *Time to Prepare the Way in the Wilderness. Papers on the Qumran Scrolls by Fellows of the Institute for Advanced Studies of the Hebrew University, Jerusalem, 1989-1990* ed. Devorah Dimant and L.H. Schiffman, Leiden: E.J. Brill, 1995, pp. 1-8

Idem, 'The Red Cow Purification Rites in Qumran Texts', *JJS* 46 (1995) 112-19

Idem, *Qumran Cave 4. XIII. The Damascus Document (4Q266-273)* (DJD XVIII), Oxford: Clarendon, 1996

Idem, 'Messianic Forgiveness of Sin in CD 14:19 (4Q266 10 i 12-13)', in *Proceedings of the International Conference on the Dead Sea Scrolls, Provo, Utah 1996* ed. D.W. Parry and E. Ulrich, Leiden: E.J. Brill, forthcoming

Beall T.S., *Josephus' Description of the Essenes Illustrated by the Dead Sea Scrolls*, Cambridge: CUP, 1988

Berger K., *Jesus and the Dead Sea Scrolls. The Truth under Lock and Key?*, Louisville: Westminster John Knox Press, 1995

Bergmeier R., *Die Essenerberichte des Flavius Josephus. Quellenstudien zu den Essenertexten im Werk des Jüdischen Historiographen*, Kampen: Kok Pharos, 1993

Betz O., 'The Qumran Halakhah Text Miqsat Ma'ase Ha-Torah (4QMMT) and Sadducean, Essene, and Early Pharisaic Tradition', in *The Aramaic Bible. Targums in Their Historical Context* ed. D.R.G. Beattie and M.J. McNamara, Sheffield: JSOT Press, 1994, pp. 176-202

Betz O. and R. Riesner, *Jesus, Qumran and the Vatican. Clarifications*, London: SCM, 1994

Bietenhardt H., 'Sabbatvorschriften von Qumran im Lichte des rabbinischen Rechts und der Evangelien', in *Qumran Probleme. Vorträge des Leipziger Symposiums über Qumran-Probleme vom 9. bis 14. Oktober 1961* ed. H. Bardtke, Berlin: Akademie, 1963, pp. 53-74

Boyce M., *The Poetry of the Damascus Document*, Edinburgh: Dissertation, 1988

Brooke G.J., 'The Temple Scroll: A Law Unto Itself?', in *Law and Religion. Essays on the Place of the Law in Israel and Early Christianity by Members of the Ehrhardt Seminar of Manchester University* ed. B. Lindars SSF, Cambridge: James Clarke, 1988, pp. 34-43

Idem, 'Levi and the Levites in the Dead Sea Scrolls and the New Testament', in *Mogilany 1989. Papers on the Dead Sea Scrolls* ed. Z.J. Kapera, Kraków: Enigma, 1993, I, pp. 105-29

Broshi M., 'Anti-Qumranic Polemics in the Talmud', in *The Madrid Qumran Congress* ed. Trebolle Barrera and Vegas Montaner, II, pp. 589-600

Burrows M., *The Dead Sea Scrolls*, London: Secker &Warburg, 1956

Callaway P.R., 'Qumran Origins: From the *Doresh* to the *Moreh*', *RQ* 14 (1990) 637-50

Campbell J.G., *The Use of Scripture in the Damascus Document 1-8, 19-20*, Berlin: De Gruyter, 1995

Carmignac J., É. Cothenet et H. Lignée eds., *Les Textes de Qumrân. Traduits et Annotés*, Paris: Letouzey et Ané, 1963

Charles R.H., *The Apocrypha and Pseudepigrapha of the Old Testament in English with Introductions and Critical and Explanatory Notes to the Several Books*, 2 Vols., Oxford: OUP, 1977

Charlesworth J.H. ed., *The Dead Sea Scrolls. Hebrew, Aramaic, and Greek Texts with English Translations*, Tübingen: J.C.B. Mohr (Paul Siebeck)/Louisville: Westminster John Knox Press, I, 1994

Idem ed., *The Dead Sea Scrolls. Hebrew, Aramaic, and Greek Texts with English Translations*, Tübingen: J.C.B. Mohr (Paul Siebeck)/Louisville: Westminster John Knox Press, II, 1995

Chazon Esther, 'Is *Divreh Ha-Me'orot* a Sectarian Prayer?', in *The Dead Sea Scrolls. Forty Years of Research* ed. Devorah Dimant and U. Rappaport, Leiden: E.J. Brill, 1992, pp. 3-17

Eadem, 'New Liturgical Manuscripts from Qumran', in *Proceedings of the Eleventh World Congress of Jewish Studies. Division A: The Bible and Its World* ed. D. Assaf, Jerusalem: World Union of Jewish Studies, 1994, pp. 207-14

Eadem, 'Prayers from Qumran and Their Historical Implications', *DSD* 1 (1994) 265-84

Collins J.J., 'Patterns of Eschatology at Qumran', in *Traditions in Transformation. Turning Points in Biblical Faith* ed. B. Halpern and J.D. Levenson, Winona Lake: Eisenbrauns, 1981, pp. 351-75

Cothenet É., 'Le Document de Damas', in *Les Textes de Qumrân*, II, pp. 129-204

Davidson M.J., *Angels at Qumran. A Comparative Study of 1 Enoch 1-36, 72-108 and Sectarian Writings from Qumran*, Sheffield: Sheffield Academic Press, 1992

Davies P.R., 'Hasidim in the Maccabean Period', *JJS* 28 (1977) 124-40

Idem, 'The Ideology of the Temple in the Damascus Document', *JJS* 33 (1982) 287—301

Idem, *The Damascus Covenant. An Interpretation of the "Damascus Document"*, Sheffield: Sheffield Academic Press, 1983
Idem, *Behind the Essenes. History and Ideology in the Dead Sea Scrolls*, Atlanta: Scholars Press, 1987
Idem, 'Halakhah at Qumran', in *A Tribute to Geza Vermes* ed. P.R. Davies and R.T. White, Sheffield: JSOT Press, 1990, pp. 37-50
Idem, 'Communities at Qumran and the Case of the Missing Teacher', *RQ* 15 (1991) 275-86
Idem, 'The Prehistory of the Qumran Community', in *The Dead Sea Scrolls. Forty Years of Research* ed. Dimant and Rappaport, pp. 116-25
Idem, 'Redaction and Sectarianism in the Qumran Scrolls', in *The Scriptures and the Scrolls. Studies in Honour of A. S. van der Woude on the Occasion of his 65th Birthday* ed. F. García Martínez, A. Hilhorst and C.J. Labuschagne, Leiden: E.J. Brill, 1992, pp. 152-63
Idem, 'The "Damascus" Sect and Judaism', in *Pursuing the Text. Studies in Honor of Ben Zion Wacholder on the Occasion of his Seventieth Birthday* ed. J.C. Reeves and J. Kampen, Sheffield: Sheffield Academic Press, 1994, pp. 70-84 reprinted in P.R. Davies, *Sects and Scrolls. Essays on Qumran and Related Topics*, Atlanta: Scholars Press, 1996, pp. 163-77
Davis R., *The History of the Composition of the Damascus Document Statutes (CD 9-16 + 4QD)*, Harvard: Dissertation, 1992
Derrett J.D.M., '"BEHUQEY HAGOYIM": Damascus Document IX,1 Again', *RQ* 11 (1982-84) 409-15
Dimant Devorah, 'Qumran Sectarian Literature', in *Jewish Writings of the Second Temple Period. Apocrypha, Pseudepigrapha, Qumran Sectarian Writings, Philo, Josephus* ed. M.E. Stone, Philadelphia: Fortress Press / Assen: Van Gorcum, 1984, pp. 483-550
Eadem, 'New Light from Qumran on the Jewish Pseudepigrapha—4Q390', in *The Madrid Qumran Congress* ed. Trebolle Barrera and Vegas Montaner, II, pp. 405-48
Dupont-Sommer A., *The Essene Writings from Qumran*, Oxford: Blackwell, 1961

Eshel Esther, '4Q477: The Rebukes by the Overseer', *JJS* 45 (1994) 111-22

Falk Z.W., '"BEHUQEY HAGOYIM" in Damascus Document IX,1', *RQ* 6 (1967-69) 569
Fishbane M., 'Use, Authority and Interpretation of Mikra at Qumran', in *Mikra. Text, Translation, Reading and Interpretation of the Hebrew Bible in Ancient Judaism and Early Christianity* ed. M.J. Mulder, Assen: Van Gorcum / Philadelphia: Fortress, 1988, pp. 339-77
Fitzmyer J.A., *Prolegomenon* to the reprint of S. Schechter, *Documents of Jewish Sectaries*, Vol. I. Fragments of a Zadokite Work, New York: Ktav, 1970, pp. 9-37
Idem,'The Use of Explicit Old Testament Quotations in Qumran Literature and in the New Testament', in *idem, Essays on the Semitic Background of the New Testament*, London: Geoffrey Chapman, 1971, pp. 3-58

Idem, The Dead Sea Scrolls. Major Publications and Tools for Study, Atlanta: Scholars Press, 1990

García Martínez F., 'Qumran Origins and Early History: A Groningen Hypothesis', *Folia Orientalia* 25 (1988) 113—36
Idem, '11Q Temple^b. A Preliminary Publication' in *The Madrid Qumran Congress* ed. Trebolle Barrera and Vegas Montaner, II, pp. 363-91
Idem, The Dead Sea Scrolls Translated. The Qumran Texts in English, Leiden: E.J. Brill, 1994
García Martínez F. and J. Trebolle Barrera, *The People of the Dead Sea Scrolls. Their Writings, Beliefs and Practices*, Leiden: E.J. Brill, 1995
García Martínez F. and A.S. van der Woude, 'A "Groningen" Hypothesis of Qumran Origins and Early History', *RQ* 56 (1990) 521-41
Gaster T.H., *The Scriptures of the Dead Sea Sect in English Translation*, London: Secker & Warburg, 1957
Ginzberg L., *An Unknown Jewish Sect*, New York City: Jewish Theological Seminary of America, 1976
Golb N., 'The Dietary Laws of the Damascus Document in Relation to Those of the Karaites', *JJS* 8 (1957) 51-69
Goodman M.D., 'A Note on the Qumran Sectarians, the Essenes and Josephus', *JJS* 46 (1995) 161-66

Harrington D.J., *Wisdom Texts from Qumran*, London: Routledge, 1996
Hempel C., 'Comments on the Translation of 4QS^d I,1', *JJS* 44 (1993) 127-28
Eadem, 'Who Rebukes in 4Q477?', *RQ* 16 (1995) 655-56
Eadem, 'The Earthly Essene Nucleus of 1QSa', *DSD* 3 (1996) 253-67
Eadem, 'The Penal Code Reconsidered', in *Legal Texts and Legal Issues: Second Meeting of the IOQS, Cambridge 1995* ed. M.J. Bernstein, F. García Martínez, and J. Kampen, Leiden: E.J. Brill, 1997, pp. 337-48
Eadem, 'Community Origins in the Damascus Document in the Light of Recent Scholarship' in *Proceedings of the International Conference on the Dead Sea Scrolls, Provo, Utah 1996*, ed. D.W. Parry and E. Ulrich, Leiden: E.J. Brill, forthcoming
Eadem, 'Community Structures in the Dead Sea Scrolls: Admission, Organization, and Disciplinary Procedures', in *The Dead Sea Scrolls after Fifty Years*, ed. P. Flint and J.C. VanderKam, Leiden: E.J. Brill, forthcoming
Eadem, 4QOrd^a (4Q159) and the Laws of the Damascus Document, in the Proceedings of the International Congress *The Dead Sea Scrolls – Fifty Years After Their Discovery*, Jerusalem: Israel Exploration Society, forthcoming.
Hoenig S.B., 'Qumran Rules of Impurities', *RQ* 6 (1967-69) 559-67
Hübner, 'Zölibat in Qumran?', *NTS* 17 (1970-71) 153-67

Jackson B.S., '*Testes Singulares* in Early Jewish Law and the New Testament', in *Idem, Essays in Jewish and Comparative Legal History*, Leiden: E.J. Brill, 1975, pp. 172-201

Idem, 'Damascus Document IX,16-23 and Parallels', *RQ* 9 (1978) 445-50
Kimbrough S.T., 'The Concept of Sabbath at Qumran', *RQ* 5 (1964-66) 483-502
Kister M., 'Some Aspects of Qumranic Halakhah', in *The Madrid Qumran Congress* ed. Trebolle Barrera and Vegas Montaner, II, pp. 571-88
Idem, 'Commentary to 4Q298', *JQR* 85 (1994) 237-49
Idem, 'Notes on Some New Texts from Qumran', *JJS* 44 (1993) 280-81
Knibb M.A., *The Qumran Community*, Cambridge: CUP, 1987
Idem, 'Jubilees and the Origins of the Qumran Community'. An Inaugural Lecture, London: King's College, 1989
Idem, 'The Place of the Damascus Document', in *Methods of Investigation of the Dead Sea Scrolls and the Khirbet Qumran Site. Present Realities and Future Prospects* ed. M.O. Wise *et al.*, New York: New York Academy of Sciences, 1994, pp. 149-62
Kosmala H., 'Maskîl', in *idem*, *Studies, Essays and Reviews*, Leiden: E.J. Brill, 1978, I, pp. 235-41
Kugel J.L., 'On Hidden Hatred and Open Reproach: Early Exegesis of Leviticus 19:17', *HTR* 80 (1987) 43-61
Idem, 'The Jubilees Apocalypse', *DSD* 1 (1994) 322-37
Kuhn K.G., *Konkordanz zu den Qumrantexten*, Göttingen: Vandenhoeck & Ruprecht, 1960

Lange A., *Weisheit und Prädestination. Weisheitliche Urordnung und Prädestination in den Textfunden von Qumran*, Leiden: E.J. Brill, 1995
Levine B.A., 'Damascus Document IX,17-22: A New Translation and Comments', *RQ* 8 (1972-75) 195-96
Idem, 'The Temple Scroll: Aspects of Its Historical Provenance and Literary Character', *BASOR* 232 (1979) 5-23
Lieberman S., 'The Discipline in the So-Called Dead Sea Manual of Discipline', *JBL* 71 (1952) 199-206
Lohse, E., *Die Texte aus Qumran*, Darmstadt: Wissenschaftliche Buchgesellschaft, 1986

Maier J., *Die Texte vom Toten Meer*, 2 Vols., München: Reinhardt, 1960
Idem, *Die Qumran-Essener: Die Texte vom Toten Meer*, 2 Vols., München: Reinhardt, 1995
Maier J. and K. Schubert, *Die Qumran-Essener*, München: Reinhardt, 1992
Mayes A.D.H., *Deuteronomy*, London: Marshall, Morgan & Scott, 1979
Metso Sarianna, 'The Primary Results of the Reconstruction of 4QS^e', *JJS* 44 (1993) 303-308
Milgrom J., '"Sabbath" and "Temple City" in the Temple Scroll', *BASOR* 232 (1978) 25-27
Idem, *Leviticus 1-16. A New Translation with Introduction and Commentary*, New York: Doubleday, 1991
Idem, 'The City of the Temple. A Response to Lawrence H. Schiffman', *JQR* 85 (1994) 125-28

Idem, 'First Day Ablutions in Qumran', in *Madrid Qumran Congress* ed. Trebolle Barrera and Vegas Montaner, II, pp. 561-70
Idem, '4QTohora[a]: An Unpublished Qumran Text on Purities', in *Time to Prepare the Way in the Wilderness* ed. Dimant and Schiffman, pp. 59-68
Milik J.T., 'Le travail d'édition des fragments manuscrits de Qûmran', *RB* 63 (1956) 49-67
Idem, *Ten Years of Discovery in the Wilderness of Judaea*, London: SCM, 1959
Idem, 'Fragment d'une source du Psautier (4QPs 89) et fragments des Jubilés, du Document de Damas, d'un Phylactère dans la Grotte 4 de Qumran', *RB* 73 (1966) 94-106
Idem, 'Milkî-sedeq et Milkî-resa[c] dans les anciens écrits juifs et chrétiens', *JJS* 23 (1972) 95-144
Milikowsky C., 'Law at Qumran. A Critical Reaction to Lawrence H. Schiffman, *Sectarian Law in the Dead Sea Scrolls: Courts, Testimony, and the Penal Code*', *RQ* 12 (1986) 237-249
Murphy-O'Connor J., 'La genèse littéraire de la Règle de la Communauté', *RB* 76 (1969) 528-49
Idem, 'An Essene Missionary Document? CD II,14-VI,1', *RB* 77 (1970) 201-29
Idem, 'A Literary Analysis of Damascus Document VI,2-VIII,3', *RB* 78 (1971) 210-32
Idem, 'The Original Text of CD 7:9-8:2 = 19:5-14', *HTR* 64 (1971) 379-86
Idem, 'The Critique of the Princes of Judah (CD VIII,3-19)', *RB* 79 (1972) 200-16
Idem, 'A Literary Analysis of Damascus Document XIX,33-XX,34', *RB* 79 (1972) 544-64
Idem, 'The Damascus Document Revisited', *RB* 92 (1985) 223-246

Nebe G.W., 'Das Sprachvermögen des Mebaqqer in Damaskusschrift XIV,10', *RQ* 16 (1993) 289-91
Neusner J., '"By the Testimony of Two Witnesses" in the Damascus Document IX,17-22 and in Pharisaic-Rabbinic Law', *RQ* 8 (1972-75) 197-217
Idem, 'Damascus Document IX,17-22 and Irrelevant Parallels', *RQ* 9 (1978) 441-44
Newsom Carol, *Songs of the Sabbath Sacrifice: A Critical Edition*, Atlanta: Scholars Press, 1985
Eadem, '"Sectually Explicit" Literature from Qumran', in *The Hebrew Bible and Its Interpreters* ed. W.H. Propp, B. Halpern, and D.N. Freedman, Winona Lake: Eisenbrauns, 1990, pp. 167-87
Eadem, 'The Sage in the Literature of Qumran: The Functions of the Maskil', in *The Sage in Israel and the Ancient Near East* ed. J.G. Gammie and L.G. Perdue, Winona Lake: Eisenbrauns, 1990, pp. 373-82
Nir-El Y. and M. Broshi, 'The Red Ink of the Dead Sea Scrolls', *Archaeometry* 38 (1996) 97-102

Nitzan Bilhah, '4QBerakhot^{a-c} (4Q286-290): A Covenantal Ceremony in the Light of Related Texts', *RQ* 16 (1995) 487-506
Noack B., 'Qumran and the Book of Jubilees', *SEA* 22-23 (1958) 191-207

Osten-Sacken P. von der, *Gott und Belial. Traditionsgeschichtliche Untersuchungen zum Dualismus in den Texten aus Qumran*, Göttingen: Vandenhoeck & Ruprecht, 1969

Pfann S., '4Q298: The Maskîl's Address to All Sons of Dawn', *JQR* 85 (1994) 203-35

Qimron E., *The Hebrew of the Dead Sea Scrolls*, Atlanta: Scholars Press, 1986
Idem, 'שבועה הבנים in the Damascus Covenant 15.1-2', *JQR* 81 (1990) 115-18
Idem, 'Notes on the 4Q Zadokite Fragments on Skin Disease', *JJS* 42 (1991) 256-59
Idem, 'The Text of CDC', in *The Damascus Document Reconsidered* ed. Broshi, pp. 9-49
Idem, 'Further Observations on the Laws of Oaths in the Damascus Document 15', *JQR* 85 (1994) 251-57
Qimron E. and J. Strugnell, *Qumran Cave 4. V.* MIQSAT MA'ASE HA-TORAH (DJD X), Oxford: Clarendon, 1994

Rabin C., *The Zadokite Documents. I. The Admonition II. The Laws*, Oxford: Clarendon, 1954
Rabinovitch N.L., 'Damascus Document IX,17-22 and Rabbinic Parallels', *RQ* 9 (1978) 113-16
Rabinowitz I., 'The Meaning and Date of "Damascus" Document IX,1', *RQ* 6 (1967-69) 433-35
Rajak Tessa, 'Ciò Che Flavio Guiseppe Vide: Josephus and the Essenes' in *Josephus and the History of the Greco-Roman Period. Essays in Memory of Morton Smith* ed. F. Parente and J. Sievers, Leiden: E.J. Brill, 1994, pp. 141-60
Reed S.A., 'Genre, Setting and Title of 4Q477', *JJS* 47 (1996) 147-48
Robinson I., 'A Note on Damascus Document IX,7', *RQ* 9 (1977) 237-40
Rubinstein A., 'Urban Halakhah and Camp Rules in the "Cairo Fragments of a Damascene Covenant"', *Sefarad* 12 (1952) 283-96

Schechter S., *Documents of Jewish Sectaries*. Vol. I. Fragments of a Zadokite Work, Cambridge: CUP, 1910
Schiffman L.H., *The Halakhah at Qumran*, Leiden: E.J. Brill, 1975
Idem, 'Legislation Concerning Relations with Non-Jews in the *Zadokite Fragments* and in Tannaitic Literature', *RQ* 11 (1982-84) 379-89
Idem, *Sectarian Law in the Dead Sea Scrolls. Courts, Testimony and the Penal Code*, Chico: Scholars Press, 1983

Idem, 'Exclusion from the Sanctuary and the City of the Sanctuary in the Temple Scroll', *HAR* 9 (1985) 301-20

Idem, 'Purity and Perfection: Exclusion from the Council of the Community in the *Serekh Ha-ʿEdah*' in *Biblical Archaeology Today* ed. Amitai, pp. 373-89

Idem, *The Eschatological Community of the Dead Sea Scrolls. A Study of the Rule of the Congregation*, Atlanta: Scholars Press, 1989

Idem, 'The Law of Vows and Oaths (*Num.* 30,3-16) in the *Zadokite Fragments* and the *Temple Scroll* ', *RQ* 15 (1991) 199-214

Idem, '4QMMT—Basic Sectarian Text' in *Qumran Cave Four. Special Report* ed. Z.J. Kapera, Krakow: Enigma, 1991, pp. 81-83

Idem, 'Pharisaic and Sadducean Halakhah in the Light of the Dead Sea Scrolls', *DSD* 1 (1994) 285-99

Idem, *Reclaiming the Dead Sea Scrolls. The History of Judaism, the Background of Christianity, the Lost Library of Qumran*, with a Foreword by Chaim Potok, Philadelphia and Jerusalem: Jewish Publication Society, 1994

Idem, 'The Theology of the Temple Scroll', *JQR* 85 (1994) 109-23

Schuller Eileen M., 'Women in the Dead Sea Scrolls', in *Methods of Investigation of the Dead Sea Scrolls and the Khirbet Qumran Site* ed. Wise *et al.*, pp. 115-31

Eadem,'Prayer, Hymnic, and Liturgical Texts from Qumran' in *The Community of the Renewed Covenant. The Notre Dame Symposium on the Dead Sea Scrolls* ed. E. Ulrich and J.C. VanderKam, Notre Dame: University of Notre Dame Press, 1994, pp. 153-71

Stegemann H., 'Das Gesetzeskorpus der "Damaskusschrift" (CD IX-XVI)', *RQ* 14 (1990) 409-34

Idem, 'The Qumran Essenes—Local Members of the Main Jewish Union in Late Second Temple Times', in *The Madrid Qumran Congress* ed. Trebolle Barrera and Vegas Montaner, I, pp. 83-166

Idem, *Die Essener, Qumran, Johannes der Täufer und Jesus*, Freiburg: Herder, 1994

Stemberger G., *Jewish Contemporaries of Jesus. Pharisees, Sadducees, Essenes*, Minneapolis: Fortress, 1995

Steudel A., 'The Houses of Prostration CD XI,21-XII,1—Duplicates of the Temple', *RQ* 16 (1993) 49-68

Strugnell J., 'MMT: Second Thoughts on a Forthcoming Edition', in *The Community of the Renewed Covenant* ed. Ulrich and VanderKam, pp. 57-73

Idem, 'More on Wives and Marriage in the Dead Sea Scrolls: (*4Q416* 2 ii [Cf. *1 Thess* 4:4] And *4QMMT* §B)', *RQ* 17 (1996) 537-47

Talmon S., 'A Further Link Between the Judean Covenanters and the Essenes?', in *idem*, *The World of Qumran From Within. Collected Studies*, Jerusalem: Magnes Press, 1989, pp. 61-67

Idem, 'Waiting for the Messiah—the Conceptual Universe of the Qumran Covenanters' in *idem*, *The World of Qumran From Within*, pp. 273-300

Idem, 'Qumran Studies: Past, Present, and Future', *JQR* 85 (1994) 1-31

Idem, 'The Community of the Renewed Covenant: Between Judaism and Christianity', in *The Community of the Renewed Covenant.* ed. Ulrich and VanderKam, pp. 3-24

Tigay J.H., 'Examination of the Accused Bride in 4Q159: Forensic Medicine at Qumran', *JANES* 22 (1993) 129-34

Tiller P., 'The Laws of the Damascus Document and Qumran', *HNTSP* 1987

Tov E. ed. with the collaboration of S.J. Pfann, *The Dead Sea Scrolls on Microfiche. A Comprehensive Facsimile Edition of the Texts from the Judean Desert*, Leiden: E.J. Brill, 1993

VanderKam J.C., *Textual and Historical Studies in the Book of Jubilees*, Missoula: Scholars Press, 1977

Idem, *The Book of Jubilees*, 2 Vols., Louvain: Peeters, 1989

Idem, 'The Jubilees Fragments from Qumran Cave 4', in *The Madrid Qumran Congress* ed. Trebolle Barrera and Vegas Montaner, II, pp. 635-48

Idem, 'Messianism in the Scrolls', in *The Community of the Renewed Covenant* ed. Ulrich and VanderKam, pp. 211-34

Vaux R. de, *Ancient Israel. Its Life and Institutions*, London: Darton, Longman & Todd, 1961

Vermes G., *The Dead Sea Scrolls. Qumran in Perspective*, Revised Third Edition, London: SCM, 1994

Idem, *The Dead Sea Scrolls in English*, Fourth Edition, London: Penguin, 1995

Idem, 'Biblical Proof-Texts in Qumran Literature', *JSS* 34 (1989) 493-508

Idem, 'Preliminary Remarks on Unpublished Fragments of the Community Rule from Qumran Cave 4', *JJS* 42 (1991) 250-55

Idem, 'Qumran Forum Miscellanea', *JJS* 43 (1992) 299-305

Idem, *The Complete Dead Sea Scrolls in English*, London: Allen Lane, The Penguin Press, 1997

Vermes G. and M.D. Goodman, *The Essenes. According to the Classical Sources*, Sheffield: JSOT Press, 1989

Wacholder B.Z., 'Rules of Testimony in Qumranic Jurisprudence: CD 9 and 11Q Torah 64', *JJS* 40 (1989) 163-74

Weinfeld M., *The Organizational Pattern and the Penal Code of the Qumran Sect. A Comparison with Guilds and Religious Associations of the Hellenistic-Roman Period*, Göttingen: Vandenhoeck & Ruprecht / Fribourg: Éditions Universitaires, 1986

Wernberg-Møller P., *The Manual of Discipline. Translated and Annotated with an Introduction*, Leiden: E.J. Brill, 1957

Wilson A. and L. Wills, 'Literary Sources of the Temple Scroll', *HTR* 75 (1982) 275-88

Winter P., 'Sadoqite Fragments IX,1', *RQ* 6 (1967-69) 131-36

Wise M.O., *A Critical Study of the Temple Scroll from Qumran Cave 11*, Chicago: The Oriental Institute of the University of Chicago, 1990

Wise M.O., M. Abegg Jr., and E. Cook, *The Dead Sea Scrolls. A New Translation*, London: Harper Collins, 1996

Yadin Y., *The Scroll of the War of the Sons of Light against the Sons of Darkness*, Oxford: OUP, 1962
Idem, *The Temple Scroll*, 3 Vols., Jerusalem: Israel Exploration Society, 1983

Zahavy T., 'The Sabbath Code of Damascus Document X,14-XI,18: Form Analytical and Redaction Critical Observations', *RQ* 10 (1979-81) 589-91

MODERN AUTHORS

Abegg M. Jr 11, 66, 132, 146, 181
Allegro J.M. 57
Amitai J. 34
Anderson A.A. 57
Assaf D. 121
Baillet M. 2, 34, 48, 57, 72, 121, 168
Bardtke H. 34
Barthélemy D. 121
Baumgarten J.M. xi, 2, 3, 7, 9, 17, 18, 20, 21, 22, 23, 26, 27, 30, 31, 32, 33, 34, 35, 37, 38, 39, 40, 41, 42, 43, 47, 48, 49, 50, 51, 52, 53, 54, 55, 56, 57, 58, 60, 61, 62, 63, 64, 65, 66, 67, 70, 71, 72, 74, 75, 79, 81, 82, 83, 86, 87, 89, 91, 92, 94, 95, 100, 103, 105, 106, 114, 116, 123, 124, 132, 141, 143, 144, 145, 149, 154, 160, 161, 163, 164, 166, 167, 168, 169, 170, 171, 173, 177, 178, 179, 180, 181, 183, 184, 192
Beall T.S. 6
Beattie D.R.G. 163
Berger K. 183
Bergmeier R. 6
Bernstein M.J. 139
Betz O. 7, 163, 166, 168
Bietenhardt H. 34, 158
Boyce M. xi, 8, 11
Brooke G.J. xi, 49, 112, 113
Broshi M. 2, 3, 51, 168
Burrows M. 77
Callaway P.R. 150
Campbell J.G. 4
Carmignac J. 77
Charles R.H. 77, 92
Charlesworth J.H. 3, 20, 21, 31, 34, 43, 47, 57, 72, 74, 75, 76, 79, 84, 87, 89, 92, 95, 100, 103, 114, 116, 120, 132, 144, 145, 163, 166, 192
Chazon E.G. 18, 19, 121, 180
Collins J.J. 110, 113
Cook E. 11, 66, 132, 146
Cothenet E. 77, 92, 106, 110, 111, 134, 154
Davidson M.J. 86

Davies P.R. 1, 2, 4, 5, 8, 25, 26, 62, 87, 89, 109, 135, 151, 190, 191, 192
Davis R. 12, 13
Derret J.D.M. 32
Dimant D. 19, 48, 87
Dupont-Sommer A. 78, 92, 134, 153, 154, 158
Eshel E. 97
Falk D. xi
Falk Z.W. 32
Fishbane M. 27, 33
Fitzmyer J.A. 2, 14, 27, 30, 31, 33, 34, 153
Flint P. 76
Freedman D.N. 18, 163
García Martínez F. xi, 2, 4, 5, 7, 14, 34, 37, 48, 49, 57, 66, 78, 84, 95, 98, 133, 144, 146, 190
Gaster T.H. 12, 78, 92, 158
Ginzberg L. 20, 35, 86, 87, 154, 156
Golb N. 160
Goodman M.D. 6, 8
Halpern B. 18, 110
Harrington D.J. 68, 102, 121
Hempel C. 37, 76, 82, 85, 97, 102, 139, 143, 144, 146, 147, 150, 188
Hilhorst A. 190
Hoenig S.B. 160
Hübner H. 156-157
Hurvitz A. 163
Jackson B.S. 95, 98
Kampen J. 135, 139
Kapera Z.J. 7, 112
Kimbrough S.T. Jr. 33, 159
Kister M. 55, 120, 121, 143, 170
Knibb M.A. xi, 7, 18, 56, 81, 109, 128, 183
Kosmala H. 106
Kugel J.L. 95, 103
Labuschagne C.J. 190
Lange A. 102, 170
Levenson J.D. 110
Levine B.A. 95, 156
Lieberman S. 99
Lignée H. 77

INDEX OF MODERN AUTHORS

Lindars B. 112
Lohse E. 78, 116
Maier J. 34, 48, 66, 77, 78, 84, 143, 146, 158
McNamara M. J. 163
Mayes A.D.H. 169
Metso S. 120
Milgrom J. 39, 48, 156, 163
Milik J.T. 2, 9, 10, 11, 12, 43, 47, 62, 86, 121, 124, 163, 168, 171, 180, 184
Milikowsky C. 26
Mulder M. J. 27
Murphy-O'Connor J. 5, 8
Nebe G. W. 75, 132, 133
Neusner J. 95
Newsom C. 18, 19, 20, 121
Nir-El Y. 51
Nitzan B. 184
Noack B. 158
Osten-Sacken P. v.d. 87
Parente F. 6
Parry D.W. 144, 150
Pfann S. 120, 121, 124, 170
Potok C. 21
Propp W. H. 18
Qimron E. 3, 7, 25, 40, 43, 47, 55, 70, 71, 73, 75, 76, 78, 79, 84, 85, 92, 94, 95, 109, 114, 116, 119, 120, 127, 132, 133, 144, 145, 161, 162, 167
Rabin C. 36, 75, 76, 78, 107, 109, 116, 122, 124, 128, 133, 134, 154, 158
Rabinovitch N.L. 95
Rabinowitz I. 31
Rajak T. 6
Rappaport U. 19
Reed S.A. 97
Reeves J. C. 135
Richter H.-P. 102
Riesner R. 7
Robinson I. 33
Rubinstein A. 9, 10, 11, 12, 37, 97
Schechter S. 1, 2, 9, 18, 21, 22, 77, 86, 101, 103, 113, 124
Schiffman L. H. 7, 9, 12, 21, 23, 25, 27, 28, 30, 33, 35, 36, 38, 48, 49, 53, 57, 70, 72, 75, 78, 86, 91, 94, 95, 96, 98, 100, 101, 102, 138, 144, 156, 158
Schubert K. 78
Schuller E. 180, 181
Sievers J. 6
Smith M. 6
Stanton G.N. xi
Stegemann H. 7, 51, 73, 102, 111, 149, 150, 184
Stemberger G. 5
Steudel A. 154
Stone M.E. 19
Strugnell J. 7, 12, 25, 55, 70, 71, 85, 102
Sussman Y. 25, 70, 71
Talmon S. 7, 8, 25, 36, 70, 143, 150, 154
Tigay J.H. 69
Tiller P. 12, 13
Trebolle Barrera J. 3, 5, 14, 48, 49, 55, 87, 95, 98, 103, 168
Ullendorff E. 75
Ulrich E. 25, 110, 143, 144, 150, 180
VanderKam J.C. 25, 76-77, 88, 89, 102, 103, 110, 143, 158, 180
Vaux R. De 2
Vegas Montaner L. 3, 48, 49, 55, 87, 103, 168
Vermes G. xi, 6, 21, 25, 27, 30, 33, 34, 42, 74, 78, 82, 84, 146, 173, 177, 178
Wacholder B. Z. 32, 95, 98, 135
Weinfeld M. 95, 142, 144, 167
Wernberg-Møller P. 107
White R. T. 26
Wills L. 168
Wilson A. 168
Winter P. 32
Wise M. O. 11, 18, 66, 132, 146, 156, 168
Woude A. S. Van der 4, 190
Wright D. P. 163
Yadin Y. 31, 95, 102, 156, 167
Zahavy T. 28

INDEX OF ANCIENT SOURCES

Hebrew Bible

Genesis
41,40	107

Exodus
18,21	108
18,25	108
19,10-15	156
35,2	158

Leviticus
1-16	39
4-5	179
5,24	31
11	161
11,41-45	161
12-15	43, 48, 49, 50
13-14	48
13,2	50
13,33	48
14-15	48
15,18	156
16	41
18,5	182
19	55
19,9	52, 59
19,17	32, 33
19,18	33, 99
19,20-22	64
19,23-25	54, 59
20,23	31
20,27	157
23,17	53, 59
23,22	52, 59
23,38	34
25	65, 67, 68, 69, 70
25,13-17	68
25,14	68
25,28	67
25,47-55	67
26,31	179
27,3	102
27,29	31

Numbers
5,11-31	64
5,13	63, 64
5,15	64
8,24-25	102
10,1-10	155
15,20	53, 59
15,35	158
30,3-16	30
30,7-9	30, 37
35,2-5	12, 96

Deuteronomy
5	169
5,12	34
7,9	127
13,6	157, 158
17,6	32, 53, 95
19,15	32, 53, 95, 96
22	65, 68, 69, 70
22,5	67, 68
22,6	167
22,10	68
22,10-11	68
22,11	68
22,13-21	68
23,24	30
24,19-21	52, 59
27	168, 169
30,4	179

1 Samuel
25,26	33
25,31	33

2 Kings
17,8	31
17,17	31

Isaiah
1,10-17	38
1,13	38
7,17	116, 127, 128, 130

17,6	53	Nahum	
58,6	122	1,2	33, 99
Jeremiah		Zechariah	
11,9-10	66	2	55
17,22	12	2,16	55
		13,7	109
Ezekiel			
20,11	182	Psalms	
20,13	182	41,1	65
20,21	182	89	43
20,38	55	90	103
22,26	161	103,13	122
34,12	122	107,40	181
45,11	57, 59	119,106	75
Hosea		Job	
5,10	182	12,24	181
5,11	122		
9,17	41	Proverbs	
		15,8	34, 37, 38
Joel			
2,12	179	Esther	
2,13	179	9,21	78
Micah			
7,2	31		

New Testament

1 Corinthians
5,11   183

Dead Sea Scrolls (Including Jubilees)

Jubilees		50,8	158
1,20	86, 158, 159	50,12-13	158
7,35-37	55		
10,12-14	86, 159	CD (Cairo Damascus Document)	
11,4-6	158	1	22, 150
11,5	87	1-8	10
15	89	1,1	22, 163, 170
15,23-24	89	1,1-2	119
15,31-32	158	1,15	181
17,16	87	1,16	182
18,9	87	2,2	163, 170
19,28	157	2,2-3	80
23	103	2,5	173
23,9-11	86, 102	2,9	88

2,9-10	119	9,2-8	32-33, 99
2,14	163, 170	9,3	173
2,14-15	119	9,5	32
3	22	9,6	33
3,12-15	88, 89	9,8	16, 26, 92
3,13-14	173	9,8-10	92, 187
3,15-16	182	9,10-12	92
3,18	66	9,10-16	13, 91-93, 113, 139, 189
3,20-4,4	1		
3,24	173	9,10-10,7	104
4	129	9,11	36, 73, 92
4,2	173	9,12-13	192
4,4	173	9,13	92
4,10	66	9,13-14	37, 92
4,12-5,15	129	9,14	92
5,7-11	168	9,15	92, 173
5,20	167, 182	9,16	92
5,20-6,1	167	9,16-20	53, 95
5,21-6,1	167	9,16-10,3	13, 32, 93-100, 182, 189
6	169		
6,5	1, 173	9,18	113, 174
6,10	79, 80	9,18-19	97
6,11-7,4	108, 127, 168	9,19	113, 174
6,14	79, 80	9,19-20	96
6,14-7,4	162	9,20	95
6,17-18	162	9,21	98
6,18-19	89	9,22	113, 174
6,19	1	9,23	94
7	128, 130	9,23-10,2	97
7,4-6	127, 128, 129	10,1	94, 98
7,5-8,21	108	10,4	26, 73, 103
7,6-8	10, 11	10,4-6	101
7,9-12	127	10,4-7	103, 189
7,10-12	127	10,4-10	13, 97, 100-104, 139
7,15	1	10,5	73, 103
7,19	1	10,5-6	96
8,4-5	80	10,6	101-102
8,9	80	10,6-7	102
8,16	173	10,7-10	35, 86, 102-104, 159, 190
8,21	1		
9	9, 22	10,8	73, 103
9-12	76	10,8-10	86
9-12,20	37	10,9-11	190
9-16	10, 73	10,10	17, 26
9,1	31-32, 36, 187	10,10-13	27, 35, 187
9,1-8	32	10,10-12,18	10, 11, 12
9,1-10,10	9, 10	10,10-12,20	13
9,1-12,18	20	10,11-13	192
9,1-12,22	12	10,12	35, 38
9,2	32, 33	10,14	17, 26
9,2-6	187	10,14-11,18	27, 33-34, 49, 187

210   INDEX OF ANCIENT SOURCES

10,18	38	12,19-23	10, 12, 161
10,19	154	12,20-21	106, 119, 120, 174
10,20	154	12,20-22	13, 105-106, 140, 189
10,21	12, 36, 96	12,21	174
10,23	36, 71, 73	12,22	127, 130
11,2	36	12,22-23	26, 101, 189, 114, 126,
11,5	36		134, 137, 140
11,7-8	12	12,22-13,7	13, 107-114
11,7-9	28	12,22-14,2	12, 134, 136
11,12	34	12,22-14,19	13
11,14-15	34	12,22-16,6	20
11,15	36	12,23	73, 79, 80
11,17	192	12,23-13,1	79, 108, 114, 129, 140,
11,17-18	192		145, 190
11,17-21	37	12,23-13,2	111
11,18-21	34, 37, 155, 187	13	82, 127
11,18-12,11	153	13,1-2	135, 137, 192
11,18-12,22	153	13,1-3	134
11,19	155, 192	13,1-7	134, 140, 189
11,20	155	13,1-16,5	10, 11
11,20-21	34, 37	13,2	101, 110, 173
11,21-12,1	153-155, 189	13,2-3	101, 110, 111, 112,
11,21-12,6	153		113, 114
11,22	154, 155, 192	13,2-7	48, 71, 93
11,23	154	13,3-4	111, 112, 113
12	105	13,3-7	114
12-14	106	13,4	36, 73
12,1	192	13,4-7	48, 112, 113
12,1-2	155-156, 157, 162, 189	13,5	36, 73, 173
12,2-3	157	13,5-6	112-113
12,2-6	86, 157-159, 162, 190	13,5-20	13
12,3	167	13,6	113, 174
12,3-6	158, 159	13,6-7	113
12,5	159	13,7	26, 36, 73, 82, 101,
12,6	36		113, 116, 117, 126,
12,6-11	35, 187		130, 138, 139, 140,
12,8	36		174
12,8-11	118	13,7-8	106, 118-121, 126, 130,
12,9	36		140, 189
12,9-10	35	13,7-14,2	97, 106, 114-130
12,10-11	135	13,8	116, 118
12,11-15	161	13,9	116
12,11-18	161, 162, 189	13,9-10	122, 123, 140, 190
12,11-20	153, 160-162	13,10	73
12,15	161	13,10-11	103, 192
12,15-18	161	13,11	73
12,16	161	13,11-12	122-123, 125, 130, 140,
12,16-17	161		190
12,17-18	161, 192	13,11-13	125
12,18	161	13,12-13	82, 117, 122, 129, 130,
12,19-20	161, 162, 190		138, 140, 174, 189

INDEX OF ANCIENT SOURCES

13,13	36, 73, 82, 103, 113, 174	14,12-16	98, 146
13,14-15	120, 123-125, 130, 140, 189	14,12-17	38
		14,12-18	138-140, 189
13,14-16	125	14,13	98, 113, 133, 139, 174
13,15	116	14,14	133
13,15-16	117, 125, 130, 138, 139, 140, 189	14,15	133
		14,16	133
13,16	36, 73, 82, 113, 139, 174	14,17	133, 140
		14,17-18	133
13,16-18	69, 126	14,18	189
13,16-19	140, 190	14,18-19	79, 110
13,16-22	126	14,18-22	141-148
13,16-14,2	114	14,19	66, 108, 144, 190
13,20	36, 73, 108, 114, 126, 128, 129, 130, 140, 189	14,20	144
		14,20-22	13, 189
13,22	106, 114, 116, 120, 126, 128, 130, 140, 174, 189	15	22, 33, 73, 86, 88, 149, 162
		15-12,22	13
		15-16	9, 88, 122
13,22-14,2	13	15,1	22
13,23	116, 130	15,1-5	13, 162, 190
13,23-14,2	126-130, 140, 190	15,3	166
14	22, 79, 127	15,5	30, 77, 78, 102
14,1	129, 130	15,5-6	77, 78, 79, 85, 90, 102, 146, 189
14,1-2	128, 130		
14,2	116, 129, 130, 140, 190	15,5-7	77, 78
14,3	36, 73, 126, 134, 136, 137, 139, 173	15,5-16,2	88, 174
		15,5-16,6	13, 73-90, 97, 117-118, 120, 122, 135, 174
14,3-6	101, 134-135, 136, 137, 140, 189		
		15,6	30, 79
14,3-10	13	15,6-7	77, 79, 81, 90, 108, 110, 190
14,3-18	131-140		
14,3-16,20	12	15,7	80, 81
14,4	123, 132, 134	15,7-16,2	85, 90, 102, 189
14,5	173	15,8	30, 81, 82, 84, 90, 113, 174, 190
14,6	132, 134, 173		
14,6-7	177	15,9	30, 75, 77
14,6-8	1-3, 136, 140, 190	15,10	75, 79
14,6-12	135-138	15,11	76, 85, 113, 174
14,7	82, 132, 136	15,12	76, 78, 79
14,7-8	101	15,13-14	83
14,8	132, 174	15,14	36, 76, 82, 83, 113, 139, 174
14,8-9	82, 113, 136, 138, 139		
14,8-12	97, 137-138, 140, 189	15,14-17	76
14,9	36, 73, 103, 132	15,15	76, 85, 174
14,10	73, 75, 103, 132	15,15-16	74
14,10-12	13	15,15-17	85, 90, 192
14,11	104, 113, 133, 174	15,16-17	85
14,12	26, 82, 138, 139, 140, 190	15,17	103, 104
		15,17-20	86
14,12-15	13	15,18	76, 85, 147

INDEX OF ANCIENT SOURCES

15,23	76	1QS (Serekh Ha-Yaḥad)	
16	30, 31, 89	1,11-13	139
16,1	76, 77, 102	1,16-2,25	87
16,1-2	86	1,16-3,12	184, 185
16,2	86, 89	1,18	87
16,2-3	192	1,23-24	87
16,2-4	86, 87	2,2	87
16,2-6	88, 89, 90, 103, 190	2,4-5	87
16,3-4	87	2,19	87, 88
16,4	76, 87	2,25-3,6	184
16,4-5	87, 88	2,26-3,1	184
16,4-6	89	3,2	139
16,6	89	3,23	87
16,6-9	13, 30, 187	5	82, 84
16,6-15	9, 10	5-9	139, 178, 191
16,10	13, 16, 26	5,1	26
16,10-12	30, 37, 187	5,1-3	139
16,12	30	5,1-4	190
16,13	16, 26, 31	5,7-9	85
16,13-17	31-32, 37, 187	5,10-20	183
16,13-9,1	31	5,14-20	183
16,14	31, 173	5,20-24	88
16,15	32	5,23	123
16,17	31	6	88
16,17-20	31, 187	6-9	81, 82, 84
16,18	31	6,2	55, 56
19	109	6,3	110, 111
19,1	127	6,3-4	101, 110
19,1-34	108	6,4	107
19,5-7	109	6,5	57
19,5-14	108	6,8	26
19,6	109	6,8-10	134
19,10	109	6,10	123
19,10-11	108, 109, 110	6,11-12	81
19,15-16	182	6,13-23	76, 99, 121, 122, 135
19,17	80	6,14	136
19,21	80	6,16	173
19,33-20,1	109	6,18-23	139
19,34	1	6,19-20	81
20,1	62, 108, 109	6,22	123
20,12	1	6,24	144, 145
20,14	62	6,24-7,25	144
20,20	173	6,26	123
20,25	182	6,26-7,8	141, 142
20,32	62	7,10-11	83
20,33	171	7,11	83, 84, 147
20,34	173	7,17-18	147
		7,21	123
1QapGen (Genesis Apocryphon)		7,24-25	183
12,13-15	55	8,15	120
		8,19	123

9	106	4Q261 (Serekh Ha-Yahad*g*)	
9,2	123	2,2	145
9,7-11	192	3,3	84, 147
9,11	120		
9,12	105, 120	4Q265 (Serekh Damascus)	
9,12-21	106		146
9,12-26	119, 120		
9,16	125	4Q266 (Damascus Document*a*)	
9,18	119	1 a-b 5	163, 170
9,22	125	2 i 6	22
10-11	122	5 i	171-174, 190
		5 i 1-7	172
1QSa (Rule of the Congregation)		5 i 8	173
1,1-3	82	5 i 8-19	172
1,7	102	5 i 9	173
2,4-9	85	5 i 10	172
2,17-21	57	5 i 11	173
		5 i 12	173
1QM (War Scroll)		5 i 13-14	173, 174
2,15-3,11	155	5 i 14	113, 174
7,4-6	85	5 i 15	173
7,12-15	155	5 i 17	106, 173, 174
10,8-12	181	5 i 18	173
13,4	87	5 i 19	173
13,11	87	5 i c-d	171
		5 i c-d 3	171
1QH (Hodayot)		5 ii	166, 173, 187
1,24	177	5 ii 1-16	39-42
2	129	5 ii 4	154
2,20-22	129	5 ii 4-5	49
		5 ii 5	36, 173
4Q159 (Ordinances*a*)		5 ii 6	154
1 ii 6	166	5 ii 7	50
1 ii 6-8	53	5 ii 8	49, 173
1 ii 13-14	57	5 ii 9	40
2-4	68	5 ii 9-10	49
2-4,7	67	5 ii 11	50
2-4,8-10	69	5 ii 12	173
		5 ii 16	42
4Q174 (Florilegium)		6 i a-c	43
1,3-5	85	6 i	47
		6 i-iii	43-50, 166, 187
4Q258 (Serekh Ha-Yahad*d*)		6 i 1	42
1	82	6 i 2	47, 50, 173
1,1	82	6 i 4	50, 173
1,1-3	42, 190	6 i 5	47
		6 i 6	50
4Q259 (Serekh Ha-Yahad*e*)		6 i 8	47
1 iii 6	120	6 i 9	50, 173
		6 i 10	50, 173
		6 i 11	47

INDEX OF ANCIENT SOURCES

6 i 12	47	10 i 4	104, 133
6 i 13	48, 173	10 i 5	82
6 i 16	48	10 i 6	133, 138
6 ii	48	10 i 7	133
6 ii 3	50	10 i 8	133
6 ii 9	50	10 i 9	133
6 ii a	43	10 i 10	133
6 iii	50, 51-54	10 i 10-11	133
6 iii-iv	187	10 i 11	133
6 iii 2	52, 53	10 i 12	79, 108
6 iii 3-4	17, 26, 50, 58	10 i 12-13	144
6 iii 3ff.	48	10 i 14	144
6 iii 4-5	17	10 ii	145
6 iii 7	52	10 ii 6-7	83
6 iii 9	52	10 ii 7	82, 83, 144, 190
6 iii a	50, 52, 53, 187	10 ii 15	144, 145
6 iii a 2	50	11	22, 82, 175-185, 190
6 iii b	58	11,1	190
6 iv	54-56	11,1-5	178-179
6 iv 3	55, 58	11,4-5	179
7 i	32, 33	11,5	177, 180
7 i-iii	32, 149	11,5-14	178, 180-182, 183
7 i 3	33	11,6	180
7 ii-iii	33	11,7	177, 181, 184
7 ii 6	73	11,7-8	181, 190
7 iii 2	113	11,8	173, 178, 183, 185
7 iii 3	73, 82, 113, 139, 174	11,9-10	181
8 i	73-90, 174	11,10-11	181
8 i-ii	9	11,10-13	181, 182
8 i 2	76	11,11	177
8 i 3	76	11,11-12	180
8 i 4	83	11,12	182
8 i 5	76	11,12-13	182
8 i 6	174	11,13-14	181
8 i 6-7	76, 85, 192	11,14	182
8 i 6-9	104	11,14-16	182-183
8 i 9	103	11,15	183
8 ii 2	31	11,16	113, 174, 177, 178, 182, 183
8 ii 7	31		
8 ii 8-9	31-32	11,16-18	183
8 iii 4-9	100-104	11,17	36, 73, 135, 178, 180, 183, 184
9 ii	107-114, 160-162		
9 ii 1-7	160	11,18-20	183-185
9 ii 7-8	105-106	11,20	177
9 iii	114-130	11,20-21	184
9 iii 7	116	12	62-64
9 iii 14	116	12-13	166
10 i	131-140	13	62
10 i-ii	141-148, 189		
10 i 1	132	4Q267 (Damascus Document[b])	
10 i 3	132, 133	2,5-6	167

5 ii	171-174	9,8	67, 82
5 ii 3	66	11 i	79, 133, 141
5 iii 1-8	39-42	11 i-ii	141-148
5 iii 6	73, 104	11 i 2	108
6	51-54		
6,4	52	4Q270 (Damascus Document^e)	
6,5	52	2 i-ii	48, 174
7	64-70	2 i 9-ii 17	164-169
8	149	2 i 9-ii 21	163-170, 190
8,4	82, 113, 139	2 i 10	166
9 i	33, 91-93	2 i 11	166
9 i 6	92	2 i 16-18	166
9 iv-v	114-130	2 ii 1	17, 26
9 iv 5	116	2 ii 5-9	17
9 iv 6	116	2 ii 5-10	166
9 v	131-140	2 ii 6	173
9 v 1	116	2 ii 12	166
9 v 3	116	2 ii 13	167
9 v 5	116	2 ii 13-14	167
9 v 6	116	2 ii 15	167
9 v 7-8	132	2 ii 16-17	167
9 v 8	132, 134	2 ii 17-18	170
9 v 10	132, 134, 135	2 ii 17-21	169-170
9 v 11	82, 132, 178	2 ii 19-21	170
9 v 12	132	3 i	50, 52, 53, 187
9 v 13	132	3 i 19	50, 51, 58
9 vi	141-148	3 i 20	50
9 vi 3	144	3 ii	51-54, 58
9 vi 4	144	3 ii 12	48, 50
		3 ii 14	52
4Q268 (Damascus Document^c)		3 ii 19	58
1,8-9	22	3 ii 21	58
1,9	119	3 ii a	58
2	131-140	3 iii	56
2,2	132	3 iii 13-15	56-57
		3 iii 19-21	59-62
4Q269 (Damascus Document^d)		3 iii 21	60
7	43-50	4	62-64, 187
7,5	47	4,1-8	62
7,6-7	47	4,5	173
8 i-ii	187	4-5	166
8 i 3	59-62	5	64-70
8 ii	60	5,17	30, 67
8 ii 1-6	59-62	5,19	67
8 ii 2	36, 60	6 i-ii	73-90
8 ii 3	60	6 i-iii	9
8 ii 4	67	6 i 5	47
8 ii 5	81	6 i 20	162
9	64-70, 126	6 ii 7	76
9,4	30, 67	6 ii 10	86
9,7	69	6 iii 13-15	31

6 iii 15-16	31-32	5 i 15	154
6 iii 17	33	5 i 15-17	153
6 iii 19	33	5 i 17-18	155
6 iv	91-93	5 i 18	167
6 iv 15-19	100-104		
6 iv 20	17, 26	4Q272 (Damascus Document^g)	
6 iv 21	35	1 i	47
6 v	34	1 i-ii	43-50
6 v 17	34	1 i 6	47
6 v 18		1 i 8	47, 173
7 i	141-148, 189	1 i 9	47
7 i-ii	175-185	1 i 13	47
7 i 4	104	1 i 17	47
7 i 9	144	1 i 20	47
7 i 11	82, 144, 190	1 ii 2	173
7 i 12-13	166	1 ii 6-18	47, 48
7 i 13-15	115		
7 i 14	73	4Q273 (Damascus Document^h)	
7 i 16	173, 177, 178	2, 1-2	39-42
7 i 19	177	4 i 5-11	39-42
7 i 21	177, 181, 183, 185	4 i 8	73
7 ii	22, 184	4 i 9-11	39
7 ii 11	135	4 ii	43-50
7 ii 14	36, 73, 177	4 ii 5	47
		4 ii 10	47
4Q271 (Damascus Document^f)		5	62
2	56, 166, 187	5,4	62
2,1-5	58		
2,1-6	56-57	4Q276 (Tohorot B^b)	
2,3	58	1	61
2,4	58		
2,7-13	59-62	4Q277 (Tohorot B^c)	
2,9	60	1	61
2,10	60		
2,12	81, 190	4Q286-290 (Berakhot^{a-e})	
3	64-70, 188		187
3,3	66		
3,3-4	67	4Q298 (Words of the Sage to Sons of Dawn)	
3,12	67		
3,14	113, 174	1-2 i 1	121
3,14-15	82		
3,15	67	4Q390 (psMoses^r)	
3,16	67	1,11	87
4 i 6-7	162		
4 ii	73-90	4Q394-399 (MMT^{a-f})	
4 ii 2-3	86	B8	26
4 ii 3	76, 86	B13	26
4 ii 12	30	B14-16	61
4 ii 12-13	16, 26	B21	26
5 i	153-159	B24	26
5 i 9	34	B38	167

B39-54	85	6Q15 (Damascus Document)	
B52	26	2	
B55	26	5	168
B62-63	55		
B63-64	166	11Q5 (Psalms^a)	
B64-72	50	26,1-5	124
B75-82	68		

4Q417 (Sapiential Work A^c)
2 i   102

4Q418 (Sapiential Work A^d)
43   102
103   68

4Q444 (Prayer)
              121

4Q513 (Ordinances^b)
1-2 i   57
4,4   72

5Q12 (Damascus Document)
              2

11Q13 (Melchizedek)
2,6   65

11Q19 (Temple Scroll^a)
45-47   156, 162
45,11-12   156
45,15-17   48
52,5   167
60,3   166
60,3-4   54, 55
63,14   99
64,6-9   167
64,6-11   32
64,8-9   32
66,15-17   168

11Q20 (Temple Scroll^b)
17   48

Rabbinic Writings

Mishnah
Peah   52

Negaim
3,1   114

Classical Authors

Josephus
The Jewish War
2,127   124

Philo
Quod omnis probus liber sit
78   124

Pliny the Elder
Natural History
5.17,4 (73)   6

Errata in *The Laws of the Damascus Document*

Page	Paragraph	Line	Change	To
142	Translation	2	Gift]	Gif[t]
187	3	6	CD 9,2–6a	CD 9,2–8a

www.ingramcontent.com/pod-product-compliance
Lightning Source LLC
Chambersburg PA
CBHW021809220426
43662CB00006B/235